D1195713

An Introduction to the Industrial and
Social History of England

New Sixteenth Century Manor House with Fields still Open, Gidea Hall, Essex

Nichols: *Progresses of Queen Elizabeth*

An Introduction

to the

Industrial and Social History of England

BY

EDWARD P. CHEYNEY

REVISED EDITION

AMS PRESS
NEW YORK

Reprinted from the edition of 1920, New York
First AMS EDITION published 1969
Manufactured in the United States of America

Library of Congress Catalogue Card Number: 79-92609

AMS PRESS, INC.
New York, N. Y. 10003

PREFACE

THIS text-book is intended for college and high-school classes. Most of the facts stated in it have become, through the researches and publications of recent years, such commonplace knowledge that a reference to authority in each case has not seemed necessary. Statements on more doubtful points, and such personal opinions as I have had occasion to express, although not supported by references, are based on a somewhat careful study of the sources. To each chapter is subjoined a bibliographical paragraph with the titles of the most important secondary authorities. These works will furnish a fuller account of the matters that have been treated in outline in this book, indicate the original sources, and give opportunity and suggestions for further study. An introductory chapter and a series of narrative paragraphs prefixed to other chapters are given with the object of correlating matters of economic and social history with other aspects of the life of the nation.

My obligation and gratitude are due, as are those of all later students, to the group of scholars who have within our own time laid the foundations of the study of economic history, and whose names and books will be found referred to in the bibliographical paragraphs.

EDWARD P. CHEYNEY.

UNIVERSITY OF PENNSYLVANIA,
January, 1901.

PREFACE TO REVISED EDITION

DURING the well-nigh twenty years that have passed since this text-book was published, events in the industrial and social world have gone far to transform modern society. An effort has been made to describe these changes of our own time in the last two chapters of this revised edition. The events of this period have also made it possible to see more clearly the character and tendency of somewhat earlier changes. The whole period since the Industrial Revolution has therefore been rewritten and rearranged chronologically in the last four chapters of the book.

Although several excellent text-books have appeared since the first edition of this, there has unfortunately been less detailed study of economic history than of some other phases. There seems, therefore, no sufficient reason for changing materially the earlier parts of the book.

EDWARD P. CHEYNEY.

UNIVERSITY OF PENNSYLVANIA,
July, 1920.

CONTENTS

CHAPTER I

GROWTH OF THE NATION TO THE MIDDLE OF THE
FOURTEENTH CENTURY

CHAPTER II

RURAL LIFE AND ORGANIZATION

CHAPTER III

TOWN LIFE AND ORGANIZATION

CHAPTER IV

MEDIÆVAL TRADE AND COMMERCE

CHAPTER V

THE BLACK DEATH AND THE PEASANTS' REBELLION

*Economic Changes of the Later Fourteenth and Early Fifteenth
Centuries*

CHAPTER VI

THE BREAKING UP OF THE MEDIÆVAL SYSTEM

*Economic Changes of the Later Fifteenth and the Sixteenth
Centuries*

Contents

xii   *Contents*

CHAPTER X

THE SPIRIT OF COMBINED ACTION, 1848–1878

CHAPTER XI

LIBERAL INFLUENCES ON INDUSTRIAL LIFE, 1878–1906

CHAPTER XII

DEMOCRATIC INFLUENCES ON INDUSTRIAL LIFE, 1906–1920

Contents   xiii

INDUSTRIAL AND SOCIAL HISTORY OF ENGLAND

CHAPTER I

GROWTH OF THE NATION

To the Middle of the Fourteenth Century

1. The Geography of England. — The British Isles lie north-west of the Continent of Europe. They are separated from it by the Channel and the North Sea, at the narrowest only twenty miles wide, and at the broadest not more than three hundred.

The greatest length of England from north to south is three hundred and sixty-five miles, and its greatest breadth some two hundred and eighty miles. Its area, with Wales, is 58,320 square miles, being somewhat more than one-quarter the size of France or of Germany, just one-half the size of Italy, and somewhat larger than either Pennsylvania or New York.

The backbone of the island is near the western coast, and consists of a body of hard granitic and volcanic rock rising into mountains of two or three thousand feet in height. These do not form one continuous chain but are in several detached groups. On the eastern flank of these mountains and under-lying all the rest of the island is a series of stratified rocks. The harder portions of these strata still stand up as long ridges, — the " wolds," " wealds," " moors," and " downs " of the more eastern and southeastern parts of England. The softer strata have been worn away into great broad valleys, furnishing the central and eastern plains or lowlands of the country.

The rivers of the south and of the far north run for the most part by short and direct courses to the sea. The rivers of the midlands are much longer and larger. As a result of the gradual sinking of the island, in recent geological periods the sea has extended some distance up the course of these rivers, making an almost unbroken series of estuaries along the whole coast.

The climate of England is milder and more equable than is indicated by the latitude, which is that of Labrador in the western hemisphere and of Prussia and central Russia on the Continent of Europe. This is due to the fact that the prevailing southwest winds drive the warmer surface waters of the south Atlantic against her shores, thus softening her climate.

These physical characteristics have been of immense influence on the destinies of England. Her position was far on the outskirts of the world as it was known to ancient and mediæval times, and England played a correspondingly inconspicuous part during those periods. In the habitable world as it has been known since the fifteenth century, on the other hand, that position is a distinctly central one, open alike to the eastern and the western hemisphere, to northern and southern lands.

Her situation of insularity and at the same time of proximity to the Continent laid her open to frequent invasion in early times, but after she secured a navy made her singularly safe from subjugation. It made the development of many of her institutions tardy, yet at the same time gave her the opportunity to borrow and assimilate what she would from the customs of foreign nations. Her separation by water from the Continent favored a distinct and continuous national life, while her nearness to it allowed her to participate in all the more important influences which affected the nations of central Europe.

Within the mountainous or elevated regions a variety of mineral resources, especially iron, copper, lead, and tin, exist in great abundance, and have been worked from the earliest

PHYSIOGRAPHIC MAP

OF

ENGLAND
AND WALES

SCALE OF ENGLISH MILES

0   20   40   60   80   100

EXPLANATION

Highlands_____

Lowlands_____

NORTH SEA

HOLY ISLE

SCOTLAND

Firth of Clyde

North Channel

Solway Firth

ISLE OF MAN

IRISH SEA

ANGLESEA

Cardigan
Bay

St. George's Channel

WALES

Bristol Channel

Land's End

ENGLISH

CHANNEL ISLANDS

CHANNEL

ISLE OF WIGHT

Beachy
Head

Dover Strait

River Thames

The Wash

R. Humber

FRANCE

R. Tweed

R. Tyne

R. Nith

R. Clyde

R. Mersey

R. Dee

R. Derwent

R. Ribble

R. Severn

R. Wye

R. Avon

R. Thames

R. Parret

R. Towy

Longitude West   2   from Greenwich   0

Wms. Eng. Co., N. Y.

3

ages. Potter's clay and salt also exist, the former furnishing the basis of industry for an extensive section of the midlands. By far the most important mineral possession of England, however, is her coal. This exists in the greatest abundance and in a number of sections of the north and west of the country. Practically unknown in the Middle Ages, and only slightly utilized in early modern times, within the eighteenth and nineteenth and twentieth centuries her coal supply has come to be the principal foundation of England's great manufacturing and commercial development.

The lowlands, which make up far the larger part of the country, are covered with soil which furnishes rich farming areas, though in many places this soil is a heavy and impervious clay, expensive to drain and cultivate. The hard ridges are covered with thin soil only. Many of them therefore remained for a long time covered with forest, and they are devoted even yet to grazing or to occasional cultivation only.

The abundance of harbors and rivers, navigable at least to the small vessels of the Middle Ages, has made a seafaring life natural to a large number of the people, and commercial intercourse comparatively easy with all parts of the country bordering on the coast or on these rivers.

Thus, to sum up these geographical characteristics, the insular situation of England, her location on the earth's surface, and the variety of her material endowments gave her a tolerably well-balanced if somewhat backward economic position during the Middle Ages, and have enabled her since the fifteenth century to pass through a continuous and rapid development, until she obtained within the nineteenth century, for the time at least, a distinct economic precedency among the nations of the world.

2. Prehistoric Britain. — The materials from which to construct a knowledge of the history of mankind before the time of written records are few and unsatisfactory. They consist for the most part of the remains of dwelling-places, fortifications, and roadways; of weapons, implements, and ornaments lost or abandoned at the time; of burial places and their contents; and of such physical characteristics of later populations as have survived from an early period. Centuries of human habitation of Britain passed away, leaving only such scanty remains and the obscure and doubtful knowledge that can be drawn from them. Through this period, however, successive races seem to have invaded and settled the country, combining with their predecessors, or living alongside of them, or in some cases, perhaps, exterminating them.

When contemporary written records begin, just before the beginning of the Christian era, one race, the Britons, was dominant, and into it had merged to all appearances all others. The Britons were a Celtic people related to the inhabitants of that part of the Continent of Europe which lies nearest to Britain. They were divided into a dozen or more separate tribes, each occupying a distinct part of the country. They lived partly by the pasturing of sheep and cattle, partly by a crude agriculture. They possessed most of the familiar grains and domestic animals, and could weave and dye cloth, make pottery, build boats, forge iron, and work other metals, including tin. They had, however, no cities, no manufactures beyond the most primitive, and but little foreign trade to connect them with the Continent. At the head of each tribe was a reigning chieftain of limited powers, surrounded by lesser chiefs. The tribes were in a state of incessant warfare one with the other.

3. Roman Britain. — This condition of insular isolation and barbarism was brought to a close in the year 55 B.C. by the invasion of the Roman army. Julius Cæsar, the Roman general who was engaged in the conquest and government of Gaul, or modern France, feared that the Britons might bring aid to certain newly subjected and still restless Gallic tribes. He therefore transported a body of troops across the Channel and fought two campaigns against the tribes in the southeast of Britain. His success in the second campaign was, however, not followed up, and he retired without leaving any permanent garrison in the country. The Britons were then left alone, so far as military invasion was concerned, for almost a century, though in the meantime trade with the adjacent parts of the Continent became more common, and Roman influence showed itself in the manners and customs of the people. In the year 44 A.D., just ninety-nine years after Cæsar's campaigns, the conquest of Britain was resumed by the Roman armies and completed within the next thirty years. Britain now became an integral part of the great, well-ordered, civilized, and wealthy Roman Empire. During the greater part of that long period, Britain enjoyed profound peace, internal and external trade were safe, and much of the culture and refinement of Italy and Gaul must have made their way even to this distant province. A part of the inhabitants adopted the Roman language, dress, customs, and manner of life. Discharged veterans from the Roman legions, wealthy civil officials and merchants settled permanently in Britain. Several bodies of turbulent tribesmen who had been defeated on the German frontier were transported by the government into Britain. The population must, therefore, have become very mixed, containing representatives of most of the races which had been conquered by the Roman armies. A permanent military force was maintained in Britain with fortified stations along the eastern and southern coast, on the Welsh frontier, and along a series of walls or dikes running across the island from the Tyne to Solway Firth. Excellent roads were constructed through the length and breadth of the land for the use of this military body and to connect the scattered stations. Along these highways population spread, and the remains of spacious villas still exist to attest the magnificence of the wealthy provincials. The roads served also as channels of trade by which goods could readily be carried from one part of the country to another. Foreign as well as internal trade became extensive, although exports were mostly of crude natural products, such as hides, skins, and furs, cattle and sheep, grain, pig-iron, lead and tin, hunting-dogs and slaves. The rapid development of towns and cities was a marked characteristic of Roman Britain. Fifty-nine towns or cities of various grades of self-government are named in the Roman survey, and many of these must have been populous, wealthy, and active, judging from the extensive ruins that remain, and the enormous number of Roman coins that have since been found. Christianity was adopted here as in other parts of the Roman Empire, though the extent of its influence is unknown.

During the Roman occupation much waste land was reclaimed. Most of the great valley regions and many of the hillsides had been originally covered with dense forests; swamps spread along the rivers and extended far inland from the coast; . so that almost the only parts capable of tillage were the high treeless plains, the hill tops, and certain favored stretches of open country. The reduction of these waste lands to human habitation has been an age-long task. It was begun in prehistoric times, it has been carried further by each successive race, and brought to final completion only within our own century. A share in this work and the great roads were the most permanent results of the Roman period of occupation and government. Throughout the fourth and fifth centuries of the Christian era the Roman administration and society in Britain were evidently disintegrating. Several successive generals of the Roman troops stationed in Britain rose in revolt with their soldiers, declared their independence of Rome, or passed over to the Continent to enter into a struggle for the control of the whole Empire. In 383 and 407 the military forces were suddenly depleted in this way and the provincial government disorganized, while the central government of the Emp're was so weak that it was unable to reëstablish a firm administration. During the same period barbarian invaders were making frequent inroads into Britain. The Picts and Scots from modern Scotland, Saxon pirates, and, later, ever increasing swarms of

Angles, Jutes, and Frisians from across the North Sea ravaged and ultimately occupied parts of the borders and the coasts. The surviving records of this period of disintegration and reorganization are so few that we are left in all but total ignorance as to what actually occurred. For more than two hundred years we can only guess at the course of events, or infer it from its probable analogy to what we know was occurring in the other parts of the Empire, or from the conditions we find to have been in existence as knowledge of succeeding times becomes somewhat more full. It seems evident that the government of the province of Britain gradually went to pieces, and that that of the different cities or districts followed. Internal dissensions and the lack of military organization and training of the mass of the population probably added to the difficulty of resisting marauding bands of barbarian invaders. These invading bands became larger, and their inroads more frequent and extended, until finally they abandoned their home lands entirely and settled permanently in those districts in which they had broken the resistance of the Roman-British natives. Even while the Empire had been strong the heavy burden of taxation and the severe pressure of administrative regulations had caused a decline in wealth and population. Now disorder, incessant ravages of the barbarians, isolation from other lands, probably famine and pestilence, brought rapid decay to the prosperity and civilization of the country. Cities lost their trade, wealth, and population, and many of them ceased altogether for a time to exist. Britain was rapidly sinking again into a land of barbarism.

4. **Early Saxon England.** — An increasing number of contemporary records give a somewhat clearer view of the condition of England toward the close of the sixth century. The old Roman organization and civilization had disappeared entirely, and a new race, with a new language, a different religion, another form of government, changed institutions and customs, had taken its place. A number of petty kingdoms had been formed

during the fifth and early sixth centuries, each under a king
or chieftain, as in the old Celtic times before the Roman invasion, but now of Teutonic or German race. The kings and
their followers had come from the northwestern portions of
Germany. How far they had destroyed the earlier inhabitants,
how far they had simply combined with them or enslaved them,
has been a matter of much debate, and one on which discordant
opinions are held, even by recent students. It seems likely
on the whole that the earlier races, weakened by defeat and
by the disappearance of the Roman control, were gradually
absorbed and merged into the body of their conquerors; so
that the petty Angle and Saxon kings of the sixth and seventh
centuries ruled over a mixed race, in which their own was the
most influential, though not necessarily the largest element.
The arrival from Rome in 597 of Augustine, the first Christian
missionary to the now heathen inhabitants of Britain, will
serve as a point to mark the completion of the Anglo-Saxon
conquest of the country. By this time the new settlers had
ceased to come in, and there were along the coast and inland
some seven or eight different kingdoms. These were, however,
so frequently divided and reunited that no fixed number remained
long in existence. The Jutes had established the kingdom of
Kent in the southeastern extremity of the island; the South and
the West Saxons were established on the southern coast and inland to the valley of the Thames; the East Saxons had a kingdom just north of the mouth of the Thames, and the Middle
Saxons held London and the district around. The rest of
the island to the north and inland exclusive of what was still
unconquered was occupied by various branches of the Angle
stock grouped into the kingdoms of East Anglia, Mercia, and
Northumbria. During the seventh and eighth centuries there
were constant wars of conquest among these kingdoms. Eventually, about 800 A.D., the West Saxon monarchy made itself
nominally supreme over all the others. Notwithstanding this
political supremacy of the West Saxons, it was the Angles who

were the most numerous and widely spread, and who gave their name, England, to the whole land.

Agriculture was at this time almost the sole occupation of the people. The trade and commerce that had centred in the towns and flowed along the Roman roads and across the Channel had long since come to an end with the Roman civilization of which it was a part. In Saxon England cities scarcely existed except as fortified places of defence. The products of each rural district sufficed for its needs in food and in materials for clothing, so that internal trade was but slight. Manufactures were few, partly from lack of skill, partly from lack of demand or appreciation; but weaving, the construction of agricultural implements and weapons, ship-building, and the working of metals had survived from Roman times, or been brought over as part of the stock of knowledge of the invaders. Far the greater part of the population lived in villages, as they probably had done in Roman and in prehistoric times. The village with the surrounding farming lands, woods, and waste grounds made up what was known in later times as the " township."

The form of government in the earlier separate kingdoms, as in the united monarchy after its consolidation, gave limited though constantly increasing powers to the king. A body of nobles known as the " witan " joined with the king in most of the actions of government. The greater part of the small group of government functions which were undertaken in these barbarous times were fulfilled by local gatherings of the principal men. A district formed from a greater or less number of townships, with a meeting for the settlement of disputes, the punishment of crimes, the witnessing of agreements, and other purposes, was known as a " hundred " or a " wapentake." A " shire " was a grouping of hundreds, with a similar gathering of its principal men for judicial, military, and fiscal purposes. Above the shire came the whole kingdom.

The most important occurrences of the early Saxon period

were the general adoption of Christianity and the organization of the church. Between A.D. 597 and 650 Christianity
gained acceptance through the preaching and influence of
missionaries, most of whom were sent from Rome, though some
came from Christian Scotland and Ireland. The organization
of the church followed closely. It was largely the work of
Archbishop Theodore, and was practically complete before the
close of the seventh century. By this organization England
was divided into seventeen dioceses or church districts, religious affairs in each of these districts being under the supervision
of a bishop. The bishop's church, called a " cathedral," was
endowed by religious kings and nobles with extensive lands, so
that the bishop was a wealthy landed proprietor, in addition to
having control of the clergy of his diocese, and exercising a
powerful influence over the consciences and actions of its lay
population. The bishoprics were grouped into two " provinces,"
those of Canterbury and York, the bishops of these two dioceses
having the higher title of archbishop, and having a certain
sort of supervision over the other bishops of their province.
Churches were gradually built in the villages, and each township usually became a parish with a regularly established priest.
He was supported partly by the produce of the " glebe," or
land belonging to the parish church, partly by tithe, a tax
estimated at one-tenth of the produce of each man's land, partly
by the offerings of the people. The bishops, the parish priests,
and others connected with the diocese, the cathedral, and the
parish churches made up the ordinary or " secular " clergy.
There were also many religious men and women who had taken
vows to live under special " rules " in religious societies withdrawn from the ordinary life of the world, and were therefore
known as " regular " clergy. These were the monks and nuns.
In Anglo-Saxon England the regular clergy lived according to
the rule of St. Benedict, and were gathered into groups, some
smaller, some larger, but always established in one building, or
group of buildings. These monasteries, like the bishoprics,

were endowed with lands which were increased from time to time by pious gifts of kings, nobles, and other laymen. Ecclesiastical bodies thus came in time to hold a very considerable share of the land of the country. The wealth and cultivation of the clergy and the desire to adorn and render more attractive their buildings and religious services fostered trade with foreign countries. The intercourse kept up with the church on the Continent also did something to lessen the isolation of England from the rest of the world. To these broadening influences must be added the effect which the Councils made up of churchmen from all England exerted in fostering the tardy growth of the unity of the country.

5. **Danish and Late Saxon England.** — At the end of the eighth century the Danes or Northmen, the barbarous and heathen inhabitants of the islands and coast-lands of Denmark, Norway, and Sweden, began to make rapid forays into the districts of England which lay near enough to the coasts or rivers to be at their mercy. Soon they became bolder or more numerous and established fortified camps along the English rivers, from which they ravaged the surrounding country. Still later, in the tenth and eleventh centuries, under their own kings as leaders, they became conquerors and permanent settlers of much of the country, and even for a time put a Danish dynasty on the throne to govern English and Danes alike. A succession of kings of the West Saxon line had struggled with varying success to drive the Danes from the country or to limit that portion of it which was under their control; but as a matter of fact the northern, eastern, and central portions of England were for more than a century and a half almost entirely under Danish rule. The constant immigration from Scandinavia during this time added an important element to the population — an element which soon, however, became completely absorbed in the mixed stock of the English people.

The marauding Danish invaders were early followed by fellow-countrymen who were tradesmen and merchants. The

Scandinavian countries had developed an early and active trade with the other lands bordering on the Baltic and North seas, and England under Danish influence was drawn into the same lines of commerce. The Danes were also more inclined to town life than the English, so that advantageously situated villages now grew into trading towns, and the sites of some of the old Roman cities began again to be filled with a busy population. With trading came a greater development of handicrafts, so that the population of later Anglo-Saxon England had somewhat varied occupations and means of support, instead of being exclusively agricultural, as in earlier centuries.

During these later centuries of the Saxon period, from 800 to 1066, the most conspicuous and most influential ruler was King Alfred. When he became king, in 871, the Danish invaders were so completely triumphant as to force him to flee with a few followers to the forest as a temporary refuge. He soon emerged, however, with the nucleus of an army and, during his reign, which continued till 901, defeated the Danes repeatedly, obtained their acceptance of Christianity, forced upon them a treaty which restricted their rule to the northeastern shires, and transmitted to his son a military and naval organization which enabled him to win back much even of this part of England. He introduced greater order, prosperity, and piety into the church, and partly by his own writing, partly by his patronage of learned men, reawakened an interest in Anglo-Saxon literature and in learning which the ravages of the Danes and the demoralization of the country had gone far to destroy. Alfred, besides his actual work as king, impressed the recognition of his fine nature and strong character deeply on the men of his time and the memory of all subsequent times.

The power of the kingship in the Anglo-Saxon system of government was strengthened by the life and work of such kings as Alfred and some of his successors. There were other causes also which were tending to make the central government more of a reality. A national taxation, the Danegeld, was introduced for the purpose of ransoming the country from the Danes; the grant of lands by the king brought many persons through the country into closer relations with him; the royal judicial powers tended to increase with the development of law and civilization; the work of government was carried on by better-trained officials.

On the other hand, a custom grew up in the tenth and early eleventh century of placing whole groups of shires under the government of great earls or viceroys, whose subjection to the central government of the king was but scant. Church bodies and others who had received large grants of land from the king were also coming to exercise over their tenants judicial, fiscal, and probably even military powers, which would seem more properly to belong to government officials. The result was that although the central government as compared with the local government of shires and hundreds was growing more active, the king's power as compared with the personal power of the great nobles was becoming less strong. Violence was common, and there were but few signs of advancing prosperity or civilization, when an entirely new set of influences came into existence with the conquest by the duke of Normandy in the year 1066.

6. The Period Following the Norman Conquest. — Normandy was a province of France lying along the shore of the English Channel. Its line of dukes and at least a considerable proportion of its people were of the same Scandinavian or Norse race which made up such a large element in the population of England. They had, however, learned more of the arts of life and of government from the more successfully preserved civilization of the Continent. The relations between England and Normandy began to be somewhat close in the early part of the eleventh century; the fugitive king of England, Ethelred, having taken refuge there, and marrying the sister of the duke. Edward the Confessor, their son, who was subsequently restored to the English throne, was brought up in Normandy, used the French language, and was accompanied on his return by Norman followers. Nine years after the accession of Edward, in 1051, William, the duke of Normandy, visited England and is said to have obtained a promise that he should receive the crown on the death of Edward, who had no direct heir. Accordingly, in 1065, when Edward died and Harold, a great English earl, was chosen king, William immediately asserted his claim and made strenuous military preparations for enforcing it. He took an army across the Channel in 1066, as Cæsar had done more than a thousand years before, and at the battle of Hastings or Senlac defeated the English army, King Harold himself being killed in the engagement. William then pressed on towards London, preventing any gathering of new forces, and obtained his recognition as king. He was crowned on Christmas Day, 1066. During the next five years he put down a series of rebellions on the part of the native English, after which he and his descendants were acknowledged as sole kings of England.

The Norman Conquest was not, however, a mere change of dynasty. It led to at least three other changes of the utmost importance. It added a new element to the population, it brought England into contact with the central and southern countries of the Continent, instead of merely with the northern as before, and it made the central government of the country vastly stronger. There is no satisfactory means of discovering how many Normans and others from across the Channel migrated into England with the Conqueror or in the wake of the Conquest, but there is no doubt that the number was large and their influence more than proportionate to their numbers. Within the lifetime of William, whose death occurred in 1087, of his two sons, William II and Henry I, and the nominal reign of Stephen extending to 1154, the whole body of the nobility, the bishops and abbots, and the government officials had come to be of Norman or other continental origin. Besides these the architects and artisans who built the castles and fortresses, and the cathedrals, abbeys, and parish churches, whose erection throughout the land was such a marked characteristic of the period, were immigrants from Normandy. Merchants from the Norman cities of Rouen and Caen came to settle in London and other English cities, and weavers from Flanders were settled in various towns and even rural districts. For a short time these newcomers remained a separate people, but before the twelfth century was over they had become for the most part indistinguishable from the great mass of the English people amongst whom they had come. They had nevertheless made that people stronger, more vigorous, more active-minded, and more varied in their occupations and interests.

King William and his successors retained their continental dominions and even extended them after their acquisition of the English kingdom, so that trade between the two sides of the Channel was more natural and easy than before. The strong government of the Norman kings gave protection and encouragement to this commerce, and by keeping down the violence of the nobles favored trade within the country. The English towns had been growing in number, size, and wealth in the years just before the Conquest. The contests of the years immediately following 1066 led to a short period of decay, but very soon increasing trade and handicraft led to still greater progress. London, especially, now made good its position as one of the great cities of Europe, and that preëminence among English cities which it has never since lost. The fishing and seaport towns along the southern and eastern coast also, and even a number of inland towns, came to hold a much more influential place in the nation than they had possessed in the Anglo-Saxon period.

The increased power of the monarchy arose partly from its military character as based upon a conquest of the country, partly from the personal character of William and his immediate successors, partly from the more effective machinery for administration of the affairs of government, which was either brought over from Normandy or developed in England. A body of trained, skilful government officials now existed, who were able to carry out the wishes of the king, collect his revenues, administer justice, gather armies, and in other ways make his rule effective to an extent unknown in the preceding period. The sheriffs, who had already existed as royal representatives in the shires in Anglo-Saxon times, now possessed far more extensive powers, and came up to Westminster to report and to present their financial accounts to the royal exchequer twice a year. Royal officials acting as judges not only settled an increasingly large number of cases that were brought before them at the king's court, but travelled through the country, trying suits and punishing criminals in the different shires. The king's income was vastly larger than that of the Anglo-Saxon monarchs had been. The old Danegeld was still collected from time to time, though under a different name, and the king's position as landlord of the men who had received the lands confiscated at the Conquest was utilized to obtain additional payments.

Perhaps the greatest proof of the power and efficiency of the government in the Norman period was the compilation of the great body of statistics known as " Domesday Book." In 1085 King William sent commissioners to every part of England to collect a variety of information about the financial conditions on which estates were held, their value, and fitness for further taxation. The information obtained from this investigation was drawn up in order and written in two large manuscript volumes which still exist in the Public Record Office at London. It is a much more extensive body of information than was collected for any other country of Europe until many centuries afterward. Yet its statements, though detailed and exact and of great interest from many points of view, are disappointing to the student of history. They were obtained for the financial purposes of government, and cannot be made to give the clear picture of the life of the people and of the relations of different classes to one another which would be so welcome, and which is so easily obtained from the great variety

c

of more private documents which came into existence a century and a half later.

The church during this period was not relatively so conspicuous as during Saxon times, but the number of the clergy, both secular and regular, was very large, the bishops and abbots powerful, and the number of monasteries and nunneries increasing. The most important ecclesiastical change was the development of church courts. The bishops or their representatives began to hold courts for the trial of churchmen, the settlement of such suits as churchmen were parties to, and the decision of cases in certain fields of law. This gave the church a new influence, in addition to that which it held from its spiritual duties, from its position as landlord over such extensive tracts, and from the superior enlightenment and mental ability of its prominent officials, but it also gave greater occasion for conflict with the civil government and with private persons.

After the death of Henry I in 1135 a miserable period of confusion and violence ensued. Civil war broke out between two claimants for the crown, Stephen the grandson, and Matilda the granddaughter, of William the Conqueror. The organization of government was allowed to fall into disorder, and but little effort was made to collect the royal revenue, to fulfil the newly acquired judicial duties, or to insist upon order being preserved in the country. The nobles took opposite sides in the contest for the crown, and made use of the weakness of government to act as if they were themselves sovereigns over their estates and the country adjacent to their castles with no ruler above them. Private warfare, oppression of less powerful men, seizure of property, went on unchecked. Every baron's castle became an independent establishment carried on in accordance only with the unbridled will of its lord, as if there were no law and no central authority to which he must bow. The will of the lord was often one of reckless violence, and there was more disorder and suffering in England than at any time since the ravages of the Danes.

In Anglo-Saxon times, when a weak king appeared, the shire moots, or the rulers of groups of shires, exercised the authority which the central government had lost. In the twelfth century, when the power of the royal government was similarly diminished through the weakness of Stephen and the confusions of the civil war, it was a certain class of men, the great nobles, that fell heir to the lost strength of government. This was because of the development of feudalism during the intervening time. The greater landholders had come to exercise over those who held land from them certain powers which in modern times belong to the officers of government only. A landlord could call upon his tenants for military service to him, and for the contribution of money for his expenses; he held a court to decide suits between one tenant and another, and frequently to punish their crimes and misdemeanors; in case of the death of a tenant leaving a minor heir, his landlord became guardian and temporary holder of the land, and if there were no heirs, the land reverted to him, not to the national government. These relations which the great landholders held toward their tenants, the latter, who often themselves were landlords over whole townships or other great tracts of land with their population, held toward their tenants. Sometimes these subtenants granted land to others below them, and over these the last landlord also exercised feudal rights, and so on till the actual occupants and cultivators of the soil were reached. The great nobles had thus come to stand in a middle position. Above them was the king, below them these successive stages of tenants and subtenants. Their tenants owed to them the same financial and political services and duties as they owed to the king. From the time of the Norman Conquest, all land in England was looked upon as being held from the king directly by a comparatively few, and indirectly through them by all others who held land at all. Moreover, from a time at least soon after the Norman Conquest, the services and payments above mentioned came to be recognized as due from all tenants to their lords, and were gradually systematized and defined. Each person or ecclesiastical body that held land from the king owed him the military service of a certain number of knights or armed horse soldiers. The period for which this service was owed was generally estimated as forty days once a year. Subtenants similarly owed military service to their landlords, though in the lesser grades this was almost invariably commuted for money. " Wardship and marriage " was the expression applied to the right of the lord to the guardianship of the estate of a minor heir of his tenant, and to the choice of a husband or wife for the heir when he came of proper age. This right also was early turned into the form of a money consideration. There were a number of money payments pure and simple. " Relief " was a payment to the landlord, usually of a year's income of the estate, made by an heir on obtaining his inheritance. There were three generally acknowledged " aids " or payments of a set sum in proportion to the amount of land held. These were on the occasion of the knighting of the lord's son, of the marriage of his daughter, and for his ransom in case he was captured in war. Land could be confiscated if the tenant violated his duties to his landlord, and it " escheated " to the lord in case of failure of heirs. Every tenant was bound to attend his landlord to help form a court for judicial work, and to submit to the judgment of a court of his fellow-tenants for his own affairs.

In addition to the relations of landlord and tenant and to the power of jurisdiction, taxation, and military service which landlords exercised over their tenants, there was considered to be a close personal relationship between them. Every tenant on obtaining his land went through a ceremony known as " homage," by which he promised faithfulness and service to his lord, vowing on his knees to be his man. The lord in return promised faithfulness, protection, and justice to his tenant. It was this combination of landholding, political rights, and sworn personal fidelity that made up feudalism. It existed in this sense in England from the later Saxon period till late in the Middle Ages, and even in some of its characteristics to quite modern times. The conquest by William of Normandy through the wholesale confiscation and regrant of lands, and through his military arrangements, brought about an almost sudden development and spread of feudalism in England, and it was rapidly systematized and completed in the reigns of his two sons. By its very nature feudalism gives great powers to the higher ranks of the nobility, the great landholders. Under the early Norman kings, however, their strength was kept in tolerably complete check. The anarchy of the reign of Stephen was an indication of the natural tendencies of feudalism without a vigorous king. This time of confusion when, as the contemporary chronicle says, "every man did that which was good in his own eyes," was brought to an end by the accession to the throne of Henry II, a man whose personal abilities and previous training enabled him to bring the royal authority to greater strength than ever, and to put an end to the oppressions of the turbulent nobles.

7. **The Period of the Early Angevin Kings, 1154–1338.** — The two centuries which now followed saw either the completion or the initiation of most of the characteristics of the English race with which we are familiar in historic times. The race, the language, the law, and the political organization have remained fundamentally the same as they became during the thirteenth and fourteenth centuries. No considerable new addition was made to the population, and the elements which it already contained became so thoroughly fused that it has always since been practically a homogeneous body. The Latin language remained through this whole period and till long afterward the principal language of records, documents, and the affairs of the church. French continued to be the language of the daily intercourse of the upper classes, of the pleadings in the law courts, and of certain documents and records. But English was taking its modern form, asserting itself as the real national language, and by the close of this period had come

into general use for the vast majority of purposes. Within the twelfth and thirteenth centuries the Universities of Oxford and Cambridge grew up, and within the fourteenth took their later shape of self-governing groups of colleges. Successive orders of religious men and women were formed under rules intended to overcome the defects which had appeared in the early Benedictine rule. The organized church became more and more powerful, and disputes constantly arose as to the limits between its power and that of the ordinary government. The question was complicated from the fact that the English Church was but one branch of the general church of Western Christendom, whose centre and principal authority was vested in the Pope at Rome. One of the most serious of these conflicts was between King Henry II and Thomas, archbishop of Canterbury, principally on the question of how far clergymen should be subject to the same laws as laymen. The personal dispute ended in the murder of the archbishop, in 1170, but the controversy itself got no farther than a compromise. A contest broke out between King John and the Pope in 1205 as to the right of the king to dictate the selection of a new archbishop of Canterbury. By 1213 the various forms of influence which the church could bring to bear were successful in forcing the king to give way. He therefore made humble apologies and accepted the nominee of the Pope for the office. Later in the thirteenth century there was much popular opposition to papal taxation of England.

In the reign of Henry II, the conquest of Ireland was begun. In 1283 Edward I, great-grandson of Henry, completed the conquest of Wales, which had remained incompletely conquered from Roman times onward. In 1292 Edward began that interference in the affairs of Scotland which led on to long wars and a nominal conquest. For a while, therefore, it seemed that England was about to create a single monarchy out of the whole of the British Islands. Moreover, Henry II was already count of Anjou and Maine by inheritance from his father when he became duke of Normandy and king of England by inheritance from his mother. He also obtained control of almost all the remainder of the western and southern provinces of France by his marriage with Eleanor of Aquitaine. It seemed, therefore, that England might become the centre of a considerable empire composed partly of districts on the Continent, partly of the British Islands. As a matter of fact, Wales long remained separated from England in organization and feeling, little progress was made with the real conquest of Ireland till in the sixteenth century, and the absorption of Scotland failed entirely. King John, in 1204, lost most of the possessions of the English kings south of the Channel and they were not regained within this period. The unification of the English government and people really occurred during this period, but it was only within the boundaries which were then as now known as England.

Henry II was a vigorous, clear-headed, far-sighted ruler. He not only put down the rebellious barons with a strong hand, and restored the old royal institutions, as already stated, but added new powers of great importance, especially in the organization of the courts of justice. He changed the occasional visits of royal officials to different parts of the country to regular periodical circuits, the kingdom being divided into districts in each of which a group of judges held court at least once in each year. In 1166, by the Assize of Clarendon, he made provision for a sworn body of men in each neighborhood to bring accusations against criminals, thus making the beginning of the grand jury system. He also provided that a group of men should be put upon their oath to give a decision in a dispute about the possession of land, if either one of the claimants asked for it, thus introducing the first form of the trial by jury. The decisions of the judges within this period came to be so consistent and so well recorded as to make the foundation of the Common Law the basis of modern law in all English-speaking countries.

Henry's successor was his son Richard I, whose government was quite unimportant except for the romantic personal adventures of the king when on a crusade and in his continental dominions. Henry's second son John reigned from 1199 to 1216. Although of good natural abilities, he was extraordinarily indolent, mean, treacherous, and obstinate. By his inactivity during a long quarrel with the king of France he lost all his provinces on the Continent, except those in the far south. His contest with the Pope had ended in failure and humiliation. He had angered the barons by arbitrary taxation and by many individual acts of outrage or oppression. Finally he had alienated the affections of the mass of the population by introducing foreign mercenaries to support his tyranny and permitting to them unbridled excess and violence. As a result of this widespread unpopularity, a rebellion was organized, including almost the whole of the baronage of England, guided by the counsels of Stephen Langton, archbishop of Canterbury, and supported by the citizens of London. The indefiniteness of feudal relations was a constant temptation to kings and other lords to carry their exactions and demands upon their tenants to an unreasonable and oppressive length. Henry I, on his accession in 1100, in order to gain popularity, had voluntarily granted a charter reciting a number of these forms of oppression and promising to put an end to them. The rebellious barons now took this old charter as a basis, added to it many points which had become questions of dispute during the century since it had been granted, and others which were of special interest to townsmen and the middle and even lower classes. They then demanded the king's promise to issue a charter containing these points. John resisted for a while, but at last gave way and signed the document which has since been known as the " Great Charter " or Magna Carta. This has always been considered as, in a certain sense, the guarantee of English liberties and the foundation of the settled constitution of the kingdom. The fact that it was forced from a reluc-

tant king by those who spoke for the whole nation, that it placed
definite limitations on his power, and that it was confirmed
again and again by later kings, has done more to give it this
position than its temporary and in many cases insignificant
provisions, accompanied only by a comparatively few statements of general principles.

The beginnings of the construction of the English parliamentary constitution fall within the next reign, that of John's
son, Henry III, 1216–1272. He was a child at his accession,
and when he became a man proved to have but few qualities
which would enable him to exercise a real control over the course
of events. Conflicts were constant between the king and con-
federations of the barons, for the greater part of the time under
the leadership of Simon de Montfort, earl of Leicester. The
special points of difference were the king's preference for foreign
adventurers in his distribution of offices, his unrestrained mu-
nificence to them, their insolence and oppression relying on the
king's support, the financial demands which were constantly
being made, and the king's encouragement of the high claims and
pecuniary exactions of the Pope. At first these conflicts took
the form of disputes in the Great Council, but ultimately they
led to another outbreak of civil war. The Great Council of
the kingdom was a gathering of the nobles, bishops, and abbots
summoned by the king from time to time for advice and participation in the more important work of government. It had
always existed in one form or another, extending back continuously to the " witenagemot " of the Anglo-Saxons. During
the reign of Henry the name " Parliament " was coming to be
more regularly applied to it, its meetings were more frequent
and its self-assertion more vigorous. But most important of
all, a new class of members was added to it. In 1265, in addition to the nobles and great prelates, the sheriffs were ordered to
see that two knights were selected from each of their shires, and
two citizens from each of a long list of the larger towns, to
attend and take part in the discussions of Parliament. This

plan was not continued regularly at first, but Henry's successor, Edward I, who reigned from 1272 to 1307, adopted it deliberately, and from 1295 forward the " Commons," as they came to be called, were always included in Parliament. Within the next century a custom arose according to which the representatives of the shires and the towns sat in a separate body from the nobles and churchmen, so that Parliament took on its modern form of two houses, the House of Lords and the House of Commons.

Until this time and long afterward the personal character and abilities of the king were far the most important single factor in the growth of the nation. Edward I was one of the greatest of English kings, ranking with Alfred, William the Conqueror, and Henry II. His conquests of Wales and of Scotland have already been mentioned, and these with the preparation they involved and a war with France into which he was drawn necessarily occupied the greater part of his time and energy. But he found the time to introduce good order and control into the government in all its branches; to make a great investigation into the judicial and administrative system, the results of which, commonly known as the " Hundred Rolls," are comparable to Domesday Book in extent and character; to develop the organization of Parliament, and above all to enact through it a series of great reforming statutes. The most important of these were the First and Second Statutes of Westminster, in 1275 and 1285, which made provisions for good order in the country, for the protection of merchants, and for other objects; the Statute of Mortmain, passed in 1279, which put a partial stop to injurious gifts of land to the church, and the Statute *Quia Emptores*, passed in 1290, which was intended to prevent the excessive multiplication of subtenants. This was done by providing that whenever in the future any landholder should dispose of a piece of land it should be held from the same lord the grantor had held it from, not from the grantor himself. He also gave more liberal charters to the towns, privileges to foreign merchants, and constant encouragement to trade. The king's firm hand and prudent judgment were felt in a wide circle of regulations applying to taxes, markets and fairs, the purchase of royal supplies, the currency, the administration of local justice, and many other fields. Yet after all it was the organization of Parliament that was the most important work of Edward's reign. This completed the unification of the country. The English people were now one race, under one law, with one Parliament representing all parts of the country. It was possible now for the whole nation to act as a unit, and for laws to be passed which would apply to the whole country and draw its different sections continually more closely together. National growth was now possible in a sense in which it had not been before.

The reign of Edward II, like his own character, was insignificant compared with that of his father. He was deposed in 1327, and his son, Edward III, came to the throne as a boy of fourteen years. The first years of his reign were also relatively unimportant. By the time he reached his majority, however, other events were imminent which for the next century or more gave a new direction to the principal interests and energies of England. A description of these events will be given in a later chapter.

For the greater part of the long period which has now been sketched in outline it is almost solely the political and ecclesiastical events and certain personal experiences which have left their records in history. We can obtain but vague outlines of the actual life of the people. An important Anglo-Saxon document describes the organization of a great landed estate, and from Domesday Book and other early Norman records may be drawn certain inferences as to the degree of freedom of the masses of the people and certain facts as to agriculture and trade. From the increasing body of public records in the twelfth century can be gathered detached pieces of information as to actual social and economic conditions, but the knowledge that can be obtained is even yet slight and uncertain. With the thirteenth century, however, all this is changed. During the latter part of the period just described, that is to say the reigns of Henry III and the three Edwards, we have almost as full knowledge of economic as of political conditions, of the life of the mass of the people as of that of courtiers and ecclesiastics. From a time for which 1250 may be taken as an approximate date, written documents began to be so numerous, so varied, and so full of information as to the affairs of private life, that it becomes possible to obtain a comparatively full and clear knowledge of the methods of agriculture, handicraft, and commerce, of the classes of society, the prevailing customs and ideas, and in general of the mode of life and social organization of the mass of the people, this being the principal subject of economic and social history. The next three chapters will therefore be devoted respectively to a description of rural life, of town life, and of trading relations, as they were during the century from 1250 to 1350, while the succeeding chapters will trace the main lines of economic and social change during succeeding periods down to the present time.

CHAPTER II

RURAL LIFE AND ORGANIZATION

8. The Mediæval Village. — In the Middle Ages in the greater part of England all country life was village life. The farmhouses were not isolated or separated from one another by surrounding fields, as they are so generally in modern times, but were gathered into villages. Each village was surrounded by arable lands, meadows, pastures, and woods which spread away till they reached the confines of the similar fields of the next adjacent village. Such an agricultural village with its population and its surrounding lands is usually spoken of as a " vill." The word " manor " is also applied to it, though this word is also used in other senses, and has differed in meaning at different periods. The word " hamlet " means a smaller group of houses separated from but forming in some respects a part of a vill or manor.

 The village consisted of a group of houses ranging in number from ten or twelve to as many as fifty or perhaps even more, grouped around what in later times would be called a " village green," or along two or three intersecting lanes. The houses were small, thatch-roofed, and one-roomed, and doubtless very miserable. Such buildings as existed for the protection of cattle or the preservation of crops were closely connected with the dwelling portions of the houses. In many cases they were under the same roof. Each vill possessed its church, which was generally, though by no means always, close to the houses of the village. There was usually a manor house, which varied in size from an actual castle to a building of a character scarcely distinguishable from the primitive houses of the villagers. This might be occupied regularly or occasionally by the lord of the manor, but might otherwise be inhabited by the steward or by a tenant, or perhaps only serve as the gathering place of the manor courts.

Connected with the manor house was an enclosure or court-yard commonly surrounded by buildings for general farm purposes and for cooking or brewing. A garden or orchard was often attached.

The location of the vill was almost invariably such that a stream with its border meadows passed through or along its

THIRTEENTH CENTURY MANOR HOUSE, MILLICHOPE, SHROPSHIRE
(Wright, *History of Domestic Manners and Sentiments.*)

confines, the mill being often the only building that lay detached from the village group. A greater or less extent of woodland is also constantly mentioned.

The vill was thus made up of the group of houses of the villagers including the parish church and the manor house, all surrounded by a wide tract of arable land, meadow, pasture, and woods. Where the lands were extensive there might perhaps be a small group of houses forming a separate hamlet at some distance from the village, and occasionally a detached mill, grange, or other building. Its characteristic appearance, however, must have been that of a close group of buildings surrounded by an extensive tract of open land.

9. The Vill as an Agricultural System. — The support of the vill was in its agriculture. The plan by which the lands of the whole group of cultivators lay together in a large tract surrounding the village is spoken of as the " open field " system. The arable portions of this were ploughed in pieces equalling approximately acres, half-acres, or quarter-acres.

The mediæval English acre was a long narrow strip forty rods in length and four rods in width, a half-acre or quarter-acre being of the same length, but of two rods or one rod in width. The rod was of different lengths in different parts of the country, depending on local custom, but the most common length was that prescribed by statute, that is to say, sixteen and a half feet. The length of the acre, forty rods, has given rise to one of the familiar units of length, the furlong, that is, a " furrow-long," or the length of a furrow. A rood is a piece of land one rod wide and forty rods long, that is, the fourth of an acre. A series of such strips were ploughed up successively, being separated from each other either by leaving the width of a furrow or two unploughed, or by marking the division with stones, or perhaps by simply throwing the first furrow of the next strip in the opposite direction when it was ploughed. When an unploughed border was left covered with grass or stones, it was called a " balk." A number of such acres or fractions of acres with their slight dividing ridges thus lay alongside of one another in a group, the number being defined by the configuration of the ground, by a traditional division among a given number of tenants, or by some other cause. Other groups of strips lay at right angles or inclined to these, so that the whole arable land of the village when ploughed or under cultivation had, like many French, German, or Swiss landscapes at the present time, something of the appearance of a great irregular checker-board or patchwork quilt, each large square being

divided in one direction by parallel lines. Usually the cultivated open fields belonging to a village were divided into three
or more large tracts or fields and these were cultivated according
to some established rotation of crops. The most common of
these was the three-field system, by which in any one year all
the strips in one tract or field would be planted with wheat,
rye, or some other crop which is planted in the fall and harvested
the next summer; a second great field would be planted with

VILLAGE WITH OPEN FIELDS, UDENHAUSEN, NEAR COBLENTZ, GERMANY
(From a photograph taken in 1894.)

oats, barley, peas, or some such crop as is planted in the spring
and harvested in the fall; the third field would be fallow, recu-
perating its fertility. The next year all the acres in the field
which had lain fallow the year before might be planted with a
fall crop, the wheat field of the previous year being planted with
a spring crop, and the oats field in its turn now lying uncultivated for a year. The third year a further exchange would
be made by which a fall crop would succeed the fallow of that
year and the spring crop of the previous year, a spring crop

would succeed the last year's fall crop, and the field from which the spring crop was taken now in its turn would enjoy a fallow year. In the fourth year the rotation would begin over again.

Agriculture was extremely crude. But eight or nine bushels of wheat or rye were expected from an acre, where now in England the average is thirty. The plough regularly required eight draught animals, usually oxen, in breaking up the ground, though lighter ploughs were used in subsequent cultivation. The breed of all farm animals was small, carts were few and cumbrous, the harvesting of grain was done with a sickle, and the mowing of grass with a short, straight scythe. The distance of the outlying parts of the fields from the farm buildings of the village added its share to the laboriousness of agricultural life.

The variety of food crops raised was small. Potatoes were of course unknown, and other root crops and fresh vegetables apparently were little cultivated. Wheat and rye of several varieties were raised as bread-stuff, barley and some other grains for the brewing of beer. Field peas and beans were raised, sometimes for food, but generally as forage for cattle. The main supply of winter forage for the farm animals had, however, to be secured in the form of hay, and for this reliance was placed entirely on the natural meadows, as no clover or grasses which could be artificially raised on dry ground were yet known. Meadow land was apt to be estimated at twice the value of arable ground or more. To obtain a sufficient support for the oxen, horses, and breeding animals through the winter required, therefore, a constant struggle. Owing to this difficulty animals that were to be used for food purposes were regularly killed in the fall and salted down. Much of the unhealthiness of mediæval life is no doubt attributable to the use of salt meat as so large a part of what was at best a very monotonous diet.

Summer pasture for the horses, cattle, sheep, and swine of the village was found partly on the arable land after the grain

D

crops had been taken off, or while it was lying fallow. Since all the acres in any one great field were planted with the same crop, this would be taken off from the whole expanse at practically the same time, and the animals of the whole village might then wander over it, feeding on the stubble, the grass of the balks, and such other growth as sprang up before the next ploughing, or before freezing weather. Pasturage was also found on the meadows after the hay had been cut. But the largest amount of all was on the " common pasture," the uncultivated land and woods which in the thirteenth century was still sufficiently abundant in most parts of England to be found in considerable extent on almost every manor. Pasturage in all these forms was for the most part common for all the animals of the vill, which were sent out under the care of shepherds or other guardians. There were, however, sometimes enclosed pieces of pasture land in the possession of the lord of the manor or of individual villagers.

The land of the vill was held and cultivated according to a system of scattered acres. That is to say, the land held by any one man was not all in one place, but scattered through various parts of the open fields of the vill. He would have an acre or two, or perhaps only a part of an acre, in one place, another strip not adjacent to it, but somewhere else in the fields, still another somewhere else, and so on for his whole holding, while the neighbor whose house was next to his in the village would have pieces of land similarly scattered through the fields, and in many cases probably have them adjacent to his. The result was that the various acres or other parts of any one man's holding were mingled apparently inextricably with those of other men, customary familiarity only distinguishing which pieces belonged to each villager.

In some manors there was total irregularity as to the number of acres in the occupation of any one man; in others there was a striking regularity. The typical holding, the group of scattered acres cultivated by one man or held by some two or

three in common, was known as a " virgate," or by some equivalent term, and although of no universal equality, was more
frequently of thirty acres than of any other number. Usually
one finds on a given manor that ten or fifteen of the villagers
have each a virgate of a given number of acres, several more
have each a half virgate or a quarter. Occasionally, on the
other hand, each of them has a different number of acres. In
almost all cases, however, the agricultural holdings of the villagers were relatively small. For instance, on a certain manor
in Norfolk there were thirty-six holdings, twenty of them below
ten acres, eight between ten and twenty, six between twenty
and thirty, and two between thirty and forty. On another,
in Essex, there were nine holdings of five acres each, two of six,
twelve of ten, three of twelve, one of eighteen, four of twenty,
one of forty, and one of fifty. Sometimes larger holdings in
the hands of individual tenants are to be found, rising to one
hundred acres or more. Still these were quite exceptional and
the mass of the villagers had very small groups of acres in their
possession.

It is to be noted next that a large proportion of the cultivated
strips were not held in virgates or otherwise by the villagers
at all, but were in the direct possession and cultivation of the
lord of the manor. This land held directly by the lord of the
manor and cultivated for him was called the " demesne," and
frequently included one-half or even a larger proportion of all
the land of the vill. Much of the meadow and pasture land, and
frequently all of the woods, was included in the demesne. Some
of the demesne land was detached from the land of the villagers
enclosed and separately cultivated or pastured; but for the
most part it lay scattered through the same open fields and was
cultivated by the same methods and according to the same
rotation as the land of the small tenants of the vill, though it
was kept under separate management.

10. Classes of People on the Manor. — Every manor was
in the hands of a lord. He might be a knight, esquire, or mere

freeman, but in the great majority of cases the lord of the manor was a nobleman, a bishop, abbot, or other ecclesiastical official, or the king. But whether the manor was the whole estate of a man of the lesser gentry, or merely one part of the possessions of a great baron, an ecclesiastical corporation, or the crown, the relation between its possessor as lord of the manor and the other inhabitants as his tenants was the same. In the former case he was usually resident upon the manor; in the latter the individual or corporate lord was represented by a steward or other official who made occasional visits, and frequently, on large manors, by a resident bailiff. There was also almost universally a reeve, who was chosen from among the tenants and who had to carry on the demesne farm in the interests of the lord.

The tenants of the manor, ranging from holders of considerable amounts of land, perhaps as much as a hundred acres, through various gradations down to mere cotters, who held no more than a cottage with perhaps a half-acre or a rood of land, or even with no land at all, are usually grouped in the " extents " or contemporary descriptions of the manors and their inhabitants into several distinct classes. Some are described as free tenants, or tenants holding freely. Others, and usually the largest class, are called villains, or customary tenants. Some, holding only a half or a quarter virgate, are spoken of as half or quarter villains. Again, a numerous class are described by some name indicating that they hold only a dwelling-house, or at least that their holding of land is but slight. These are generally spoken of as cotters.

All these tenants hold land from the lord of the manor and make payments and perform services in return for their land. The free tenants most commonly make payments in money only. At special periods in the year they give a certain number of shillings or pence to the lord. Occasionally they are required to make some payment in kind, a cock or a hen, some eggs, or other articles of consumption. These money payments and payments of articles of money value are called " rents of assize," or established rents. Not unusually, however, the free tenant has to furnish *precariæ* or " boon-works " to the lord. That is, he must, either in his own person or through a man hired for the purpose, furnish one or more days' labor at the specially busy seasons of the year, at fall and spring ploughing, at mowing or harvest time. Free tenants were also frequently bound to pay relief and heriot. Relief was a sum of money paid to the lord by an heir on obtaining land by inheritance. Custom very generally established the amount to be paid as the equivalent of one year's ordinary payments. Heriot was a payment made in kind or in money from the property left by a deceased tenant, and very generally consisted by custom of the best animal which had been in the possession of the man, or its equivalent in value. On many manors heriot was not paid by free tenants, but only by those of lower rank.

The services and payments of the villains or customary tenants were of various descriptions. They had usually to make some money payments at regular periods of the year, like the free tenants, and, even more frequently than they, some regular payments in kind. But the fine paid on the inheritance of their land was less definitely restricted in amount, and heriot was more universally and more regularly collected. The greater part of their liability to the lord of the manor was, however, in the form of personal, corporal service. Almost universally the villain was required to work for a certain number of days in each week on the demesne of the lord. This " week-work " was most frequently for three days a week, sometimes for two, sometimes for four ; sometimes for one number of days in the week during a part of the year, for another number during the remainder. In addition to this were usually the *pro cariæ* or boon-works already referred to. Sometimes as part of, sometimes in addition to, the week-work and the boon-work, the villain was required to plough so many acres in the fall and spring; to mow, toss, and carry in the hay from so many acres; to haul and scatter so many loads of manure; carry grain to the barn or the market, build hedges, dig ditches, gather brush, weed grain, break clods, drive sheep or swine, or any other of the forms of agricultural labor as local custom on each manor had established his burdens. Combining the week-work, the regular boon-works, and the extra specified services, it will be seen that the labor required from the customary tenant was burdensome in the extreme. Taken on the average, much more than half of the ordinary villain's time must have been given in services to the lord of the manor.

The cotters made similar payments and performed similar labors, though less in amount. A widespread custom required them to work for the lord one day a week throughout the year, with certain regular payments, and certain additional special services.

Besides the possession of their land and rights of common pasture, however, there were some other compensations and alleviations of the burdens of the villains and cotters. At the boon-works and other special services performed by the tenants, it was a matter of custom that the lord of the manor provide food for one or two meals a day, and custom frequently defined the kind, amount, and value of the food for each separate meal; as where it is said in a statement of services: " It is to be known that all the above customary tenants ought to reap one day in autumn at one boon-work of wheat, and they shall have among them six bushels of wheat for their bread, baked in the manor, and broth and meat, that is to say, two men have one portion of beef and cheese, and beer for drinking. And the aforesaid customary tenants ought to work in autumn at two boon-works of oats. And they shall have six bushels of rye for their bread as described above, broth as before, and herrings, viz. six herrings for each man, and cheese as before, and water for drinking."

Thus the payments and services of the free tenants were

principally of money, and apparently not burdensome; those
of the villains were largely in corporal service and extremely
heavy; while those of the cotters were smaller, in correspondence with their smaller holdings of land and in accordance with
the necessity that they have their time in order to make their
living by earning wages.

The villains and cotters were in bondage to the lord of the
manor. This was a matter of legal status quite independent
of the amount of land which the tenant held or of the services
which he performed, though, generally speaking, the great
body of the smaller tenants and of the laborers were of servile
condition. In general usage the words *villanus, nativus, servus,
custumarius*, and *rusticus* are synonymous, and the cotters
belonged legally to the same servile class.

The distinction between free tenants and villains, using
this word, as is customary, to include all those who were legally
in servitude, was not a very clearly marked one. Their economic
position was often so similar that the classes shaded into one
another. But the villain was, as has been seen, usually burdened with much heavier services. He was subject to special
payments, such as " merchet," a payment made to the lord of
the manor when a woman of villain rank was married, and
" leyr," a payment made by women for breach of chastity.
He could be " tallaged " or taxed to any extent the lord saw fit.
He was bound to the soil. He could not leave the manor to
seek for better conditions of life elsewhere. If he ran away,
his lord could obtain an order from a court and have him brought
back. When permission was obtained to remain away from
the manor as an inhabitant of another vill or of a town, it was
only upon payment of a periodical sum, frequently known as
" chevage " or head money. He could not sell his cattle without paying the lord for permission. He had practically no
standing in the courts of the country. In any suit against
his lord the proof of his condition of villainage was sufficient
to put him out of court, and his only recourse was the local

court of the manor, where the lord himself or his representative presided. , Finally, in the eyes of the law, the villain had no property of his own, all his possessions being, in the last resort, the property of his lord. This legal theory, however, apparently had but little application to real life; for in the ordinary course of events the customary tenant, if only by custom, not by law, yet held and bequeathed to his descendants his land and his chattels quite as if they were his own.

Serfdom, as it existed in England in the thirteenth century, can hardly be defined in strict legal terms. It can be described most correctly as a condition in which the villain tenant of the manor was bound to the locality and to his services and payments there by a legal bond, instead of merely by an economic bond, as was the case with the small free tenant.

There were commonly a few persons in the vill who were not in the general body of cultivators of the land and were not therefore in the classes so far described. Since the vill was generally a parish also, the village contained the parish priest, who, though he might usually hold some acres in the open fields, and might belong to the peasant class, was of course somewhat set apart from the villagers by his education and his ordination. The mill was a valued possession of the lord of the manor, for by an almost universal custom the tenants were bound to have their grain ground there, paying the usual tolls, and this monopoly enabled the miller to pay a substantial rent to the lord while keeping enough profit for himself to become proverbially well-to-do.

There was often a blacksmith, whom we find sometimes exempted from other services on condition of keeping the demesne ploughs and other iron implements in order. A chance weaver or other craftsman is sometimes found, and when the vill was near sea or river or forest some who made their living by industries dependent on the locality. In the main, however, the whole life of the vill gathered around the arable, meadow, and pasture land, and the social position of the tenants, except for the cross division of serfdom, depended upon the respective amounts of land which they held.

11. **The Manor Courts.** — The manor was the sphere of operations of a manor court. On every manor the tenants

INTERIOR OF FOURTEENTH CENTURY MANOR HOUSE, GREAT MALVERN, WORCESTERSHIRE

(*Domestic Architecture in the Fourteenth Century.*)

gathered at frequent periods for a great amount of petty judicial and regulative work. The most usual period for the meeting of the manor court was once every three weeks, though in some manors no trace of a meeting is found more frequently than three times, or even twice, a year. In these cases, however, it is quite probable that less formal meetings occurred of which no regular record was kept. Different kinds of gatherings of the tenants are usually distinguished according to the authority under which they were held, or the class of tenants of which they were made up. If the court was held by the lord simply because of his feudal rights as a landholder, and was busied only with matters of the inheritance, transfer, or grant of lands, the fining of tenants for the breach of manorial custom, or failure to perform their duties to the lord of the manor, the election of tenants to petty offices on the manor, and such matters, it was described in legal language as a court baron. If a court so occupied was made up of villain tenants only, it was called a customary court. If, on the other hand, the court also punished general offences, petty crimes, breaches of contract, breaches of the assize, that is to say, the established standard of amount, price, or quality of bread or beer, the lord of the manor drawing his authority to hold such a court either actually or supposedly from a grant from the king, such a court was called a court leet. With the court leet was usually connected the so-called view of frank pledge. Frank pledge was an ancient system, according to which all men were obliged to be enrolled in groups, so that if any one committed an offence, the other members of the group would be obliged to produce him for trial. View of frank pledge was the right to punish by fine any who failed so to enroll themselves. In the court baron and the customary court it was said by lawyers that the body of attendants were the judges, and the steward, representing the lord of the manor, only a presiding official; while in the court leet the steward was the actual judge of the tenants. In practice, however, it is probable that not much was made of these distinctions, and that the periodic gatherings were made to do duty for all business of any kind that needed attention, while the procedure was that which had become customary on that special manor, irrespective of the particular form of authority for the court.

The manor court was presided over by a steward or other officer representing the lord of the manor. Apparently all adult male tenants were expected to be present, and any inhabitant was liable to be summoned. A court was usually held in each manor, but sometimes a lord of several neighboring manors would hold the court for all of these in some one place. As most manors belonged to lords who had many manors in their possession, the steward or other official commonly proceeded from one manor or group of manors to another, holding the courts in each. Before the close of the thirteenth century the records of the manor courts, or at least of the more important of them, began to be kept with very great regularity and fulness, and it is to the mass of these manor court rolls which still remain that we owe most of our detailed knowledge of the condition of the body of the people in the later Middle Ages. The variety and the amount of business transacted at the court were alike considerable. When a tenant had died it was in the meeting of the manor court that his successor obtained a regrant of the land. The required relief was there assessed, and the heriot from the property of the deceased recorded. New grants of land were made, and transfers, leases, and abandonments by one tenant and assignments to another announced. For each of these processes of land transfer a fine was collected for the lord of the manor. Such entries as the following are constantly found: " John of Durham has come into court and taken one bond-land which Richard Avras formerly held but gave up because of his poverty; to have and hold for his lifetime, paying and doing the accustomed services as Richard paid and did them. He gives for entrance 6s. 8d."; " Agnes Mabeley is given possession of a quarter virgate of land which her mother held, and gives the lord 33s. 4d. for entrance."

Disputes as to the right of possession of land and questions of dowry and inheritance were decided, a jury being granted in many cases by the lord at the petition of a claimant and on payment of a fee. Another class of cases consisted in the imposition of fines or amerciaments for the violation of the customs of the manor, of the rules of the lord, or of the requirements of the culprit's tenure; such as a villain marrying without leave, failure to perform boon-works or bad performance of work, failure to place the tenant's sheep in the lord's fold, cutting of wood or brush, making unlawful paths across the fields, the meadows, or the common, encroachment in ploughing upon other men's land or upon the common, or failure to send grain to the lord's mill for grinding. Sometimes the offence was of a more general nature, such as breach of assize, breach of contract, slander, assault, or injury to property. Still another part of the work of the court was the election of petty manorial officers; a reeve, a reaper, ale-tasters, and perhaps others. The duty of filling such offices when elected by the tenants and approved by the lord or his steward was, as has been said, one of the burdens of villainage. However, when a villain was fulfilling the office of reeve, it was customary for him to be relieved of at least a part of the payments and services to which he would otherwise be subject. Finally the manor court meetings were employed for the adoption of general regulations as to the use of the commons and other joint interests, and for the announcement of the orders of the steward in the keeping of the peace.

12. The Manor as an Estate of a Lord. — The manor was profitable to the lord in various ways. He received rents in money and kind. These included the rents of assize from free and villain land tenants, rent from the tenant of the mill, and frequently from other sources. Then came the profits derived from the cultivation of the demesne land. In this the lord of the manor was simply a large farmer, except that he had a supply of labor bound to remain at hand and to give service without wages almost up to his needs. Finally there were the profits of the manor courts. As has been seen, these consisted of a great variety of fees, fines, amerciaments, and collections made by the steward or other official. Such varied payments and profits combined to make up the total value of the manor to the landowner. Not only the slender income of the country squire or knight whose estate consisted of a single manor of some ten or twenty pounds yearly value, but the vast wealth of the great noble or of the rich monastery or powerful bishopric was principally made up of the sum of such payments from a considerable number of manors. An appreciable part of the income of the government even was derived from the manors still in the possession of the crown.

The mediæval manor was a little world in itself. The large number of scattered acres which made up the demesne farm cultivated in the interests of the lord of the manor, the small groups of scattered strips held by free holders or villain tenants who furnished most of the labor on the demesne farm, the little patches of ground held by mere laborers whose living was mainly gained by hired service on the land of the lord or of more prosperous tenants, the claims which all had to the use of the common pasture for their sheep and cattle and of the woods for their swine, all these together made up an agricultural system which secured a revenue for the lord, provided food and the raw material for primitive manufactures for the inhabitants of the vill, and furnished some small surplus which could be sold.

Life on the mediæval manor was hard. The greater part of the population was subject to the burdens of serfdom, and all, both free and serf, shared in the arduousness of labor, coarseness and lack of variety of food, unsanitary surroundings, and liability to the rigor of winter and the attacks of pestilence. Yet the average condition of comfort of the mass of the rural inhabitants of England was probably as high as at any subsequent time. Food in proportion to wages was very cheap, and the almost universal possession of some land made it possible for the very poorest to avoid starvation. Moreover, the great extent to which custom governed all payments, services, and rights must have prevented much of the extreme suffering which has occasionally existed in subsequent periods in which greater competition has distinguished more clearly the capable from the incompetent. The habit of living in a close village must also have given much opportunity for sociability, and it freed country life from the loneliness which has characterized it in some other times and places.

From the social rather than from the economic point of view the life of the mediæval manor was perhaps most clearly marked by this predominance of custom and by a second characteristic nearly related. This was the singularly close relationship in which all the inhabitants of the manor were bound to one another, and their correspondingly complete separation from the outside world. The common pasture, the intermingled strips of the holdings in the open fields, the necessary coöperation in the performance of their daily labor on the demesne land, the close contiguity of their dwellings, their universal membership in the same parish church, their common attendance and action in the manor courts, all must have combined to make the vill an organization of singular unity. This self-centred life, economically, judicially, and ecclesiastically so nearly independent of other bodies, put obstacles in the way of change. It prohibited intercourse beyond the manor, and opposed the growth of a feeling of common national life. The manorial life lay at the base of the stability which marked the mediæval period.

13. BIBLIOGRAPHY

GENERAL WORKS

Certain general works which refer to long periods of economic history will be mentioned here and not again referred to, excepting in special cases. It is to be understood that they contain valuable matter on the subject, not only of this, but of succeeding chapters. They should therefore be consulted in addition to the more specific works named under each chapter.

Cunningham, William: *Growth of English Industry and Commerce,* two volumes. The most extensive and valuable work that covers the whole field of English economic history.

Ashley, W. J.: *English Economic History,* two volumes. The first volume is a full and careful analysis of mediæval economic conditions, with detailed notes and references to the primary sources. The second volume is a work of original investigation, referring particularly to conditions in the fifteenth and sixteenth centuries, but it does not give such a clear analysis of the conditions of its period as the first volume.

Lipson, E.: *Economic History of England,* Vol. I. *The Middle Ages.*

Traill, H. D.: *Social England,* six volumes. A composite work including a great variety of subjects, but seldom having the most satisfactory account of any one of them.

Rogers, J. E. T.: *History of Agriculture and Prices; Six Centuries of Work and Wages; Economic Interpretation of History.* Professor Rogers' work is very extensive and detailed, and his books were largely pioneer studies. His statistical and other facts are useful, but his general statements are not very valuable, and his conclusions are not convincing.

Palgrave, R. H. I.: *Dictionary of Political Economy.* Many of the articles on subjects of economic history are the best and most recent studies on their respective subjects, and the bibliographies contained in them are especially valuable.

Several single-volume text-books have been published on this general subject. Among them are: —

Usher, A. P.: *Industrial History of England.*

Cunningham, William, and McArthur, E. A.: *Outlines of English Industrial History.*

Gibbins, H. de B.: *Industry in England.*

Warner, George Townsend: *Landmarks in English Industrial History.*

Price, L. L.: *A Short History of English Commerce and Industry.*

Ashley, W. J.: *The Economic Organization of England*.
Innes, A. D.: *England's Industrial Development*.

SPECIAL WORKS

Seebohm, Frederic: *The English Village Community*. Although written for another purpose, — to suggest a certain view of the origin of the mediæval manor, — the first five chapters of this book furnish the clearest existing descriptive account of the fundamental facts of rural life in the thirteenth century. Its publication marked an era in the recognition of the main features of manorial organization. Green, for instance, the historian of the English people, seems to have had no clear conception of many of those characteristics of ordinary rural life which Mr. Seebohm has made familiar.

Gray, H. L.: *English Field Systems*.

Vinogradoff, Paul: *Villainage in England, English Society in the Eleventh Century*.

Pollock, Sir Frederick, and Maitland, F. W.: *History of English Law*, Vol. I.

Maitland, F. W.: *Domesday Book and Beyond*.

These three works are of especial value for the organization of the manor courts and the legal condition of the population.

SOURCES

Much that can be explained only with great difficulty becomes clear to the student immediately when he reads the original documents. Concrete illustrations of general statements, moreover, make the work more interesting and real. It has therefore been found desirable by many teachers to bring their students into contact with at least a few typical illustrative documents. The sources for the subject generally are given in the works named above. A full and admirable bibliography has been published by Gross, Charles: *The Sources and Literature of English History from the Earliest Times to about 1485*. References to abundant material for the illustration or further investigation of the subject of this chapter will be found in the following pamphlet : —

Davenport, Frances G. : *A Classified List of Printed Original Materials for English Manorial and Agrarian History.*

Sources for the mediæval period are almost all in Latin or French. Some of them, however, have been made more accessible by being translated into English and reprinted in convenient form. A few of these are given in E. P. Cheyney : *Readings in English History;* C. W. Colby : *Selections from the Sources of English History;* and G. C. Lee : *Source Book of English History.*

In the series of *Translations and Reprints from the Original Sources of European History*, published by the Department of History of the University of Pennsylvania, several numbers include documents in this field. Vol. III, No. 5, is devoted entirely to manorial documents.

DISCUSSIONS OF THE ORIGIN OF THE MANOR

The question of the origin of the mediæval manorial organization, whether it is principally of native English or of Roman origin, or hewn from still other materials, although not treated in this text-book, has been the subject of much interest and discussion. One view of the case is the thesis of Seebohm's book, referred to above. Other books treating of it are the following : —

Earle, John : *Land Charters and Saxonic Documents*, Introduction.

Gomme, G. L. : *The Village Community.*

Ashley, W. J. : A translation of Fustel de Coulanges, *Origin of Property in Land*, Introduction.

Andrews, Charles M. : *The Old English Manor*, Introduction.

Maitland, F. W. : *Domesday Book and Beyond.*

Meitzen, August : *Siedelung und Agrarwesen*, Vol. II, Chap. 7.

The writings of Kemble and of Sir Henry Maine belong rather to a past period of study and speculation, but their ideas still lie at the base of discussions on the subject.

E

CHAPTER III

TOWN LIFE AND ORGANIZATION

14. The Town Government. — In the middle of the thirteenth century there were some two hundred towns in England distinguishable by their size, form of government, and the occupations of their inhabitants, from the rural agricultural villages which have just been described. London probably had more than 25,000 inhabitants; York and Bristol may each have had as many as 10,000. The population of the others varied from as many as 6000 to less than 1000. Perhaps the most usual population of an English mediæval town lay between 1500 and 4000. They were mostly walled, though such protection was hardly necessary, and the military element in English towns was therefore but slightly developed. Those towns which contained cathedrals, and were therefore the seats of bishoprics, were called cities. All other organized towns were known as boroughs, though this distinction in the use of the terms city and borough was by no means always preserved. The towns differed widely in their form of government; but all had charters from the king or from some nobleman, abbey, or bishopric on whose lands they had grown up. Such a charter usually declared the right of the town to preserve the ancient customs which had come to be recognized among its inhabitants, and granted to it certain privileges, exemptions, and rights of self-government. The most universal and important of these privileges were the following: the town paid the tolls and dues owed to the king or other lord by its inhabitants in a lump sum, collecting the amount from its own citizens as the latter or their own authorities saw fit; the town courts had jurisdiction over most suits and offences, relieving the townsmen frcm answering at hundred and county court suits which concerned matters within their own limits; the townsmen, where the king granted the charter, were exempt from the payment of tolls of various kinds throughout his dominions; they could pass ordinances and regulations controlling the trade of the town the administration of its property, and its internal affairs generally, and could elect officials to carry out such regulations. These officials also corresponded and negotiated in the name of the town with the authorities of other towns and with the government. From the close of the thirteenth century all towns of any importance were represented in Parliament. These elements of independence were not all possessed by every town, and some had special privileges not enumerated in the above list. The first charter of a town was apt to be vague and inadequate, but from time to time a new charter was obtained giving additional privileges and defining the old rights more clearly. Nor had all those who dwelt within the town limits equal participation in its advantages. These were usually restricted to those who were known as citizens or burgesses; full citizenship depending primarily on the possession of a house and land within the town limits. In addition to the burgesses there were usually some inhabitants·of the town— strangers, Jews, fugitive villains from the rural villages, or perhaps only poorer natives of the town—who did not share in these privileges. Those who did possess all civil rights of the townsmen were in many ways superior in condition to men in the country. In addition to the advantages of the municipal organization mentioned above, all burgesses were personally free, there was entire exemption from the vexatious petty payments of the rural manors, and burgage tenure was the nearest to actual land ownership existent during the Middle Ages.

15. The Gild Merchant. — The town was most clearly marked off from the country by the occupations by which its people earned their living. These were, in the first place, trading; secondly, manufacturing or handicrafts. Agriculture of course existed also, since most townsmen possessed some lands lying outside of the enclosed portions of the town. On these they raised crops and pastured their cattle. Of these varied occupations, however, it was trade which gave character and, indeed, existence itself to the town. Foreign goods were brought to the towns from abroad for sale, the surplus products of rural manors found their way there for marketing; the products of one part of the country which were needed in other parts were sought for and purchased in the towns. Men also sold the products of their own labor, not only food products, such as bread, meat, and fish, but also objects of manufacture, as cloth, arms, leather, and goods made of wood, leather, or metal. For the protection and regulation of this trade the organization known as the gild merchant had grown up in each town. The gild merchant seems to have included all of the population of the town who habitually engaged in the business of selling, whether commodities of their own manufacture or those they had previously purchased. Membership in the gild was not exactly coincident with burgess-ship; persons who lived outside of the town were sometimes admitted into that organization, and, on the other hand, some inhabitants of the town were not included among its members. Nevertheless, since practically all of the townsmen made their living by trade in some form or another, the group of burgesses and the group of gild members could not have been very different. The authority of the gild merchant within its field of trade regulations seems to have been as complete as that of the town community as a whole in its field of judicial, financial, and administrative jurisdiction. The gild might therefore be defined as that form of organization of the inhabitants of the town which controlled its trade and industry. The principal reason for the existence of the gild was to preserve to its own members the monopoly of trade. No one not in the gild merchant of the town could buy or sell there except under conditions imposed by the gild. Foreigners coming from other countries or traders from other English towns were prohibited from buying or selling in any way that might interfere with the interest of the gildsmen. They must buy and sell at such times and in such places and only such articles as were provided for by the gild regulations. They must in all cases pay the town tolls, from which members of the gild were exempt. At Southampton, for instance, we find the following provisions: "And no one in the city of Southampton shall buy anything to sell again in the same city unless he is of the gild merchant or of the franchise." Similarly at Leicester, in 1260, it was ordained that no gildsman should form a partnership with a stranger, allowing him to join in the profits of the sale of wool or other merchandise.

As against outsiders the gild merchant was a protective body, as regards its own members it was looked upon and constantly spoken of as a fraternity. Its members must all share in the common expenditures, they are called brethren of the society, their competition with one another is reduced to its lowest limits. For instance, we find the provision that "any one who is of the gild merchant may share in all merchandise which another gildsman shall buy."

The presiding officer was usually known as the alderman, while the names given to other officials, such as stewards, deans, bailiffs, chaplains, skevins, and ushers, and the duties they performed, varied greatly from place to place.

Meetings were held at different periods, sometimes annually, in many cases more frequently. At these meetings new ordinances were passed, officers elected, and other business transacted. It was also a convivial occasion, a gild feast preceding or following the other labors of the meeting. In some gilds the meeting was regularly known as "the drinking." There were likewise frequent sittings of the officials of the fraternity, devoted to the decision of disputes between brethren, the admission of new members, the fining or expulsion of offenders against the gild ordinances, and other routine work. These meetings were known as "morrowspeches."

The great part of the activity of the gild merchant consisted in the holding of its meetings with their accompanying feasts, and in the enforcement of its regulations upon its members and upon outsiders. It fulfilled, however, many fraternal duties for its members. It is provided in one set of statutes that, "If a gildsman be imprisoned in England in time of peace, the alderman, with the steward and with one of the skevins, shall go, at the cost of the gild, to procure the deliverance of the one who is in prison." In another, "If any of the brethren shall fall into poverty or misery, all the brethren are to assist him by common consent out of the chattels of the house or fraternity, or of their proper own." The funeral rites, especially, were attended by the man's gild brethren. "And when a gildsman dies, all those who are of the gild and are in the city shall attend the service for the dead, and gildsmen shall bear the body and bring it to the place of burial." The gild merchant also sometimes fulfilled various religious, philanthropic, and charitable duties, not only to its members, but to the public generally, and to the poor. The time of the fullest development of the gild merchant varied, of course, in different towns, but its widest expansion was probably in the early part of the period we are studying, that is, during the thirteenth century. Later it came to be in some towns indistinguishable from the municipal government in general, its members the same as the burgesses, its officers represented by the officers of the town. In some other towns the gild merchant gradually lost its control over trade, retaining only its fraternal, charitable, and religious features. In all other cases the expression gradually lost all definite significance and its meaning became a matter for antiquarian dispute.

16. The Craft Gilds. — By the fourteenth century the gild merchant of the town was a much less conspicuous institution than it had previously been. Its decay was largely the result of the growth of a group of organizations in each town which were spoken of as crafts, fraternities, gilds, misteries, or often merely by the name of their occupation, as "the spurriers,"

" the dyers," "the fishmongers." These organizations are usually described in later writings as craft gilds. It is not to be understood that the gild merchant and the craft gilds never existed contemporaneously in any town. The former began earlier and decayed before the craft gilds reached their height, but there was a considerable period when it must have been a common thing for a man to be a member both of the gild merchant of the town and of the separate organization of his own trade. The later gilds seem to have grown up in response to the needs of handicraft much as the gild merchant had grown up to regulate trade, though trading occupations also were eventually drawn into the craft gild form of organization. The weavers seem to have been the earliest occupation to be organized into a craft gild; but later almost every form of industry which gave employment to a handful of craftsmen in any town had its separate fraternity. Since even nearly allied trades, such as the glovers, girdlers, pocket makers, skinners, white tawyers, and other workers in leather; or the fletchers, the makers of arrows, the bowyers, the makers of bows, and the stringers, the makers of bowstrings, were organized into separate bodies, the number of craft gilds in any one town was often very large. At London there were by 1350 at least as many as forty, at York, some time later, more than fifty.

The craft gilds existed usually under the authority of the town government, though frequently they obtained authorization or even a charter from the crown. They were formed primarily to regulate and preserve the monopoly of their own occupations in their own town, just as the gild merchant existed to regulate the trade of the town in general. No one could carry on any trade without being subject to the organization which controlled that trade. Membership, however, was not intentionally restricted. Any man who was a capable workman and conformed to the rules of the craft was practically a member of the organization of that industry. It is a common requirement in the earliest gild statutes that every man who wishes to carry on that

particular industry should have his ability testified to by some
known members of the craft.   But usually full membership and
influence in the gild was reached as a matter of course by the
artisans passing through the successive grades of apprentice,
journeyman, and master.   As an apprentice he was bound to a
master for a number of years, living in his house and learning
the trade in his shop.   There was usually a signed contract
entered into between the master and the parents of the apprentice, by which the former agreed to provide all necessary
clothing, food, and lodging, and teach to the apprentice all he
himself knew about his craft.   The latter, on the other hand,
was bound to keep secret his master's affairs, to obey all his
commandments, and to behave himself properly in all things.
After the expiration of the time agreed upon for his apprenticeship, which varied much in individual cases, but was apt to be
about seven years, he became free of the trade as a journeyman,
a full workman.   The word " journeyman " may refer to the
engagement being by the day, from the French word *journée*,
or to the habit of making journeys from town to town in search
of work, or it may be derived from some other origin.   As a
journeyman he served for wages in the employ of a master.   In
many cases he saved enough money for the small requirements of
setting up an independent shop.   Then as full master artisan
or tradesman he might take part in all the meetings and general
administration of the organized body of his craft, might hold
office, and would himself probably have one or more journeymen
in his employ and apprentices under his guardianship.   As
almost all industries were carried on in the dwelling-houses of
the craftsmen, no establishments could be of very considerable
size, and the difference of position between master, journeyman,
and apprentice could not have been great.   The craft gild was
organized with its regular rules, its officers, and its meetings.
The rules or ordinances of the fraternity were drawn up at some
one time and added to or altered from time to time afterward.
The approval of the city authorities was frequently sought for

such new statutes as well as for the original ordinances, and in many towns appears to have been necessary. The rules provided for officers and their powers, the time and character of meetings, and for a considerable variety of functions. These varied, of course, in different trades and in different towns, but some characteristics were almost universal. Provisions were always either tacitly or formally included for the preservation of the monopoly of the crafts in the town. The hours of labor were regulated. Night work was very generally prohibited, apparently because of the difficulty of oversight at that time, as was work on Saturday afternoons, Sundays, and other holy days. Provisions were made for the inspection of goods by the officers of the gild, all workshops and goods for sale being constantly subject to their examination, if they should wish it. In those occupations that involved buying and selling the necessities of life, such as those of the fishmongers and the bakers, the officers of the fraternity, like the town authorities, were engaged in a continual struggle with "regrators," "forestallers," and "engrossers," which were appellations as odious as they were common in the mediæval town. Regrating meant buying to sell again at a higher price without having made any addition to the value of the goods; forestalling was going to the place of production to buy, or in any other way trying to outwit fellow-dealers by purchasing things before they came into the open market where all had the same opportunity; engrossing was buying up the whole supply, or so much of it as not to allow other dealers to get what they needed, the modern "cornering of the market." These frequent practices, which were so objectionable in the eyes of mediæval traders, were frequently nothing more than what would be considered commendable enterprise in a more competitive age. Another class of rules was for mutual assistance, for kindliness among members, and for the obedience and faithfulness of journeymen and apprentices. There were provisions for assistance to members of the craft when in need, or to their widows and orphans, for the visitation of those sick or in prison, for common attendance at the burial services of deceased members, and for other charitable and philanthropic objects. Thus the craft gild, like the gild merchant, combined close social relationship with a distinctly recognized and enforced regulation of the trade. This regulation provided for the protection of members of the organization from outside competition, and it also prevented any considerable amount of competition among members; it supported the interests of the full master members of the craft as against those in the journeyman stage, and enforced the custom of the trade in hours, materials, methods of manufacture, and often in prices.

The officers were usually known as masters, wardens, or stewards. Their powers extended to the preservation of order among the master members of the craft at the meetings, and among the journeymen and apprentices of the craft at all times; to the supervision, either directly or through deputies, of the work of the members, seeing that it conformed to the rules and was not false in any way; to the settlement, if possible, of disputes among members of the craft; to the administration of its charitable work; and to the representation of the organized body of the craft before town or other authorities.

Common religious observances were held by the craftsmen not only at the funerals of members, but on the day of the saint to which the gild was especially dedicated. Most fraternities kept up a shrine or chapel in some parish church. Fines for the breach of gild rules were often ordered to be paid in wax that the candles about the body of dead brethren and in the gild chapel should never be wanting. All the brethren of the gild, dressed in common suits of livery, walked in procession from their hall or meeting room to the church, performed their devotions, and joined in the services in commemoration of the dead. Members of the craft frequently bequeathed property for the partial support of a chaplain and payment of other expenses connected with their " obits," or masses for the repose of their souls and those of their relatives.

Closely connected with the religious observances was the convivial side of the gild's life. On the annual gild day, or more frequently, the members all gathered at their hall or some inn to a feast, which varied in luxuriousness according to the wealth of the fraternity, from bread, cheese, and ale to all the exuberance of which the Middle Ages were capable.

Somewhat later, we find the craft gilds taking entire charge of the series or cycles of " mystery plays," which were given in various towns. The words of the plays produced at York, Coventry, Chester, and Woodkirk have come down to us and are of extreme interest as embryonic forms of the drama and examples of purely vernacular language. It is quite certain that such groups of plays were given by the crafts in a number of other towns. They were generally given on Corpus Christi day, a feast which fell in the early summer time, when out-door pleasures were again enjoyable after the winter's confinement. A cycle consisted of a series of dialogues or short plays, each based upon some scene of biblical story, so arranged that the whole Bible narrative should be given consecutively from the Creation to the Second Advent. One of the crafts, starting early in the morning, would draw a pageant, consisting of a platform on wheels, to a regularly appointed spot in a conspicuous part of the town, and on this platform, with some rude scenery, certain members of the gild or men employed by them would proceed to recite a dialogue in verse representative of some early part of the Bible story. After they had finished, their pageant would be dragged to another station, where they repeated their performance. In the meantime a second company had taken their former place, and recited a dialogue representative of a second scene. So the whole day would be occupied by the series of performances. The town and the craftsmen valued the celebration because it was an occasion for strangers visiting their city and thus increasing the volume of trade, as well as because it furnished an opportunity for the gratification of their social and dramatic instincts.

It was not only at the periodical business meetings, or on the feast days, or in the preparation for the dramatic shows, that the gildsmen were thrown together. Usually all the members of one craft lived on the same street or in the same part of the town, and were therefore members of the same parish church and constantly brought under one another's observation in all the daily concerns of life. All things combined to make the craft a natural and necessary centre for the interest of each of its members.

17. Non-industrial Gilds. — Besides the gild merchant, which included persons of all industrial occupations, and the craft gilds, which were based upon separate organizations of each industry, there were gilds or fraternities in existence which had no industrial functions whatever. These are usually spoken of as "religious" or "social" gilds. It would perhaps be better to describe them simply as non-industrial gilds; for their religious and social functions they had in common, as has been seen, both with the gild merchant and the craft organizations. They only differed from these in not being based upon or interested in the monopoly or oversight of any kind of trade or handicraft. They differed also from the craft gilds in that all their members were on an equal basis, there being no such industrial grades as apprentice, journeyman, and master; and from both of the organizations already discussed in the fact that they existed in small towns and even in mere villages, as well as in industrial centres.

In these associations the religious, social, and charitable elements were naturally more prominent than in those fraternities which were organized primarily for some kind of economic regulation. They were generally named after some saint. The ordinances usually provided for one or more solemn services in the year, frequently with a procession in livery, and sometimes with a considerable amount of pantomime or symbolic show. For instance, the gild of St. Helen at Beverly, in their procession to the church of the Friars Minors on the day of their patron saint, were preceded by an old man carrying a cross; after him a fair young man dressed as St. Helen; then another old man carrying a shovel, these being intended to typify the finding of the cross. Next came the sisters, two and two, after them the brethren of the gild, and finally the officers. There were always provisions for solemnities at the funerals of members, for burial at the expense of the gild if the member who had died left no means for a suitable ceremony, and for prayers for deceased members. What might be called the insurance feature was also much more nearly universal than in the case of the industrial fraternities. Help was given in case of theft, fire, sickness, or almost any kind of loss which was not chargeable to the member's own misdoing. Finally it was very customary for such gilds to provide for the support of a certain number of dependents, aged men or women, cripples, or lepers, for charity's sake; and occasionally educational facilities were also provided by them from their regular income or from bequests made for the purpose. The social-religious gilds were extremely numerous, and seem frequently to have existed within the limits of a craft, including some of its members and not others, or within a certain parish, including some of the parishioners, but not all.

Thus if there were men in the mediæval town who were not members of some trading or craft body, they would in all probability be members of some society based merely on religious or social feeling. The whole tendency of mediæval society was toward organization, combination, close union with one's fellows. It might be said that all town life involved membership in some organization, and usually in that one into which a man was drawn by the occupation in which he made his living. These gilds or the town government itself controlled even the affairs of private economic life in the city, just as the customary agriculture of the country prevented much freedom of action there. Methods of trading, or manufacture, the kind and amount of material to be used, hours of labor, conditions of employment, even prices of work, were regulated by the gild ordinances.   The individual gildsman had as little opportunity to emancipate himself from the controlling force of the association as the individual tenant on the rural manor had to free himself from the customary agriculture and the customary services. Whether we study rural or urban society, whether we look at the purely economic or at the broader social side of existence, life in the thirteenth and fourteenth centuries was corporate rather than individual.

18. BIBLIOGRAPHY

Gross, Charles: *The Gild Merchant,* two volumes.   The first volume consists of a full account and discussion of the character and functions of the gild merchant, with a number of appendices on cognate subjects.   The second volume contains the documents on which the first is based.

Seligman, E. R. A.: *Two Chapters on Mediæval Gilds.*

Unwin, G.: *The Guilds and Companies of London.*

Brentano, L.: *The History and Development of English Gilds.*   An essay prefixed to a volume of ordinances of English Gilds, edited by T. Smith.   Brentano's essay is only referred to because of the paucity of works on the subject, as it is fanciful and unsatisfactory.   No thorough and scholarly description of the craft gilds exists.   On the other hand, a considerable body of original materials is easily accessible in English, as in the following works: —

Riley: *Memorials of London and London Life.*

Smith, Toulmin: *English Gilds.*

Various documents illustrative of town and gild history will also be found in Vol. II, No. 1, of the *Translations and Reprints,* published by the Department of History of the University of Pennsylvania.

Better descriptions exist for the position of the gilds in special towns than for their general character, especially in London by Herbert, in Hull by Lambert, in Shrewsbury by Hibbert, and in Coventry by Miss Harris.

CHAPTER IV

MEDIÆVAL TRADE AND COMMERCE

19. Markets and Fairs. — Within the towns, in addition to the ordinary trading described in the last chapter, much buying and selling was done at the weekly or semi-weekly markets. The existence of a market in a town was the result of a special grant from the king, sometimes to the burgesses themselves, sometimes to a neighboring nobleman or abbey. In the latter case the tolls paid by outsiders who bought or sold cattle or victuals in the markets did not go to the town or gild authorities, but to the person who was said to " own " the market. Many places which differed in scarcely any other way from agricultural villages possessed markets, so that " market towns " became a descriptive term for small towns midway in size between the larger boroughs or cities and mere villages. The sales at markets were usually of the products of the surrounding country, especially of articles of food consumption, so that the fact of the existence of a market on one or more days of the week in a large town was of comparatively little importance from the point of view of more general trade.

Far more important was the similar institution of periodical fairs. Fairs, like markets, existed only by grant from the king. They differed from markets, however, in being held only once a year or at most semi-annually or quarterly, in being invariably in the possession of private persons, never of town governments, and in the fact that during their continuance as a rule all buying and selling except at the fairs was suspended within a considerable circuit. Several hundred grants of fairs are recorded on the rolls of royal charters, most of them to abbeys, bishoprics, and noblemen; but comparatively few of them were of sufficient size or importance to play any considerable part in the trade and commerce of the country. Moreover, the development of the towns with their continuous trade tended to draw custom away from all the fairs except those which had obtained some especial importance and an international reputation. Of these, however, there was still a considerable number whose influence was very great. The best known were those of Winchester, of Stourbridge near Cambridge, of St. Ives belonging to the abbot of Ramsay, and of Boston. In early times fairs were frequently held in the churchyards, but this came to be looked upon as a scandal, and was prohibited by a law of 1285. The fairs were in many cases held just beyond the limits of a town in an open field or on a smooth hillside. Each year, some time before the opening day of the fair, this ground was formally occupied by the servants of the owner of the fair, wooden booths were erected or ground set apart for those who should put up their own tents or prefer to sell in the open. Then as merchants appeared from foreign or English towns they chose or were assigned places which they were bound to retain during the continuance of the fair. By the time of the opening of the fair those who expected to sell were arranged in long rows or groups, according to the places they came from, or the kind of goods in which they dealt. After the opening had been proclaimed no merchant of the near-by town could buy or sell, except within the borders of the fair. The town authorities resigned their functions into the hands of the officials whom the lord of the fair had placed in charge of it, and for the time for which the fair was held, usually from six to twelve days, everything within the enclosure of the fair, within the town, and in the surrounding neighborhood was under their control.

Tolls were collected for the advantage of the lord of the fair from all goods as they were brought into or taken out from the bounds of the fair, or at the time of their sale; stallage was paid for the rent of booths, fees were charged for the

LOCATION OF SOME

OF THE

PRINCIPAL FAIRS

IN THE

THIRTEENTH CENTURY

SCALE OF MILES

0   20   40   60   80   100

ENGRAVED BY BORMAY & CO., N.Y.

use of space, and for using the lord's weights and scales. Good order was preserved and fair dealing enforced by the officials of the lord. To prevent offences and settle disputes arising in the midst of the busy trading the officials of the lord formed a court which sat continually and followed a summary procedure. This was known as a court of " pie-powder," that is *pied poudré*, or *dusty foot*, so called, no doubt, from its readiness to hear the suits of merchants and wayfarers, as they were, without formality or delay. At this court a great variety of cases came up, such as disputes as to debts, failure to perform contracts of sale or purchase, false measurements, theft, assault, defamation, and misdemeanors of all kinds. Sometimes the court decided offhand, sometimes compurgation was allowed immediately or on the next day, sometimes juries were formed and gave decisions. The law which the court of pie-powder administered was often referred to as the " law merchant," a somewhat less rigid system than the common law, and one whose rules were generally defined, in these courts and in the king's courts, by juries chosen from among the merchants themselves.

At these fairs, even more than in the towns, merchants from a distance gathered to buy the products peculiar to the part of England where the fair was held, and to sell their own articles of importation or production. The large fairs furnished by far the best markets of the time. We find mention made in the records of one court of pie-powder of men from a dozen or twenty English towns, from Bordeaux, and from Rouen. The men who came from any one town, whether of England or the Continent, acted and were treated as common members of the gild merchant of that town, as forming a sort of community, and being to a certain extent responsible for one another. They did their buying and selling, it is true, separately, but if disputes arose, the whole group were held responsible for each member. For example, the following entry was made in the roll of the fair of St. Ives in the year 1275 : " William of Fleetbridge and Anne his wife complain of Thomas Coventry of Leicester for unjustly withholding from them 55*s*. 2½*d*. for a sack of wool. . . . Elias is ordered to attach the community of Leicester to answer . . . and of the said community Allan Parker, Adam Nose and Robert Howell are attached by three bundles of ox-hides, three hundred bundles of sheep skins and six sacks of wool."

20. Trade Relations between Towns. — The fairs were only temporary selling places. When the time for which the fair was held had expired the booths were removed, the merchants returned to their native cities or travelled away to some other fair, and the officials were withdrawn. The place was deserted until the next quarter or year. But in the towns, as has been already stated, more or less continuous trade went on; not only petty retail trade and that of the weekly or semi-weekly markets between townsmen or countrymen coming from the immediate vicinity, but a wholesale trade between the merchants of that town and those from other towns in England or on the Continent.

It was of this trade above all that the gild merchant of each town possessed the regulation. Merchants from another town were treated much the same, whether that town was English or foreign. In fact, " foreigner " or " alien," as used in the town records, of Bristol, for instance, may apply to citizens of London or Oxford just as well as to those of Paris or Cologne. Such " foreign " merchants could deal when they came to a town only with members of the gild, and only on the conditions required by the gild. Usually they could buy or sell only at wholesale, and tolls were collected from them upon their sales or purchases. They were prohibited from dealing in some kinds of articles altogether, and frequently the duration of their stay in the town was limited to a prescribed period. Under such circumstances the authorities of various towns entered into trade agreements with those of other towns providing for mutual concessions and advantages. Correspondence was also constantly going on between the officials of various towns for the settlement of individual points of dispute, for the return of fugitive apprentices, asking that justice might be done to aggrieved citizens, and on occasion threatening reprisal. Southampton had formal agreements with more than seventy towns or other trading bodies. During a period of twenty years the city authorities of London sent more than 300 letters on such matters to the officials of some 90 other towns in England and towns on the Continent. The merchants from any one town did not therefore trade or act entirely as separate individuals, but depended on the prestige of their town, or the support of the home authorities, or the privileges already agreed upon by treaty. The non-payment of a debt by a merchant of one town usually made any fellow-townsman liable to seizure where the debt was owed, until the debtor could be made to pay. In 1285, by a law of Edward I, this was prohibited as far as England was concerned, but a merchant from a French town might still have his person and property seized for a debt of which he may have had no previous knowledge. External trade was thus not so much individual, between some Englishmen and others; or international, between Englishmen and Frenchmen, Flemings, Spaniards, or Germans, as it was intermunicipal, as it has been well described. Citizens of various towns, London, Bristol, Venice, Ghent, Arras, or Lubeck, for instance, carried on their trade under the protection their city had obtained for them.

21. Foreign Trading Relations. — The regulations and restrictions of fairs and town markets and gilds merchant must have tended largely to the discouragement of foreign trade. Indeed, the feeling of the body of English town merchants was one of strong dislike to foreigners and a desire to restrict their trade within the narrowest limits. In addition to the burdens and limitations placed upon all traders not of their own town, it was very common in the case of merchants from abroad to require that they should only remain within the town for the purpose of selling for forty days, and that they should board not at an inn but in the household of some town merchant, who could thus keep oversight of their movements, and who would be held responsible if his guests violated the law in any way. This was called the custom of " hostage."

The king, on the other hand, and the classes most influential in the national government, the nobility and the churchmen, favored foreign trade. A series of privileges, guarantees, and concessions were consequently issued by the government to individual foreign merchants, to foreign towns, and even to foreigners generally, the object of which was to encourage their coming to England to trade. The most remarkable instance of this was the so-called *Carta Mercatoria* issued by Edward I in 1303. It was given, according to its own terms, for the peace and security of merchants coming to England from Germany, France, Spain, Portugal, Navarre, Lombardy, Tuscany, Provence, Catalonia, Aquitaine, Toulouse, Quercy, Flanders, Brabant, and all other foreign lands. It allowed such merchants to bring in and sell almost all kinds of goods, and freed them from the payment of many tolls and payments habitually exacted by the towns; it gave them permission to sell to strangers as well as to townsmen, and to retail as well as sell by wholesale. It freed them from the necessity of dwelling with native merchants, and of bringing their stay to a close within a restricted time. Town and market authorities were required by it to give prompt justice to foreigners according to the law merchant, and it was promised that a royal judge would be specially appointed to listen to appeals. It is quite evident that if this charter had been enforced some of the most familiar and valued customs of the merchants of the various English towns would have been abrogated. In consequence of vigorous protests and bitter resistance on the part of the townsmen its provisions were partly withdrawn, partly ignored, and the position of foreign merchants in England continued to depend on the tolerably consistent support of the crown. Even this was modified by the steady policy of hostility, limitation, and control on the part of the native merchants.

With the exception of some intercourse between the northern towns and the Scandinavian countries, the foreign trade of England was carried on almost entirely by foreigners. English merchants, until after the fourteenth century, seem to have had neither the ability, the enterprise, nor the capital to go to continental cities in any numbers to sell the products of their own country or to buy goods which would be in demand when imported into England. Foreigners were more enterprising. From Flemish, French, German, Italian, and even Spanish cities merchants came over as traders. The product of England which was most in demand was wool. Certain parts of England were famous throughout all Europe for the quality and quantity of the wool raised there. The relative good order of England and its exemption from civil war made it possible to raise sheep more extensively than in countries where foraging parties from rival bodies of troops passed frequently to and fro. Many of the monasteries, especially in the north and west, had large outlying wastes of land which were regularly used for the raising of sheep. The product of these northern and western pastures as well as the surplus product of the demesnes and larger holdings of the ordinary manors was brought to the fairs and towns for sale and bought up readily by foreign merchants. Sheepskins, hides, and tanned leather were also exported, as were certain coarse woven fabrics. Tin and lead were well-known products, at that time almost peculiar to England, and in years of plentiful production, grain, salt meat, and dairy products were exported. England was far behind most of the Continent in industrial matters, so that there was much that could be brought into the country that would be in demand, both of the natural productions of foreign countries and of their manufactured articles.

Trade relations existed between England and the Scandinavian countries, northern Germany, southern Germany, the Netherlands, northeastern, northwestern, and southern France, Spain and Portugal, and various parts of Italy. Of these lines of trade the most important were the trade with the Hanse cities of northern Germany, with the Flemish cities, and with those in Italy, especially Venice.

22. The Italian and Eastern Trade. — The merchandise which Venice had to offer was of an especially varied nature. Her prosperity had begun with a coastwise trade along the shores of the Adriatic. Later, especially during the period of the Crusades, her trading had been extended to the eastern Mediterranean, where she obtained trading concessions from the Greek Emperor and formed a half commercial, half political empire of her own among the island cities and coast districts of the Ionian Sea, along the Dardanelles and the Sea of Marmora, and finally in the Black Sea. From these regions she brought the productions peculiar to the eastern Mediterranean: wines, sugar, dried fruits and nuts, cotton, drugs, dyestuffs, and certain kinds of leather and other manufactured articles.

Eventually Venice became the special possessor of a still more distant trade, that of the far East. The products of Arabia and Persia, India and the East Indian Islands, and even of China, all through the Middle Ages, as in antiquity, made their way by long and difficult routes to the western countries of Europe. Silk and cotton, both raw and manufactured into fine goods, indigo and other dyestuffs, aromatic woods and gums, narcotics and other drugs, pearls, rubies, diamonds, sapphires, turquoises, and other precious stones, gold and silver, and, above all, the edible spices, pepper, ginger, cinnamon, cloves, and allspice, could be obtained only in Asia. There were three principal routes by which these goods were brought into Europe: first, along the Red Sea and overland across Egypt; second, up the Persian Gulf to its head, and then either along the Euphrates to a certain point whence the caravan route turned westward to the Syrian coast, or along the Tigris to its upper waters, and then across to the Black Sea at Trebizond; third, by caravan routes across Asia, then across the Caspian Sea, and overland again, either to the Black Sea or through Russia to the Baltic. A large part of this trade was gathered up by the Italian cities, especially Venice, at its various outlets upon the Mediterranean or adjacent waters. She had for exportation therefore, in addition to her own manufactures, merchandise which had been gathered from all parts of the then known world. The Venetian laws regulated commerce with the greatest minuteness. All goods purchased by Venetian traders must as a rule be brought first to the city and unloaded and stored in the city warehouses. A certain amount of freedom of export by land or water was then allowed, but by far the greater proportion of the goods remained under the partial control of the government. When conditions were considered favorable, the Senate voted a certain number of government galleys for a given voyage. There were several objective points for these voyages, but one was regularly England and Flanders, and the group of vessels sent to those countries was known as the " Flanders Fleet." Such an expedition was usually ordered about once a year, and consisted of two to five galleys. These were put under the charge of an admiral and provided with sailing masters, crews of rowers, and armed men to protect them, all at the expense of the merchants who should send goods in the vessels. Stringent regulations were also imposed upon them by the government, defining the length of their stay and appointing a series of stopping places, usually as follows: Capo d' Istria, Corfu, Otranto, Syracuse, Messina, Naples, Majorca, certain Spanish ports, Lisbon; then across the Bay of Biscay to the south coast of England, where usually the fleet divided, part going to Sluys, Middleburg, or Antwerp, in the Netherlands; the remainder going to Southampton, Sandwich, London, or elsewhere in England. At one or other of the southern ports of England the fleet would reassemble on its return, the whole outward and return voyage usually taking about a year.

The merchants who had come with the fleet thereupon proceeded to dispose of their goods in the southern towns and fairs of England and to buy wool or other goods which might be taken back to Venice or disposed of on the way. A somewhat similar trade was kept up with other Italian cities, especially with Genoa and Florence, though these lines of trade were more extensive in the fifteenth century than in the fourteenth.

23. The Flanders Trade and the Staple. — A trade of greater bulk and greater importance, though it did not include articles from such a distance as that of Italy, was the trade with the Flemish cities. This was more closely connected with English wool production than was that with any other country. Ghent, Bruges, Ypres, Courtrai, Arras, and a number of other cities in Flanders and the adjacent provinces of the Netherlands and France had become populous and rich, principally from their weaving industry. For their manufacture of fine fabrics they needed the English wool, and in turn their fine woven goods were in constant demand for the use of the wealthier classes in England. English skill was not yet sufficient to produce anything more than the crudest and roughest of textile fabrics. The fine cloths, linens, cambrics, cloth of gold and silver, tapestries and hangings, were the product of the looms of the Flemish cities. Other fine manufactured goods, such as armor and weapons, glass and furniture, and articles which had been brought in the way of trade to the Netherlands, were all exported thence and sold in England.

The Flemish dealers who habitually engaged in the English trade were organized among themselves in a company or league known as the " Flemish Hanse of London." A considerable number of towns held such membership in the organization that their citizens could take part in the trade and share in the benefits and privileges of the society, and no citizen of these towns could trade in England without paying the dues and submitting himself to the rules of the Hanse. The export trade from England to the Netherlands was controlled from the English side by the system known as the " Staple." From early times it had been customary to gather English standard products in certain towns in England or abroad for sale. These towns were known as " staples " or " staple towns," and wool, woolfells, leather, tin, and lead, the goods most extensively exported, were known as " staple goods." Subsequently the government took control of the matter, and appointed a certain town

THE PRINCIPAL WOOL-RAISING DISTRICTS OF ENGLAND AND WOOL-MANU-
FACTURING TOWNS OF FLANDERS AND BRABANT

in the Netherlands to which staple goods must be sent in the first place when they were exported from England. Later certain towns in England were appointed as staple towns, where all goods of the kinds mentioned above should be taken to be registered, weighed, and taxed before exportation. Just at the close of the period under discussion, in 1354, a careful organization was given to the system of staple towns in England, by which in each of the ten or twelve towns to which staple goods must be brought for exportation, a Mayor of the Staple and two Constables were elected by the " merchants of the staple," native and foreign. These officials had a number of duties, some of them more particularly in the interest of the king and treasury, others in the interest of the foreign merchants, still others merely for the preservation of good order and the enforcement of justice. The law merchant was made the basis of judgment, and every effort made to grant protection to foreigners and at the same time secure the financial interests of the government. But the policy of the government was by no means consistent. Both before and after this date, the whole system of staples was repeatedly abolished for a time and the whole trade in these articles thrown open. Again, the location of the staple towns was shifted from England to the Continent and again back to England. Eventually, in 1363, the staple came to be established at Calais, and all " staplers," or exporters of staple goods from England, were forced to give bonds that their cargoes would be taken direct to Calais to be sold.

24. The Hanse Trade. — The trade with Germany was at this time almost all with the group of cities which made up the German Hanse or League. This was a union of a large number of towns of northern Germany, such as Lubeck, Hamburg, Bremen, Dantzig, Brunswick, and perhaps sixty or eighty others. By a series of treaties and agreements among themselves, these towns had formed a close confederation which acted as a single whole in obtaining favorable trading concessions and privileges in various countries. There had been a considerable trade between the merchants of these towns and England from an early time. They brought the products of the Baltic lands, such as lumber, tar, salt, iron, silver, salted and smoked fish, furs, amber, certain coarse manufactures, and goods obtained by Hanseatic merchants through their more distant trade connections, such as fine woven goods, armor and other metal goods, and even spices and other Eastern goods, obtained from the great Russian fairs. The Hanse cities had entered into treaties with the English government, and possessed valuable concessions and privileges, and imported and exported quite extensively. The term " sterling," as applied to standard English money, is derived from the word " Easterling," which was used as synonymous with " German," " Hansard," " Dutch," and several other names descriptive of these traders.

The trade with the cities of northeastern France was similar to that with the neighboring towns of Flanders. That with northwestern France consisted especially of salt, sail-cloth, and wine. The trade with Poitou, Gascony, and Guienne was more extensive, as was natural from their long political connection with England. The chief part of the export from southern France was wine, though a variety of other articles, including fruits and some manufactured articles, were sent to England. A trade of quite a varied character also existed between England and the various countries of the Spanish Peninsula, including Portugal. Foreign trade with all of these countries was destined to increase largely during the later fourteenth and the fifteenth century, but its foundations were well laid within the first half of the fourteenth. Vessels from all these countries appeared from time to time in the harbors of England, and their merchants traded under government patronage and support in many English towns and fairs.

25. Foreigners Settled in England. — The fact that almost all of the foreign trade of England was in the hands of aliens necessarily involved their presence in the country temporarily or permanently in considerable numbers. The closely related fact that the English were distinctly behind the people of the Continent in economic knowledge, skill, and wealth also led foreigners to seek England as a field for profitable exercise of their abilities in finance, in trade, and manufactures. The most conspicuous of these foreigners at the close of the thirteenth century and during the early part of the fourteenth were the Italian bankers. Florence was not only a great trading and manufacturing city, but a money centre, a capitalist city. The Bardi, Peruzzi, Alberti, Frescobaldi, and other banking companies received deposits from citizens of Florence and other Italian cities, and loaned the money, as well as their own capital, to governments, great nobles, and ecclesiastical corporations in other countries. When the Jews were expelled from England in 1290, there being no considerable amount of money among native Englishmen, the Italian bankers were the only source from which the government could secure ready money. When a tax had been authorized by Parliament, but the product of it could be obtained only after a year or more spent in its collection, the Florentines were at hand to offer the money at once, receiving security for repayment when the receipts from the tax should come in. Government monopolies like the Cornwall tin mines were leased to them for a lump sum; arrangements were made by which the bankers furnished a certain amount of money each day during a campaign or a royal progress. The immediate needs of an impecunious king were regularly satisfied with money borrowed to be repaid some months afterward. The equipment for all of the early expeditions of the Hundred Years' War was obtained with money borrowed from the Florentines. Payments abroad were also made by means of bills of exchange negotiated by the same money-lenders. Direct payment of interest was forbidden by law, but they seem to have been rewarded by valuable government concessions, by the profits on exchange, and no doubt by the indirect payment of interest, notwithstanding its illegality.

The Italian bankers evidently loaned to others besides the king, for in 1327 the Knights Hospitallers in England repaid to the Society of the Bardi £848 5d., and to the Peruzzi £551 12s. 11d. They continued to loan freely to the king, till in

1348 he was indebted to one company alone to the extent of
more than £50,000, a sum equal in modern value to about
$3,000,000. The king now failed to repay what he had prom-
ised, and the banking companies fell into great straits. Defal-
cations having occurred in other countries also, some of them
failed, and after the middle of the century they never held so
conspicuous a place, though some Italians continued to act as
bankers and financiers through the remainder of the fourteenth
and fifteenth centuries. Many Italian merchants who were

THE STEELYARD IN THE SEVENTEENTH CENTURY
(Herbert: *History of London Livery Companies.*)

not bankers, especially Venetians and Genoese, were settled in
England, but their occupation did not make them so conspicuous
as the financiers of the same nation.

The German or Hanse merchants had a settlement of their
own in London, known as the " Steelyard," " Gildhall of the
Dutch," or the " Easterling's House." They had similar establishments on a smaller scale in Boston and Lynn, and perhaps
in other towns. Their permission to own property and to live
in their own house instead of in the houses of native merchants,
as was the usual custom, was derived, like most privileges of

foreigners, from the gift of the king. Little by little they had purchased property surrounding their original grants until they had a great group of buildings, including a meeting and dining hall, tower, kitchen, storage house, offices and other warehouses, and a considerable number of dwelling-houses, all enclosed by a wall and fences. It was located immediately on the Thames just above London Bridge so that their vessels unloaded at their own wharf. The merchants or their agents lived under strict rules, the gates being invariably closed at nine o'clock, and all discords among their own nation were punished by their own officers. Their trade was profitable to the king through payment of customs, and after the failure of the Italian bankers the merchants of the Steelyard made considerable loans to the English government either directly or acting for citizens at home. In 1343, when the king had been granted a tax of 40s. a sack on all wool exported, he immediately borrowed the value of it from Tiedemann van Limberg and Johann van Wolde, Easterlings. Similarly in 1346 the Easterlings loaned the king money for three years, holding his second crown as security. Like the Florentines, at one time they took the Cornwall tin mines at farm. They had many privileges not accorded generally to foreigners, but were exceedingly unpopular alike with the population and the authorities of the city of London. There were some other Germans domiciled in England, but nowhere else were they so conspicuous or influential as at the Steelyard.

The trade with Flanders brought Flemish merchants into England temporarily, but they do not seem to have formed any settlement or located permanently in any one place. Flemish artisans, on the other hand, had migrated to England from early times and were scattered here and there in several towns and villages. In the early part of the fourteenth century Edward III made it a matter of deliberate policy to encourage the immigration of Flemish weavers and other handicraftsmen, with the expectation that they would teach their art to the more backward native English. In 1332, he issued a charter of protection and privilege to a Fleming named John Kempe, a weaver of woollen cloth, offering the same privilege and protection to all other weavers, dyers, and fullers who should care to come to England to live. In 1337 a similar charter was given to a body of weavers coming from Zealand to England. It is believed that a considerable number of immigrants from the Netherlands came in at this period, settled largely in the smaller towns and rural villages, and taking English apprentices brought about a great improvement in the character of English manufactures. Flemings are also met with in local records in various occupations, even in agriculture.

There were other foreigners resident in England, especially Gascons from the south of France, and Spaniards; but the main elements of alien population in the thirteenth and fourteenth centuries were those which have just been described, Italians, Germans from the Hanse towns, and Flemings. These were mainly occupied as bankers, merchants, and handicraftsmen.

26. BIBLIOGRAPHY

Dr. Cunningham's *Growth of English Industry and Commerce* is particularly full and valuable on this subject. He has given further details on one branch of it in his *Alien Immigrants in England*.

Schanz, Georg: *Englische Handelspolitik gegen Ende des Mittelalters*. This work refers to a later period than that included in this chapter, but the summaries which the author gives of earlier conditions are in many cases the best accounts that we have.

Jenckes, A. L.: *Organization and Location of the Staple of England*.

Day, C.: *History of Commerce*.

Ashley, W. J.: *Early History of the Woolen Industry in England*.

Pauli, R.: *Pictures from Old England.* Contains an interesting account of the Steelyard.

Pirenne, Henri: *La Hanse flamande de Londres.*

Von Ochenkowski, W.: *England's Wirthsschaftliche Entwickelung im Ausgange des Mittelalters.*

Schultz, F.: *Die Hanse und England.*

Gross, C.: *Select Cases on the Law Merchant.*

CHAPTER V

THE BLACK DEATH AND THE PEASANTS' REBELLION

Economic Changes of the Later Fourteenth and Early Fifteenth Centuries

27. National Affairs from 1338 to 1461.—For the last century or more England had been standing with her back to the Continent. Deprived of most of their French possessions, engaged in the struggle to bring Wales, Scotland, and Ireland under the English crown, occupied with repeated conflicts with their barons or with the development of the internal organization of the country, John, Henry III, and the two Edwards had had less time and inclination to interest themselves in continental affairs than had Henry II and Richard. But after 1337 a new influence brought England for the next century into close connection with the rest of Europe. This was the "Hundred Years' War" between England and France. Several causes had for years combined to make this war unavoidable: the interference of France in the dispute with Scotland, the conflicts between the rising fishing and trading towns on the English and the French side of the Channel, the desire of the French king to drive the English kings from their remaining provinces in the south of France, and the reluctance of the English kings to accept their dependent position in France. Edward III commenced the war in 1338 with the invasion of France, and it was continued with comparatively short intervals of peace until 1452. During its progress the English won three of the most brilliant military victories in their history, at Crécy, Poitiers, and Agincourt, in 1346, 1356, and 1415. But most of the campaigns were characterized by brutality, destructive ravaging, and the reduction of cities by famine. The whole contest indeed often degenerated into desultory, objectless warfare. A permanent settlement was attempted at Bretigny in 1360. The English required the dismemberment of France by the surrender of almost one-third of the country and the payment by the French of a large ransom for their king, who had been captured by the English. In return King Edward withdrew any other claims he might have to territory, or the French crown. These terms were, however, so humiliating to the French that they did not adhere to them, the war soon broke out again, and finally terminated in the driving out of the English from all of France except the city of Calais, in the middle years of the next century.

The many alliances, embassies, exchanges of visits, and other international intercourse which the prosecution of the Hundred Years' War involved brought England into a closer participation in the general life of Europe than ever before, and caused the ebb and flow of a tide of influences between England and the Continent which deeply affected economic, political, and religious life on both sides of the Channel.

The Universities continued to flourish during almost the whole of this period. It was from Oxford as a centre, under the influence of John Wycliffe, a lecturer there, that a great revival and reforming movement in the church emanated. From about 1370 Wycliffe and others began to agitate for a more earnest religious life. They translated the Bible into English, wrote devotional and polemic tracts, preached throughout the country, spoke and wrote against the evils in the church at the time, then against its accepted form of organization, and finally against its official teachings. They thus became heretics. Thousands were influenced by their teachings, and a wave of religious revival and ecclesiastical rebellion spread over the country. The powers of the church and the civil government were ultimately brought to bear to crush out the "Lollards," as those who held heretical beliefs at that time were called. New and stringent laws were passed in 1401 and 1415, several persons were burned at the stake, and a large number forced to recant, or frightened into keeping their opinions secret. This religious movement gradually died out, and by the middle of the fifteenth century nothing more is heard of Lollardry.

Wycliffe had been not only a religious innovator, but a writer of much excellent English. Contemporary with him or slightly later were a number of writers who used the native language and created permanent works of literature. *The Vision of Piers Plowman* is the longest and best of a number of poems written by otherwise unknown men. Geoffrey Chaucer, one of England's greatest poets, wrote at first in French, then in English; his *Canterbury Tales* showing a perfected English form, borrowed originally, like so much of what was best in England at the time, from Italy or France, but assimilated, improved, and reconstructed until it seemed a purely English production. During the reign of Edward III English became the official language of the courts and the usual language of conversation, even among the higher classes.

Edward III lived until 1377. Through his long reign of half a century, during which he was entirely dependent on the grants of Parliament for the funds needed to carry on the war against France, this body obtained the powers, privileges, and organization which made it thereafter such an influential part of the government. His successor, Richard II, after a period of moderate government tried to rule with a high hand, but in 1399 was deposed through the influence of his cousin, Henry of Lancaster, who was crowned as Henry IV. Henry's title to the throne, according to hereditary principles, was defective, for the grandson of an older brother was living. But he was a mere child, and there was no considerable opposition to Henry's accession. Under the Lancastrian line, as Henry IV, Henry V, and Henry VI, who now reigned successively, are called, Parliament reached the highest position which it had yet attained, a position higher in fact than it held for several centuries after-

ward. Henry VI was a child at the death of his father in 1422.
On coming to be a man he proved too mild in temper to control
the great nobles who, by the chances of inheritance, had become
almost as powerful as the great feudal barons of early Norman
times. The descendants of the older branch of the royal family
were now represented by a vigorous and capable man, the duke
of York. An effort was therefore made about 1450 by one
party of the nobles to depose Henry VI in favor of the duke of
York. A number of other nobles took the side of the king, and
civil war broke out. After a series of miserable contests known
as the "Wars of the Roses" the former party was successful, at
least temporarily, and the duke of York became king in 1461
as Edward IV.

28. The Black Death and its Effects. — During the earlier
mediæval centuries the most marked characteristic of society
was its stability. Institutions continued with but slight changes
during a long period. With the middle of the fourteenth century changes become more prominent. Some of the most
conspicuous of these gather around a series of attacks of epidemic
disease during the latter half of the century.

From the autumn of 1348 to the spring of 1350 a wave of
pestilence was spreading over England from the southwest
northward and eastward, progressively attacking every part of
the country. The disease was new to Europe. Its course in
the individual case, like its progress through the community,
was very rapid. The person attacked either died within two
or three days or even less, or showed signs of recovery within
the same period. The proportion of cases which resulted
fatally was extremely large; the infectious character of the disease quite remarkable. It was, in fact, an extremely violent
epidemic attack, the most violent in history, of the bubonic
plague, with which we have unfortunately become again familiar
within recent years.

From much careful examination of several kinds of contemporary evidence it seems almost certain that as each locality was

successively attacked in 1348 and 1349 something like a half of the population died. In other words, whereas in an ordinary year at that time perhaps one-twentieth of the people died, in the plague year one-half died. Such entries as the following are frequent in the contemporary records. At the abbey of Newenham, "in the time of this mortality or pestilence there died in this house twenty monks and three lay brothers, whose names are entered in other books. And Walter, the abbot, and two monks were left alive there after the sickness." At Leicester, " in the little parish of St. Leonard there died more than 380, in the parish of Holy Cross more than 400, in that of St. Margaret more than 700; and so in every parish great numbers." The close arrangement of houses in the villages, the crowding of dwellings along narrow streets in the towns, the promiscuous life in the monasteries and in the inns, the uncleanly habits of living universally prevalent, all helped to make possible this sweeping away of perhaps a majority of the population by an attack of epidemic disease. It had devastated several of the countries of Europe before appearing in England, having been introduced into Europe apparently along the great trade routes from the far East. Within a few months the attack in each successive district subsided, the disease in the southwestern counties of England having run its course between August, 1348, and May, 1349; in and about London between November, 1348, and July, 1349; in the eastern counties in the summer of 1349; and in the more northern counties through the last months of that year or within the spring of 1350. Pestilence was frequent throughout the Middle Ages, but this attack was not only vastly more destructive and general than any which had preceded it, but the disease when once introduced became a frequent scourge in subsequent times, especially during the remainder of the fourteenth century. In 1361, 1368, and 1396 attacks are noticed as occurring more or less widely through the country, but none were so extensive as that which is usually spoken of as the "Black Death" of 1348–1349. The term "Black Death" was not used contemporaneously, nor until comparatively modern times. The occurrence of the pestilence, however, made an extremely strong impression on men's minds, and as "the great mortality," "the great pestilence," or "the great death," it appears widely in the records and the literature of the time.

Such an extensive and sudden destruction of life could not take place without leaving its mark in many directions. Monasteries were depopulated, and the value of their property and the strictness of their discipline diminished. The need for priests led to the ordination of those who were less carefully prepared and selected. The number of students at Oxford and Cambridge was depleted; the building and adornment of many churches suspended. The war between England and France, though promptly renewed, involved greater difficulty in obtaining equipment, and ultimately required new devices to meet its expense. Many of the towns lost numbers and property that were never regained, and the distribution of population throughout England was appreciably changed.

But the most evident and far-reaching results of the series of pestilences occurring through the last half of the fourteenth century were those connected with rural life and the arrangement of classes described in Chapter II.

The lords of manors might seem at first thought to have reaped advantage from the unusually high death rate. The heriots collected on the death of tenants were more numerous; reliefs paid by their successors on obtaining the land were repeated far more frequently than usual; much land escheated to the lord on the extinction of the families of free tenants, or fell into his hands for redisposal on the failure of descendants of villains or cotters. But these were only temporary and casual results. In other ways the diminution of population was distinctly disadvantageous to the lords of manors. They obtained much lower rents for mills and other such monopolies, because there were fewer people to have their grain ground and the ten-

ants of the mills could therefore not make as much profit.   The
rents of assize or regular periodical payments in money and in
kind made by free and villain tenants were less in amount, since
the tenants were fewer and much land was unoccupied.   The
profits of the manor courts were less, for there were not so many
suitors to attend, to pay fees, and to be fined.   The manor
court rolls for these years give long lists of vacancies of holdings,
often naming the days of the deaths of the tenants.   Their
successors are often children, and in many cases whole families
were swept away and the land taken into the hands of the lord
of the manor.   Juries appointed at one meeting of the manor
court are sometimes all dead by the time of the next meeting.
There are constant complaints by the stewards that certain
land "is of no value because the tenants are all dead"; in one
place that a water-mill is worthless because "all the tenants
who used it are dead," in another that the rents are £7 14s.
less than in the previous year because fourteen holdings, consisting of 102 acres of land, are in the hands of the lord; in still
another that the rents of assize which used to be £20 are now
only £2 and the court fees have fallen from 40 to 5 shillings
"because the tenants there are dead."   There was also less
required service performed on the demesne lands, for many of
the villain holdings from which it was owed were now vacant.
Last, and most seriously of all, the lords of manors suffered as
employers of labor.   It had always been necessary to hire
additional labor for the cultivation of the demesne farm and for
the personal service of the manor, and through recent decades
somewhat more had come to be hired because of a gradual
increase of the practice of commutation of services.   That is,
villain tenants were allowed to pay the value of their required
days' work in money instead of in actual service.   The bailiff or
reeve then hired men as they were wanted, so that quite an appreciable part of the work of the manor had come to be done by
laborers hired for wages.

After the Black Death the same demesne lands were to be

cultivated, and in most cases the larger holdings remained or descended or were regranted to those who would expect to continue their cultivation. Thus the demand for laborers remained approximately as great as it had been before. The number of laborers, on the other hand, was vastly diminished. They were therefore eagerly sought for by employers. Naturally they took advantage of their position to demand higher wages, and in many cases combined to refuse to work at the old accustomed rates. A royal ordinance of 1349 states that, "because a great part of the people, especially of workmen and servants, have lately died in the pestilence, many, seeing the necessity of masters and great scarcity of servants, will not serve unless they may receive excessive wages." A contemporary chronicler says that "laborers were so elated and contentious that they did not pay any attention to the command of the king, and if anybody wanted to hire them he was bound to pay them what they asked, and so he had his choice either to lose his harvest and crops or give in to the proud and covetous desires of the workmen." Thus, because of this rise in wages, at the very time that many of the usual sources of income of the lords of manors were less remunerative, the expenses of carrying on their farming operations were largely increased. On closer examination, therefore, it becomes evident that the income of the lords of manors, whether individuals or corporations, was not increased, but considerably diminished, and that their position was less favorable than it had been before the pestilence.

The freeholders of land below lords of manors were disadvantageously affected in as far as they had to hire laborers, but in other ways were in a more favorable position. The rent which they had to pay was often reduced. Land was everywhere to be had in plenty, and a threat to give up their holdings and go to where more favorable terms could be secured was generally effective in obtaining better terms where they were.

The villain holders legally of course did not have this opportunity, but practically they secured many of its advantages.

It is probable that many took up additional land, perhaps on an improved tenure.   Their payments and their labor, whether done in the form of required "week-work," or, if this were commuted, done for hire, were much valued, and concessions made to them accordingly.   They might, as they frequently did, take to flight, giving up their land and either obtaining a new grant somewhere else or becoming laborers without lands of their own.

This last-named class, made up of those who depended entirely on agricultural labor on the land of others for their support, was a class which had been increasing in numbers, and which was the most distinctly favored by the demand for laborers and the rise of wages.   They were the representatives of the old cotter class, recruited from those who either inherited no land or found it more advantageous to work for wages than to take up small holdings with their burdens.

But the most important social result of the Black Death and the period of pestilence which followed it was the general shock it gave to the old settled life and established relations of men to one another.   It introduced many immediate changes, and still more causes of ultimate change; but above all it altered the old stability, so that change in future would be easy.

29. The Statutes of Laborers. — The change which showed itself most promptly, the rise in the prevailing rate of wages, was met by the strenuous opposition of the law.   In the summer of 1349, while the pestilence was still raging in the north of England the king, acting on the advice of his Council, issued a proclamation to all the sheriffs and the officials of the larger towns, declaring that the laborers were taking advantage of the needs of their lords to demand excessive wages, and prohibiting them from asking more than had been due and accustomed in the year before the outbreak of the pestilence or for the preceding five or six years.   Every laborer when offered service at these wages must accept it; the lords of manors having the first right to the labor of those living on their manors, provided they did not insist on retaining an unreasonable number. If any laborers, men or women, bond or free, should refuse to accept such an offer of work, they were to be imprisoned till they should give bail to serve as required. Commissioners were then appointed by the king in each county to inquire into and punish violations of this ordinance.

When Parliament next met, in February, 1351, the Commons sent a petition to the king stating that his ordinance had not been obeyed and that laborers were claiming double and treble what they had received in the years before the pestilence. In response to the petition what is usually called the " First Statute of Laborers " was enacted. It repeated the requirement that men must accept work when it was offered to them, established definite rates of wages for various classes of laborers, and required all such persons to swear twice a year before the stewards, bailiffs, or other officials that they would obey this law. If they refused to swear or disobeyed the law, they were to be put in the stocks for three days or more and then sent to the nearest jail till they should agree to serve as required. It was ordered that stocks should be built in each village for this purpose, and that the judges should visit each county twice a year to inquire into the enforcement of the law. In 1357 the law was reënacted, with some changes of the destination of the fines collected for its breach. In 1361 there was a further reënactment of the law with additional penalties. If laborers will not work unless they are given higher wages than those established by law, they can be taken and imprisoned by lords of manors for as much as fifteen days, and then be sent to the next jail to await the coming of the justices. If any one after accepting service leaves it, he is to be arrested and sued before the justices. If he cannot be found, he is to be outlawed and a writ sent to every sheriff in England ordering that he should be arrested, sent back, and imprisoned till he pays his fine and makes amends to the party injured; "and besides for the falsity he shall be burnt in the forehead with an iron made and formed to this letter F in token of Falsity, if the party aggrieved shall ask for it." This last provision, however, was probably intended as a threat rather than an actual punishment, for its application was suspended for some months, and even then it was to be inflicted only on the advice of the judges, and the iron was to remain in the custody of the sheriff. The statute was reënacted with slight variations thirteen times within the century after its original introduction; namely, in addition to the dates already mentioned, in 1362, 1368, 1378, 1388, 1402, 1406, 1414, 1423, 1427, 1429, and 1444.

The necessity for these repeated reissues of the statutes of laborers indicates that the general rise of wages was not prevented. Forty years after the pestilence the law of 1388 is said to be passed, "because that servants and laborers are not, nor by a long time have been willing to serve and labor without outrageous and excessive hire." Direct testimony also indicates that the prevailing rate of wages was much higher, probably half as much again, as it had been before the pestilence. Nevertheless, the enforcement of the law in individual cases must have been a very great hardship. The fines which were collected from breakers of the law were of sufficient amount to be estimated at one time as part payment of a tax, at another as a valuable source of income to the lords of manors. Their enforcement was intrusted at different times to the local justices of the peace, the royal judges on circuit, and special commissioners.

The inducement to the passage of the laws prohibiting a rise in wages was no doubt partly the self-interest of the employing classes who were alone represented in Parliament, but partly also the feeling that the laboring class were taking advantage of an abnormal condition of affairs to change the well-established customary rates of remuneration of labor. The most significant fact indicated by the laws, however, was the existence of a distinct class of laborers. In earlier times, when almost all rural dwellers held some land, this can hardly have been the case; it is quite evident that there was now an increasing class who made their living simply by working for wages. Another fact frequently referred to in the laws is the frequent passage of laborers from one district to another; it is evident that the population was becoming somewhat less stationary. Therefore while the years following the great pestilence were a period of difficulty for the lords of manors and the employing classes, for the lower classes the same period was one of increasing opportunity and a breaking down of old restrictions. Whether or not the statutes had any real effect in keeping the rate of wages lower than it would have otherwise become is hard to determine, but there is no doubt that the efforts to enforce the law and the frequent punishment of individuals for its violation embittered the minds of the laborers and helped to throw them into opposition to the government and to the upper classes generally. The statutes of laborers thus became one of the principal causes of the growth of that hostility which culminated in the Peasants' Rebellion.

30. The Peasants' Rebellion of 1381. — From the scanty contemporary records still remaining we can obtain glimpses of a widespread restlessness among the masses of the English people during the latter half of the fourteenth century. According to a petition submitted to Parliament in 1377 the villains were refusing to pay their customary services to their lords and to acknowledge the requirements of their serfdom. They were also gathering together in great bodies to resist the efforts of the lords to collect from them their dues and to force them to submit to the decisions of the manor courts. The ready reception given to the religious revival preached by the Lollards throughout the country indicates an attitude of independence and of self-assertion on the part of the people of which there had been no sign during earlier times. The writer who represents most nearly popular feeling, the author of the *Vision of Piers Plowman*, reflects a certain restless and questioning mysticism which has no particular plan of reform to propose, but is nevertheless thoroughly dissatisfied with the world as it is. Lastly, a series of vague appeals to revolt, written in the vernacular, partly in prose, partly in doggerel rhyme, have been preserved and seem to testify to a deliberate propaganda of lawlessness. Some of the general causes of this rising tide of discontent are quite apparent. The efforts to enforce the statutes of laborers, as has been said, kept continual friction between the employing and the employed class. Parliament, which kept petitioning for reënactments of these laws, the magistrates and special commissioners who enforced them, and the land-owners who appealed to them for relief, were alike engaged in creating class antagonism and multiplying individual grievances. Secondly, the very improvement in the economic position of the lower classes, which was undoubtedly in progress, made them doubly impatient of the many burdens which still pressed upon them. Another cause for the prevalent unrest may have lain in the character of much of the teaching of the time. Undisguised communism was preached by a wandering priest, John Ball, and the injustice of the claims of the property-holding classes was a very natural inference from much of the teachings of Wycliffe and his "poor priests." Again, the corruption of the court, the incapacity of the ministers, and the failure of the war in France were all reasons for popular anger, if the masses of people can be supposed to have had any knowledge of such distant matters.

But the most definite and widespread cause of discontent was probably the introduction of a new form of taxation, the general poll tax. Until this time taxes had either been direct taxes laid upon land and personal property, or indirect taxes laid upon various objects of export and import. In 1377, however, Parliament agreed to the imposition of a tax of four pence a head on all laymen, and Convocation soon afterward taxed all the clergy, regular and secular, the same amount. Notwithstanding this grant and increased taxes of the old forms, the government still needed more money for the expenses of the war with France, and in April, 1379, a graduated poll tax was laid on all persons above sixteen years of age. This was regulated according to the rank of the payer from mere laborers, who were to pay four pence, up to earls, who must pay £4. But this only produced some £20,000, while more than £100,000 were needed; therefore in November of 1380 a third poll tax was laid in the following manner. The tax was to be collected at the rate of three groats or one shilling for each person over fifteen years of age. But although the total amount payable from any town or manor was to be as many shillings as there were inhabitants over fourteen years of age, it was to be assessed in each manor upon individuals in proportion to their means, the more well-to-do paying more, the poorer paying less; but with the limits that no one should have to pay more than £1 for himself and his wife, and no one less than four pence for himself and his wife.

The poll tax was extremely unpopular. In the first place, it was a new tax, and to all appearances an additional weight given to the burden of contributing to the never ending expenses of the government of which the people were already weary. Moreover, it fell upon everybody, even upon those who from their lack of property had probably never before paid any tax. The inhabitants of every cottage were made to realize, by the payment of what amounted to two or three days' wages, that they had public and political as well as private and economic burdens. Lastly, the method of assessing the tax gave scope for much unfairness and favoritism.

In addition to this general unpopularity of the poll tax there was a special reason for opposition in the circumstances of that imposed in 1380. As the returns began to come in they were extremely disappointing to the government. Therefore in March, 1381, the king, suspecting negligence on the part of the collectors, appointed groups of commissioners for a number of different districts who were directed to go from place to place investigating the former collection and enforcing payment from any who had evaded it before. This no doubt seemed to many of the ignorant people the imposition of a second tax. The first rumors of disorder came in May from some of the villages of

DISTRIBUTION

OF POPULATION

According to the Poll-tax of

1377

Below 40 to the square mile

Between 40 and 60 per sq. mile

Above 60 to the square mile

SCALE OF MILES

0   20   40   60   80

Essex, where the tax-collectors and the commissioners who followed them were driven away violently by the people. Finally, during the second week in June, rioting began in several parts of England almost simultaneously. In Essex those who had refused to pay the poll tax and driven out the collectors now went from village to village persuading or compelling the people to join them. In Kent the villagers seized pilgrims on their way to Canterbury and forced them to take an oath to resist any tax except the old taxes, to be faithful to "King Richard and the Commons," to join their party when summoned and never to allow John of Gaunt to become king. A riot broke out at Dartford in Kent, then Canterbury was overrun, and the sheriff was forced to give up the tax rolls to be destroyed. They proceeded to break into Maidstone jail and release the prisoners there, and subsequently entered Rochester. These Kentish insurgents then set out toward London, wishing no doubt to obtain access to the young king, who was known to be there, but also directed by an instinctive desire to strike at the capital of the kingdom. By Wednesday, the 12th of June, they had formed a rendezvous at Blackheath some five miles below the city. Some of the Essex men had crossed the river and joined them, others had also taken their way toward London, marching along the northern side of the Thames. At the same time, or by the next day, another band was approaching London from Hertfordshire on the north. The body of insurgents gathered at Blackheath, who were stated by contemporary chroniclers, no doubt with the usual exaggeration, to have numbered 60,000, succeeded in communicating with King Richard, a boy of fourteen years, who was residing at the Tower of London with his mother and principal ministers and several great nobles, asking him to come to meet them. On the next day, Corpus Christi day, June 12th, he was rowed with a group of nobles to the other bank of the river, where the insurgents were crowding to the water side. The confusion and danger were so great that the king did not land, and the conference amounted to nothing.

During the same day, however, the rebels pressed on to the city, and a part of the populace of London having left the drawbridge open for them, they made their way in. The evening of the same day the men from Essex entered through one of the city gates which had also been opened for them by connivance from within. There had already been much destruction of property and of life. As the rebels passed along the roads, the villagers joined them and many of the lower classes of the town population as well. In several cases they burned the houses of the gentry and of the great ecclesiastics, destroyed tax and court rolls and other documents, and put to death persons connected with the law. When they had made their way into London they burned and pillaged the Savoy palace, the city house of the duke of Lancaster, and the houses of the Knights Hospitallers at Clerkenwell and at Temple Bar. By this time leaders had arisen among the rebels. Wat Tyler, John Ball, and Jack Straw were successful in keeping their followers from stealing and in giving some semblance of a regular plan to their proceedings. On the morning of Friday, the 14th, the king left the Tower, and while he was absent the rebels made their way in, ransacked the rooms, seized and carried out to Tower Hill Simon Sudbury, archbishop of Canterbury, who was Lord Chancellor, Robert Hales, Grand Master of the Hospitallers, who was then Lord Treasurer, and some lower officials. These were all put through the hasty forms of an irregular trial and then beheaded. There were also many murders throughout the city. Foreigners especially were put to death, probably by Londoners themselves or by the rural insurgents at their instigation. A considerable number of Flemings were assassinated, some being drawn from one of the churches where they had taken refuge. The German merchants of the Steelyard were attacked and driven through the streets, but took refuge in their well-defended buildings.

During the same three days, insurrection had broken out in several other parts of England. Disorders are mentioned in Kent, Essex, Hertfordshire, Middlesex, Suffolk, Norfolk,

EXTENSION

OF THE

PEASANTS' INSURRECTION

OF

1381

SCALE OF MILES

0   20   40   60   80   100

ENGRAVED BY BORMAY & CO., N.Y.

Cambridge, Huntingdon, Hampshire, Sussex, Somerset, Leicester, Lincoln, York, Bedford, Northampton, Surrey, and Wiltshire. There are also indications of risings in nine other counties. In Suffolk the leadership was taken by a man named John Wrawe, a priest like John Ball. On June 12th, the same day that the rendezvous was held on Blackheath, a great body of peasants under Wrawe attacked and pillaged a manor house belonging to Richard Lyons, an unpopular minister of the last days of Edward III. The next day they looted a parish church where were stored the valuables of Sir John Cavendish, Chief Justice of the Court of King's Bench and Chancellor of the town of Cambridge. On the 14th they occupied Bury, where they sacked the houses of unpopular men and finally captured and put to death Cavendish himself, John of Cambridge, prior of the St. Edmund's Abbey, and John of Lakenheath, an officer of the king. The rioters also forced the monks of the abbey to hand over to them all the documents giving to the monastery power over the townsmen. There were also a large number of detached attacks on persons and on manor houses, where manor court rolls and other documents were destroyed and property carried off. There was more theft here than in London; but much of the plundering was primarily intended to settle old disputes rather than for its own sake. In Norfolk the insurrection broke out a day or two later than in Suffolk, and is notable as having among its patrons a considerable number of the lesser gentry and other well-to-do persons. The principal leader, however, was a certain Geoffrey Lister. This man had issued a proclamation calling on all the people to meet on the 17th of June on Mushold Heath, just outside the city of Norwich. A great multitude gathered, and they summoned Sir Robert Salle, who was in the military service of the king, but was living at Norwich, and who had risen from peasant rank to knighthood, to come out for a conference. When he declined their request to become their leader they assassinated him, and subsequently made their way into the city, of which they kept control for several days.

Throughout Norfolk and Cambridgeshire we hear of the same murders of men who had obtained the hatred of the lower classes in general, or those of individuals who were temporarily influential with the insurgents. There were also numerous instances of the destruction of court rolls found at the manor houses of lay lords of manors or obtained from the muniment rooms of the monasteries. It seems almost certain that there was some agreement beforehand among the leaders of the revolt in the eastern districts of England, and probably also with the leaders in Essex and Kent.

Another locality where we have full knowledge of the occurrences during the rebellion is the town and monastery of St. Albans, just north of London. The rising here was either instigated by, or, at least, drew its encouragement from, the leaders who gathered at London. The townsmen and villains from surrounding manors invaded the great abbey, opened the prison, demanded and obtained all the charters bearing on existing disputes, and reclaimed a number of millstones which were kept by the abbey as a testimony to the monopoly of all grinding by the abbey mill. In many other places disorders were in progress. For a few days in the middle of June a considerable part of England was at the mercy of the revolted peasants and artisans, under the leadership partly of men who had arisen among their own class, partly of certain persons of higher position who had sufficient reason for throwing in their lot with them.

The culmination of the revolt was at the time of the execution of the great ministers of government on Tower Hill on the morning of the 14th. At that very time the young king had met a body of the rebels, mostly made up of men from Essex and Hertfordshire at Mile End, just outside of one of the gates of London. In a discussion in which they stated their grievances, the king, apparently in good faith, but as it afterward proved in bad, promised to give them what they demanded, begged them to disperse and go to their homes, only leaving representatives from each village to take back the charters of emancipation which he proceeded to have prepared and issued to them. There had been no intentional antagonism to the king himself, and a great part of the insurgents took him at his word and scattered to their homes. The charters which they took with them were of the following form : —

"Richard, by the grace of God, King of England and France, and Lord of Ireland, to all his bailiffs and faithful ones, to whom these present letters shall come, greeting. Know that of our special grace, we have manumitted all of our lieges and each of our subjects and others of the County of Hertford; and them and each of them have made free from all bondage, and by these presents make them quit. And moreover we pardon our same lieges and subjects for all kinds of felonies, treasons, transgressions, and extortions, however done or perpetrated by them or any of them, and also outlawry, if any shall have been promulgated on this account against them or any of them; and our most complete peace to them and each of them we concede in these matters. In testimony of which things we have caused these our letters to be made patent. Witness, myself, at London, on the fifteenth day of June, in the fourth year of our reign."

The most prominent leaders remained behind, and a large body of rioters spent the rest of Friday and the following night in London. The king, after the interview at Mile End, had returned to the Tower, then to the Queen's Wardrobe, a little palace at the other side of London, where he spent the night with his mother. In the morning he mounted his horse, and with a small group of attendants rode toward the Tower. As he passed through the open square of Smithfield he met Wat Tyler, also on horseback, accompanied by the great body of rebels. Tyler rode forward to confer with the king, but an altercation having broken out between him and some of the king's attendants, the mayor of London, Sir William Walworth, suddenly dashed forward, struck him from his horse with the blow of a sword, and while on the ground he was stabbed to death by the other attendants of the king. There was a moment of extreme danger of an attack by the leaderless rebels on the king and his companions, but the ready promises of the king, his natural gifts of pretence, and the strange attachment which the peasants showed to him through all the troubles, tided over a little time until they had been led outside of the city gates, and the armed forces which many gentlemen had in their houses in the city had at last been gathered together and brought to where they had the disorganized body of rebels at their mercy. These were then disarmed, bidden to go to their homes, and a proclamation issued that if any stranger remained in London over Sunday he would pay for it with his life.

The downfall of Tyler and the dispersion of the insurgents at London turned the tide of the whole revolt. In the various districts where disorders were in progress the news of that failure came as a blow to all their own hopes of success. The revolt had been already disintegrating rather than gaining in strength and unity; and now its leaders lost heart, and local bodies of gentry proportionately took courage to suppress revolt in their own localities. The most conspicuous and influential of such efforts was that of Henry de Spencer, bishop of Norwich. This warlike prelate was in Rutlandshire when the news of the revolt came. He hastened toward Norwich; on his way met an embassy from the rioters to the king; seized and beheaded two of its peasant members, and still pushing on met the great body of the rebels near Walsham, where after a short conflict and some parleying the latter were dispersed, and their leaders captured and hanged without any ceremony other than the last rites of religion. As a matter of fact the rising had no cohesion sufficient to withstand attack from any constituted authority or from representatives of the dominant classes.

The king's government acted promptly. On the 17th of June, two days after the death of Tyler, a proclamation was issued forbidding unauthorized gatherings of people; on the

23d a second, requiring all tenants, villains, and freemen alike to perform their usual services to their lords; and on the 2d of July a third, withdrawing the charters of pardon and manumission which had been granted on the 15th of June. Special sessions of the courts were organized in the rebellious districts, and the leaders of the revolt were searched out and executed by hanging or decapitation.

On the 3d of November Parliament met. The king's treasurer explained that he had issued the charters under constraint, and recognizing their illegality, with the expectation of withdrawing them as soon as possible, which he had done. The suggestion of the king that the villains should be regularly enfranchised by a statute was declined in vigorous terms by Parliament. Laws were passed relieving all those who had made grants under compulsion from carrying them out, enabling those whose charters had been destroyed to obtain new ones under the great seal, granting exemption from prosecution to all who had exercised illegal violence in putting down the late insurrection, and finally granting a general pardon, though with many exceptions, to the late insurgents.

Thus the rising of June, 1381, had become a matter of the past by the close of the year. The general conditions which brought about a popular uprising have already been discussed. The specific objects which the rioters had in view in each part of the country are a much more obscure and complicated question.

There is no reason to believe that there was any general political object, other than opposition to the new and burdensome taxation, and disgust with the existing ministry. Nor was there any religious object in view. No doubt a large part of the disorder had no general purpose whatever, but consisted in an attempt, at a period of confusion and relaxation of the law, to settle by violence purely local or personal disputes and grievances.

Apart from these considerations the objects of the rioters were of an economic nature. There was a general effort to destroy the rolls of the manor courts. These rolls, kept either in manor houses, or in the castles of great lords, or in the monasteries, were the record of the burdens and payments and disabilities of the villagers. Previous payments of heriot, relief, merchet, and fines, acknowledgments of serfdom, the obtaining of their land on burdensome conditions, were all recorded on the rolls and could be produced to prove the custom of the manor to the disadvantage of the tenant. It is true that these same rolls showed who held each piece of ground and defined the succession to it, and that they were long afterward to be recognized in the national courts as giving to the customary holder the right of retaining and of inheriting the land, so that it might seem an injury to themselves to destroy the manor court records. But in that period, when tenants were in such demand, their hold on their land had been in no danger of being disturbed. If these records were destroyed, the villains might well expect that they could claim to be practically owners of the houses and little groups of acres which they and their ancestors had held from time immemorial; and this without the necessity for payments and reservations to which the rolls testified.

Again, lawyers and all connected with the law were the objects of special hostility on the part of insurgents. This must have been largely from the same general cause as that just mentioned. It was lawyers who acted as stewards for the great lords, it was through lawyers that the legal claims of lords of manors were enforced in the king's courts. It was also the judges and lawyers who put in force the statutes of laborers, and who so generally acted as collectors of the poll tax.

More satisfactory relations with their lords were demanded by insurgents who were freeholders, as well as by those who were villains. Protests are recorded against the tolls on sales and purchases, and against attendance at the manorial courts, and a maximum limit to the rent of land is asked for. Finally, the removal of the burdens of serfdom was evidently one of the general objects of the rebels, though much of the initiative of the revolt was taken by men from Kent, where serfdom did not exist. The servitude of the peasantry is the burden of the sermon of John Ball at Blackheath, its abolition was demanded in several places by the insurgents, and the charters of emancipation as given by the king professed to make them " free from all bondage."

These objects were in few if any cases obtained. It is extremely difficult to trace any direct results from the rising other than those involved in its failure, the punishment of the leaders, and the effort to restore everything to its former condition. There was indeed a conservative reaction in several directions. The authorities of London forbade the admission of any former villain to citizenship, and the Commons in Parliament petitioned the king to reduce the rights of villains still further. On the whole, the revolt is rather an illustration of the general fact that great national crises have left but a slight impress on society, while the important changes have taken place slowly and by an almost imperceptible development. The results of the rising are rather to be looked for in giving increased rapidity and definite direction to changes already in progress, than in starting any new movement or in obtaining the results which the insurgents may have wished.

31. Commutation of Services. — One of these changes, already in progress long before the outbreak of the revolt, has already been referred to. A silent transformation was going on inside of the manorial life in the form of a gradual substitution of money payments by the villain tenants for the old labor for two, three, or four days a week, and at special times during the year. This was often described as " selling to the tenants their services." They " bought " their exemption from furnishing actual work by paying the value of it in money to the official representing the lord of the manor.

This was a mutually advantageous arrangement. The villain's time would be worth more to himself than to his lord; for if he had sufficient land in his possession he could occupy himself profitably on it, or if he had not so much land he could choose his time for hiring himself out to the best advantage. The lord, on the other hand, obtained money which could be spent in paying men whose services would be more willing and interested, and who could be engaged at more available times. It is not, therefore, a matter of surprise that the practice of allowing tenants to pay for their services arose early. Commutation is noticeable as early as the thirteenth century and not very unusual in the first half of the fourteenth. After the pestilence, however, there was a very rapid substitution of money payments for labor payments. The process continued through the remainder of the fourteenth century and the early fifteenth, and by the middle of that century the enforcement of regular labor services had become almost unknown. The boon-works continued to be claimed after the week-work had disappeared, since labor was not so easy to obtain at the specially busy seasons of the year, and the required few days' services at ploughing or mowing or harvesting were correspondingly valuable. But even these were extremely unusual after the middle of the fifteenth century.

This change was dependent on at least two conditions, an increased amount of money in circulation and an increased number of free laborers available for hire. These conditions were being more and more completely fulfilled. Trade at fairs and markets and in the towns was increasing through the whole fourteenth century. The increase of weaving and other handicrafts produced more wealth and trade. Money coming from abroad and from the royal mints made its way into circulation and came into the hands of the villain tenants through the sale of surplus products or as payment for their labor. The sudden destruction of one-half of the population by the Black Death while the amount of money in the country remained the same, doubled the circulation *per capita.* Tenants were thus able to offer regular money payments to their lords in lieu of their personal services.

During the same period the number of free laborers who could be hired to perform the necessary work on the demesne was increasing. Even before the pestilence there were men and women on every manor who held little or no land and who could be secured by the lord for voluntary labor if the compulsory labor of the villains was given up. Some of these laborers were fugitive villains who had fled from one manor to another to secure freedom, and this class became much more numerous under the circumstances of disorganization after the Black Death. Thus the second condition requisite for the extensive commutation was present also.

It might be supposed that after the pestilence, when wages were high and labor was so hard to procure, lords of manors would be unwilling to allow further commutation, and would even try to insist on the performance of actual labor in cases where commutation had been previously allowed. Indeed, it has been very generally stated that there was such a reaction. The contrary, however, was the case. Commutation was never more rapid than in the generation immediately after the first attack of the pestilence. The laborers seem to have been in so favorable a position, that the dread of their flight was a controlling inducement to the lords to allow the commutation of their services if they desired it. The interest of the lords in their labor services was also, as will be seen, becoming less.

When a villain's labor services had been commuted into money, his position must have risen appreciably. One of the main characteristics of his position as a villain tenant had been the uncertainty of his services, the fact that during the days in which he must work for his lord he could be put to any kind of labor, and that the number of days he must serve was itself only restricted by the custom of the manor. His services once commuted into a definite sum of money, all uncertainty ceased. Moreover, his money payments to the lord, although rising from an entirely different source, were almost indistinguishable from the money rents paid by the freeholder.

Therefore, serf though he might still be in legal status, his position was much more like that of a freeman.

32. The Abandonment of Demesne Farming. — A still more important change than the commutation of services was in progress during the fourteenth and fifteenth centuries. This was the gradual withdrawal of the lords of manors from the cultivation of the demesne farms. From very early times it had been customary for lords of manors to grant out small portions of the demesne, or of previously uncultivated land, to tenants at a money rent. The great demesne farm, however, had been still kept up as the centre of the agricultural system of the vill. But now even this was on many manors rented out to a tenant or group of tenants. The earliest known instances are just at the beginning of the fourteenth century, but the labor troubles of the latter half of the century made the process more usual, and within the next hundred years the demesne lands seem to have been practically all rented out to tenants. In other words, whereas, during the earlier Middle Ages lords of manors had usually carried on the cultivation of the demesne lands themselves, under the administration of their bailiffs and with the labor of the villains, making their profit by obtaining a food supply for their own households or by selling the surplus products, now they gave up their cultivation and rented them out to some one else, making their profit by receiving a money payment as rent. They became therefore landlords of the modern type. A typical instance of this change is where the demesne land of the manor of Wilburton in Cambridgeshire, consisting of 246 acres of arable land and 42 acres of meadow, was rented in 1426 to one of the villain tenants of the manor for a sum of £8 a year. The person who took the land was usually either a free or a villain tenant of the same or a neighboring manor. The land was let for a certain number of years, but afterward was usually relet either to the same or to another tenant. The word *farmer* originally meant one of these tenants who took the demesne or some other piece of land, paying for it a " farm " or *firma*, that is, a settled established sum, in place of the various forms of profit that might have been secured from it by the lord of the manor. The free and villain holdings which came into the hands of the lord by failure of heirs in those times of frequent extinction of families were also granted out very generally at a money rent, so that a large number of the cultivators of the soil came to be tenants at a money rent, that is, leaseholders or " farmers." These free renting farmers, along with the smaller freeholders, made up the " yeomen " of England.

33. The Decay of Serfdom. — It is in the changes discussed in the last two paragraphs that is to be found the key to the disappearance of serfdom in England. Men had been freed from villainage in individual cases by various means. Manumission of serfs had occurred from time to time through all the mediæval centuries. It was customary in such cases either to give a formal charter granting freedom to the man himself and to his descendants, or to have entered on the manor court roll the fact of his obtaining his enfranchisement. Occasionally men were manumitted in order that they might be ordained as clergymen. In the period following the pestilences of the fourteenth century the difficulty in recruiting the ranks of the priesthood made the practice more frequent. The charters of manumission issued by the king to the insurgents of 1381 would have granted freedom on a large scale had they not been disowned and subsequently withdrawn. Still other villains had obtained freedom by flight from the manors where they had been born. When a villain who had fled was discovered he could be reclaimed by the lord of the manor by obtaining a writ from the court, but many obstacles might be placed in the way of obtaining this writ, and it must always have involved so much difficulty as to make it doubtful whether it was worth while. So long as a villain was anywhere else than on the manor to which he belonged, he was practically a free man, but few of the disabilities of villainage existing except as between him and his own lord. Therefore, if a villain was willing to sacrifice his little holding and make the necessary break with his usual surroundings, he might frequently escape into a veritable freedom.

The attitude of the common law was favorable to liberty as against servitude, and in cases of doubt the decisions of the royal courts were almost invariably favorable to the freedom of the villain.

But all these possibilities of liberty were only for individual cases. Villainage as an institution continued to exist and to characterize the position of the mass of the peasantry. The number of freemen through the country was larger, but the serfdom of the great majority can scarcely have been much influenced by these individual cases. The commutation of services, however, and still more the abandonment of demesne farming by the lords of manors, were general causes conducive to freedom. The former custom indicated that the lords valued the money that could be paid by the villains more than they did their compulsory services. That is, villains whose services were paid for in money were practically renters of land from the lords, no longer serfs on the land of the lords. The lord of the manor could still of course enforce his claim to the various payments and restrictions arising from the villainage of his tenants, but their position as payers of money was much less servile than as performers of forced labor. The willingness of the lords to accept money instead of service showed, as before stated, that there were other persons who could be hired to do the work. The villains were valued more as tenants now that there were others to serve as laborers. The occupants of customary holdings were a higher class and a class more worth the lord's consideration and favor than the mere laborers. The villains were thus raised into partial freedom by having a free class still below them.

The effect of the relinquishment of the old demesne farms by the lords of the manors was still more influential in destroying serfdom. The lords had valued serfdom above all because it furnished an adequate and absolutely certain supply of labor. The villains had to stay on the manor and provide the labor necessary for the cultivation of the demesne. But if the demesne was rented out to a farmer or divided among several holders, the interest of the lord in the labor supply on the manor was very much diminished. Even if he agreed in his lease of the demesne to the new farmer that the villains should perform their customary services in as far as these had not been commuted, yet the farmer could not enforce this of himself, and the lord of the manor was probably languid or careless or dilatory in doing so. The other payments and burdens of serfdom were not so lucrative, and as the ranks of the old villain class were depleted by the extinction of families, and fewer inhabitants were bound to attend the manor courts, they became less so. It became, therefore, gradually more common, then quite universal, for the lords of manors to cease to enforce the requirements of serfdom. A legal relation of which neither party is reminded is apt to become obsolete; and that is what practically happened to serfdom in England. It is true that many persons were still legally serfs, and occasionally the fact of their serfdom was asserted in the courts or inferred by granting them manumission. These occasional enfranchisements continued down into the second half of the sixteenth century, and the claim that a certain man was a villain was pleaded in the courts as late as 1618. But long before this time serfdom had ceased to have much practical importance. It may be said that by the middle of the fifteenth century the mass of the English rural population were free men and no longer serfs. With their labor services commuted to money and the other conditions of their villainage no longer enforced, they became an indistinguishable part either of the yeomanry or of the body of agricultural laborers.

34. Changes in Town Life and Foreign Trade. — The changes discussed in the last three sections apply in the main

I

to rural life. The economic and social history of the towns
during the same period, except in so far as it was part of the
general national experience, consisted in a still more complete
adoption of those characteristics which have already been
described in Chapter III. Their wealth and prosperity became
greater, they were still more independent of the rural districts
and of the central government, the intermunicipal character
of their dealings, the closeness of connection between their

AN OLD STREET IN WORCESTER
(Britton: *Picturesque Antiquities of English Cities.*)

industrial interests and their government, the completeness
with which all occupations were organized under the "gild
system," were all of them still more marked in 1450 than they
had been in 1350. It is true that far-reaching changes were
beginning, but they were only beginning, and did not reach
an important development until a time later than that included
in this chapter. The same thing is true in the field of foreign
trade. The latter part of the fourteenth and the early fifteenth
century saw a considerable increase and development of the

trade of England, but it was still on the same lines and carried on by the same methods as before. The great proportion of it was in the hands of foreigners, and there was the same inconsistency in the policy of the central government on the occasions when it did intervene or take any action on the subject. The important changes in trade and in town life which have their beginning in this period will be discussed in connection with those of the next period in Chapter VI.

35. BIBLIOGRAPHY

Jessop, Augustus: *The Coming of the Friars and other Essays.* Two interesting essays in this volume are on *The Black Death in East Anglia.*

Gasquet, F. A.: *The Great Pestilence of 1349.*

Creighton, C.: *History of Epidemics in Britain*, two volumes. This gives especial attention to the nature of the disease.

Trevelyan, G. M.: *England in the Age of Wycliffe.* This book, published in 1899, gives by far the fullest account of the Peasant Rising which has so far appeared in English.

Petit-Dutaillis, C., et Reville, A.: *Le Soulèvement des Travailleurs d'Angleterre en 1381.* The best account of the Rebellion.

Powell, Edgar: *The Peasant Rising in East Anglia in 1381.* Especially valuable for its accounts of the poll tax.

Powell, Edgar, and Trevelyan, G. M.: *Documents Illustrating the Peasants' Rising and the Lollards.*

Page, Thomas Walker: *The End of Villainage in England.* This monograph, published in 1900, is particularly valuable for the new facts which it gives concerning the rural changes of the fourteenth century.

CHAPTER VI

THE BREAKING UP OF THE MEDIÆVAL SYSTEM

Economic Changes of the Later Fifteenth and the Sixteenth Centuries

36. National Affairs from 1461 to 1603. — The close of the fifteenth and the opening of the sixteenth century has been by universal consent settled upon as the passage from one era to another, from the Middle Ages to modern times. This period of transition was marked in England by at least three great movements: a new type of intellectual life, a new ideal of government, and the Reformation. The greatest changes in English literature and intellectual interests are traceable to foreign influence. In the fifteenth century the paramount foreign influence was that of Italy. From the middle of the fifteenth century an increasing number of young Englishmen went to Italy to study, and brought back with them an interest in the study of Greek and of other subjects to which this led. Somewhat later the social intercourse of Englishmen with Italy exercised a corresponding influence on more courtly literature. In 1491 the teaching of Greek was begun at Oxford by Grocyn, and after this time the passion for classical learning became deep, widespread, and enthusiastic. But not only were the subjects of intellectual interest different, but the attitude of mind in the study of these subjects was much more critical than it had been in the Middle Ages. The discoveries of new routes to the far East and of America, as well as the new speculations in natural science which came at this time, reacted on the minds of men and broadened their whole mental outlook. The production of works of pure literature had suffered a decline after the time of Wycliffe and Chaucer, from which there was no considerable revival till the early part of the sixteenth century. Sir Thomas More's *Utopia*, written in Latin in 1514, was a philosophical work thrown into the form of a literary dialogue and description of an imaginary commonwealth. But writing became constantly more abundant and more varied through the reigns of Henry VIII, 1509–1547, Edward VI, 1547–1553, and Mary, 1553–1558, until it finally blossomed out into the splendid Elizabethan literature, just at the close of our period.

A stronger royal government had begun with Edward IV. The conclusion of the war with France made the king's need for money less, and at the same time new sources of income appeared. Edward, therefore, from 1461, neglected to call Parliament annually, as had been usual, and frequently allowed three or more years to go by without any consultation with it. He also exercised very freely what was called the dispensing power, that is, the power to suspend the law in certain cases, and in other ways asserted the royal prerogative as no previous king had done for two hundred years. But the true founder of the almost absolute monarchy of this period was Henry VII, who reigned from 1485 to 1509. He was not the nearest heir to the throne, but acted as the representative of the Lancastrian line, and by his marriage with the lady who represented the claim of the York family joined the two contending factions. He was the first of the Tudor line, his successors being his son, Henry VIII, and the three children of Henry VIII, Edward VI, Mary, and Elizabeth. Henry VII was an able, shrewd, far-sighted, and masterful man. During his reign he put an end to the disorders of the nobility; made Parliament relatively insignificant by calling it even less frequently than Edward IV had done, and by initiating its legislation when it did meet. He also increased and regulated the income of the crown, and rendered its expenditures subject to control. He was able to keep ambassadors regularly abroad, for the first time, and in many other ways to support a more expensive administration, though often by unpopular and illegal means of extortion from the people. He formed foreign political and commercial treaties in all directions, and encouraged the voyages of the Cabots to America. He brought a great deal of business constantly before the Royal Council, but chose its members for their ability rather than for their high rank. In these various ways he created a strong personal government, which left but little room for Parliament or people to do anything except carry out his will. In these respects Henry's immediate successors and their ministers followed the same policy. In fact, the Reformation in the reign of Henry VIII, and new internal and foreign difficulties in the reign of Elizabeth, brought the royal power into a still higher and more independent position.

The need for a general reformation of the church had long been recognized. More than one effort had been made by the ecclesiastical authorities to insist on higher intellectual and moral standards for the clergy and to rid the church of various evil customs and abuses. Again, there had been repeated efforts to clothe the king, who was at the head of all civil government, with extensive control and oversight of church affairs also. Men holding different views on questions of church government and religious belief from those held by the general Christian church in the Middle Ages, had written and taught and found many to agree with them. Thus efforts to bring about changes in the established church had not been wanting, but they had produced no permanent result. In the early years of the sixteenth century, however, several causes combined to bring about a movement of this nature extending over a number of years and profoundly affecting all subsequent history. This is known as the Reformation. The first steps of the Reformation in England were taken as the result of a dispute between King Henry VIII and the Pope. In the first place, several laws were passed through Parliament, beginning with the year 1529, abolishing a number of petty evils and abusive practices in the church courts. The Pope's income from England was then cut off, and his jurisdiction and all other forms of authority in England brought to an end. Finally, the supremacy of the king over the church and clergy and over all ecclesiastical affairs was declared and enforced. By the year 1535 the ancient connection between the church in England and the Pope was severed. Thus in England, as in many continental countries at about the same time, a national church arose independent of Rome. Next, changes began to be made in the doctrine and practices of the church. The organization under bishops was retained, though they were now appointed by the king. Pilgrimages and the worship of saints were forbidden, the Bible translated into English, and other changes gradually introduced. The monastic life came under the condemnation of the reformers. The monasteries were therefore dissolved and their property confiscated and sold, between the years 1536 and 1542. In the reign of Edward VI, 1547–1553, the Reformation was carried much further. An English prayer book was issued which was to be used in all religious worship, the adornments of the churches were removed, the services made more simple, and doctrines introduced which assimilated the church of England to the contemporary Protestant churches on the Continent.

Queen Mary, who had been brought up in the Roman faith, tried to make England again a Roman Catholic country, and in the later years of her reign encouraged severe persecutions, causing many to be burned at the stake, in the hope of thus crushing out heresy. After her death, however, in 1558, Queen Elizabeth adopted a more moderate position, and the church of England was established by law in much the form it had possessed at the death of Henry VIII.

In the meantime, however, there had been growing up a far more spontaneous religious movement than the official Reformation which has just been described. Many thousands of persons had become deeply interested in religion and enthusiastic in their faith, and had come to hold different views on church government, doctrines, and practices from those approved of either by the Roman Catholic church or by the government of England. Those who held such views were known as Puritans, and throughout the reign of Elizabeth were increasing in numbers and making strenuous though unsuccessful efforts to introduce changes in the established church.

The reign of Elizabeth was marked not only by the continuance of royal despotism, by brilliant literary production, and by the struggle of the established church against the Catholics on the one side and the Puritans on the other, but by difficult and dangerous foreign relations.

More than once invasion by the continental powers was imminent. Elizabeth was threatened with deposition by the English adherents of Mary, Queen of Scots, supported by France and Spain. The English government pursued a policy of interference in the internal conflicts of other countries that brought it frequently to the verge of war with their governments and sometimes beyond. Hostility bordering on open warfare was therefore the most frequent condition of English foreign relations. Especially was this true of the relations with Spain. The most serious contest with that country was the war which culminated in the battle of the Armada in 1588. Spain had organized an immense fleet which was intended to go to the Netherlands and convoy an army to be taken thence for the invasion of England. While passing through the English Channel, a storm broke upon them, they were attacked and harried by the English and later by the Dutch, and the whole fleet was eventually scattered and destroyed. The danger of invasion was greatly reduced after this time and until the end of Elizabeth's reign in 1603.

37. Enclosures. — The century and a half which extends from the middle years of the fifteenth century to the close of the sixteenth was, as has been shown, a period remarkable for the extent and variety of its changes in almost every aspect of society. In the political, intellectual, and religious world the sixteenth century seemed far removed from the fifteenth. It is not therefore a matter of surprise that economic changes were numerous and fundamental, and that social organization in town and country alike was completely transformed.

During the period last discussed, the fourteenth and the early fifteenth century, the manorial system had changed very considerably from its mediæval form. The demesne lands had been quite generally leased to renting farmers, and a new class of tenants was consequently becoming numerous; serfdom had fallen into decay; the old manorial officers, the steward, the bailiff, and the reeve had fallen into unimportance; the manor courts were not so active, so regular, or so numerously attended. These changes were gradual and were still uncompleted at the middle of the fifteenth century; but there was already showing itself a new series of changes, affecting still other parts of manorial life, which became steadily more extensive during the remainder of the fifteenth and through much of the sixteenth century. These changes are usually grouped under the name " enclosures."

The enclosure of land previously open was closely connected with the increase of sheep-raising. The older form of agriculture, grain-raising, labored under many difficulties. The price of labor was high, there had been no improvement in the old crude methods of culture, nor, in the open fields and under the customary rules, was there opportunity to introduce any. On the other hand, the inducements to sheep-raising were numerous. There was a steady demand at good prices for wool, both for export, as of old, and for the manufactures within England, which were now increasing. Sheep-raising required fewer hands and therefore high wages were less an obstacle, and it gave opportunity for the investment of capital and for comparative freedom from the restrictions of local custom. Therefore, instead of raising sheep simply as a part of ordinary farming, lords of manors, freeholders, farming tenants, and even customary tenants began here and there to raise sheep for wool as their principal or sole production. Instances are mentioned of five thousand, ten thousand, twenty thousand, and even twenty-four thousand sheep in the possession of a single person. This custom spread more and more widely, and so attracted the attention of observers as to be frequently mentioned in the laws and literature of the time.

But sheep could not be raised to any considerable extent on land divided according to the old open field system. In a vill whose fields all lay open, sheep must either be fed with those of other men on the common pasture, or must be kept in small groups by shepherds within the confines of the various acres or other small strips of the sheep-raiser's holding. No large number could of course be kept in this way, so the first thing to be done by the sheep-raiser was to get enough strips together in one place to make it worth while to put a hedge or other fence around them, or else to separate off in the same way a part or the whole of the open pastures or meadows. This was the process known as enclosing. Separate enclosed fields, which had existed only occasionally in mediæval farming, became numerous in this time, as they have become practically universal in modern farming in English-speaking countries.

But it was ordinarily impracticable to obtain groups of adjacent acres or sufficiently extensive rights on the common pasture for enclosing without getting rid of some of the other tenants. In this way enclosing led to evictions. Either the lord of the manor or some one or more of the tenants enclosed the lands which they had formerly held and also those which were formerly occupied by some other holders, who were evicted from their land for this purpose.

Some of the tenants must have been protected in their holdings by the law. As early as 1468 Chief Justice Bryan had declared that " tenant by the custom is as well inheritor to have his land according to the custom as he which hath a freehold at the common law." Again, in 1484, another chief justice declared that a tenant by custom who continued to pay his service could not be ejected by the lord of the manor. Such tenants came to be known as copyholders, because the proof of their customary tenure was found in the manor court rolls, from which a copy was taken to serve as a title. Subsequently copyhold became one of the most generally recognized forms of land tenure in England, and gave practically as secure title as did a freehold. At this time, however, notwithstanding the statements just given, the law was probably not very definite or not very well understood, and customary tenants may have had but little practical protection of the law against eviction. Moreover, the great body of the small tenants were probably no longer genuine customary tenants. The great proportion of small farms had probably not been inherited by a long line of tenants, but had repeatedly gone back into the hands of the lords of the manors and been subsequently rented out again, with or without a lease, to farmers or rent-paying tenants. These were in most cases probably the tenants who were now evicted to make room for the new enclosed sheep farms.

By these enclosures and evictions in some cases the open lands of whole vills were enclosed, the old agriculture came to an end, and as the enclosers were often non-residents, the whole farming population disappeared from the village. Since sheep-raising required such a small number of laborers, the farm laborers also had to leave to seek work elsewhere, and the whole village, therefore, was deserted, the houses fell into ruin, and the township lost its population entirely. This was commonly spoken of at the time as " the decaying of towns," and those who were responsible for it were denounced as enemies of their country. In most cases, however, the enclosures and depopulation were only partial. A number of causes combined to carry this movement forward. England was not yet a wealthy country, but such capital as existed, especially in the towns, was utilized and made remunerative by investment in the newly enclosed farms and in carrying on the expenses of enclosure. The dissolution of the monasteries between 1536 and 1542 brought the lands which they had formerly held into the possession of a class of men who were anxious to make them as remunerative as possible, and who had no feeling against enclosures.

Nevertheless, the changes were much disapproved. Sir Thomas More condemns them in the *Utopia*, as do many other writers of the same period and of the reign of Elizabeth. The landlords, the enclosers, the city merchants who took up country lands, were preached against and inveighed against by such preachers as Latimer, Lever, and Becon, and in a dozen or more pamphlets still extant. The government also put itself into opposition to the changes which were in progress. It was believed that there was danger of a reduction of the population and thus of a lack of soldiers; it was feared that not enough grain would be raised to provide food for the people; the dangerous masses of wandering beggars were partly at least recruited from the evicted tenants; there was a great deal of discontent in the country due to the high rents, lack of occupation, and general dislike of change. A series of laws were therefore carried through Parliament and other measures taken, the object of which was to put a stop to the increase of sheep-farming and its results. In 1488 a statute was enacted prohibiting the turning of tillage land into pasture. In 1514 a new law was passed reënacting this and requiring the repair by their owners of any houses which had fallen into decay because of the substitution of pasture for tillage, and their reoccupation with tenants. In 1517 a commission of investigation into enclosures was appointed by the government. In 1518 the Lord Chancellor, Cardinal Wolsey, issued a proclamation requiring all those who had enclosed lands since 1509 to throw them open again, or else give proof that their enclosure was for the public advantage. In 1534 the earlier laws were reënacted and a further provision made that no person holding rented lands should keep more than twenty-four hundred sheep. In 1548 a new commission on enclosures was appointed which made extensive investigations, instituted prosecutions, and recommended new legislation. A law for more careful enforcement was passed in 1552, and the old laws were reënacted in 1554 and 1562. This last law was repealed in 1593, but in 1598 others were enacted and later extended. In 1624, however, all the laws on the subject were repealed. As a matter of fact, the laws seem to have been generally ineffective. The nobility and gentry were in the main in favor of the enclosures, as they increased their rents even when they were not themselves the enclosers; and it was through these classes that legislation had to be enforced at this time if it was to be effective.

Besides the official opposition of the government, there were occasional instances of rioting or violent destruction of hedges and other enclosures by the people who felt themselves aggrieved by them. Three times these riots rose to the height of an insurrection. In 1536 the so-called "Pilgrimage of Grace" was a rising of the people partly in opposition to the introduction of the Reformation, partly in opposition to enclosures. In 1549 a series of risings occurred, the most serious of which was the "camp" under Kett in Norfolk, and in 1552 again there was an insurrection in Buckinghamshire. These risings were harshly repressed by the government. The rural changes, therefore, progressed steadily, notwithstanding the opposition of the law, of certain forms of public opinion, and of the violence of mobs. Probably enclosures more or less complete were made during this period in as many as half the manors of England. They were at their height in the early years of the sixteenth century, during its latter half they were not so numerous, and by its close the enclosing movement had about run its course, at least for the time.

38. Internal Divisions in the Craft Gilds. — Changes in town life occurred during this period corresponding quite closely to the enclosures and their results in the country. These consisted in the decay of the gilds, the dispersion of certain town industries through the rural districts, and the loss of prosperity of many of the old towns. In the earlier craft gilds each man had normally been successively an apprentice, a journeyman, and a full master craftsman, with a little establishment of his own and full participation in the administration of the fraternity. There was coming now to be a class of artisans who remained permanently employed and never attained to the position of master craftsmen. This was sometimes the result of a deliberate process of exclusion on the part of those who were already masters. In 1480, for instance, a new set of ordinances given to the Mercers' Gild of Shrewsbury declares that the fines assessed on apprentices at their entry to be masters had been excessive and should be reduced. Similarly, the Oxford Town Council in 1531 restricts the payment required from any person who should come to be a full brother of any craft in that town to twenty shillings, a sum which would equal perhaps fifty dollars in modern value. In the same year Parliament forbade the collection of more than two shillings and sixpence from any apprentice at the time of his apprenticeship, and of more than three shillings and fourpence when he enters the trade fully at the expiration of his time. This indicates that the fines previously charged must have been almost prohibitive. In some trades the masters required apprentices at the time of indenture to take an oath that they would not set up independent establishments when they had fulfilled the years of their apprenticeship, a custom which was forbidden by Parliament in 1536. In other cases it was no doubt the lack of sufficient capital and enterprise which kept a large number of artisans from ever rising above the class of journeymen.

Under these circumstances the journeymen evidently ceased

to feel that they enjoyed any benefits from the organized crafts, for they began to form among themselves what are generally described as " yeomen gilds " or " journeymen gilds." At first the masters opposed such bodies and the city officials supported the old companies by prohibiting the journeymen from holding assemblies, wearing a special livery, or otherwise acting as separate bodies. Ultimately, however, they seem to have made good their position, and existed in a number of different crafts in more or less subordination to the organizations of the masters. The first mention of such bodies is soon after the Peasants' Rebellion, but in most cases the earliest rise of a journeyman gild in any industry was in the latter part of the fifteenth or in the sixteenth century. They were organizations quite similar to the older bodies from which they were a split, except that they had of course no general control over the industry. They had, however, meetings, officers, feasts, and charitable funds. In addition to these functions there is reason to believe that they made use of their organization to influence the rates of wages and to coerce other journeymen. Their relations to the masters' companies were frequently defined by regular written agreements between the two parties. Journeymen gilds existed among the saddlers, cordwainers, tailors, blacksmiths, carpenters, drapers, ironmongers, founders, fishmongers, cloth-workers, and armorers in London, among the weavers in Coventry, the tailors in Exeter and in Bristol, the shoemakers in Oxford, and no doubt in some other trades in these and other towns.

Among the masters also changes were taking place in the same direction. Instead of all master artisans or tradesmen in any one industry holding an equal position and taking an equal part in the administration of affairs of the craft, there came, at least in some of the larger companies, to be quite distinct groups usually described as those " of the livery " and those " not of the livery." The expression no doubt arose from the former class being the more well-to-do and

active masters who had sufficient means to purchase the suits
of livery worn on state occasions, and who in other ways
were the leading and controlling members of the organization.
This came, before the close of the fifteenth century, in many
crafts to be a recognized distinction of class or station in the company.   A statement of the members in one of the London fraternities made in 1493 gives a good instance of this distinction of
classes, as well as of the subordinate body last described.   There
were said to be at that date in the Drapers' Company, of the
craft of drapers in the clothing, including the masters and four
wardens, one hundred and fourteen; of the brotherhood out
of the clothing one hundred and fifteen; of the bachelors'
company sixty.   It was from this prominence of the liveried
gildsmen that the term " Livery Companies " came to be
applied to the greater London gilds.   It was the wealthy merchants and the craftsmen of the livery of the various fraternities
who rode in procession to welcome kings or ambassadors at
their entrance into the city, to add lustre to royal wedding
ceremonies, or give dignity to other state occasions.   In 1483
four hundred and six members of livery companies riding
in mulberry colored coats attended the coronation procession of Richard III.   The mayors and sheriffs and aldermen
of London were almost always livery men in one or another of
the companies.   A substantial fee had usually to be paid when
a member was chosen into the livery, which again indicates
that they were the wealthier members.   Those of the livery
controlled the policy of the gild to the exclusion of the less
conspicuous members, even though these were also independent
masters with journeymen and apprentices of their own.

But the practical administration of the affairs of the wealthier
companies came in many cases to be in the hands of a still
smaller group of members.   This group was often known as the
" Court of Assistants," and consisted of some twelve, twenty, or
more members who possessed higher rights than the others, and,
with the wardens or other officials, decided disputes, negotiated

with the government or other authorities, disposed of the funds, and in other ways governed the organized craft or trade. At a general meeting of the members of the Mercers of London, for instance, on July 23, 1463, the following resolution was passed: " It is accorded that for the holding of many courts and congregations of the fellowship, it is odious and grievous to the body of the fellowship and specially for matters of no great effect, that hereafter yearly shall be chosen and associated to the wardens for the time being twelve other sufficient persons to be assistants to the said wardens, and all matters by them finished to be holden firm and stable, and the fellowship to abide by them." Sixteen years later these assistants with the wardens were given the right to elect their successors.

Thus before the close of the sixteenth century the craft and trading organizations had gone through a very considerable internal change. In the fourteenth century they had been bodies of masters of approximately equal position, in which the journeymen participated in some of the elements of membership, and would for the most part in due time become masters and full members. Now the journeymen had become for the most part a separate class, without prospect of mastership. Among the masters themselves a distinct division between the more and the less wealthy had taken place, and an aristocratic form of government had grown up which put the practical control of each of the companies in the hands of a comparatively small, self-perpetuating ruling body. These developments were all more marked, possibly some of them were only true, in the case of the London companies. London, also, so far as known, is the only English town in which the companies were divided into two classes, the twelve " Greater Companies," and the fifty or more " Lesser Companies "; the former having practical control of the government of the city, the latter having no such influence.

39. Change of Location of Industries. — The changes described above were, as has been said, the result of develop-

K

ment from within the craft and trading organizations themselves, resulting probably in the main from increasing wealth. There were other contemporary changes in these companies which were rather the result of external influences. One of these external factors was the old difficulty which arose from artisans and traders who were not members of the organized companies. There had always been men who had carried on work surreptitiously outside of the limits of the authorized organizations of their respective industries. They had done this from inability or unwillingness to conform to the requirements of gild membership, or from a desire to obtain more employment by underbidding in price, or additional profit by using unapproved materials or methods. Most of the bodies of ordinances mention such workmen and traders, men who have not gone through a regular apprenticeship, " foreigners " who have come in from some other locality and are not freemen of the city where they wish to work, irresponsible men who will not conform to the established rules of the trade. This class of persons was becoming more numerous through the fifteenth and sixteenth centuries, notwithstanding the efforts of the gilds, supported by municipal and national authority. The prohibition of any workers setting up business in a town unless they had previously obtained the approval of the officials of their trade was more and more vigorous in the later ordinances; the fines imposed upon masters who engaged journeymen who had not paid the dues, newcomers into the town, were higher. The complaints of the intrusion of outsiders were more loud and frequent. There was evidently more unsupervised, unregulated labor.

But the increase in the number of these unorganized laborers, these craftsmen and traders not under the control of the gilds, was most marked in the rural districts, that is to say, in market towns and in villages entirely outside of the old manufacturing and trading centres. Even in the fourteenth century there were a number of weavers, and probably of other craftsmen, who worked in the villages in the vicinity of the larger towns, such as London, Norwich, and York, and took their products to be sold on fair or market days in these towns. But toward the end of the fifteenth century this rural labor received a new kind of encouragement and a corresponding extension far beyond anything before existing. The English cloth-making industry at this period was increasing rapidly. Whereas during the earlier periods, as we have seen, wool was the greatest of English exports, now it was coming to be manufactured within the country. In connection with this manufacture a new kind of industrial organization began to show itself which, when it was completed, became known as the " domestic system." A class of merchants or manufacturers arose who are spoken of as " clothiers," or " merchant clothiers," who bought the wool or other raw material, and gave it out to carders or combers, spinners, weavers, fullers, and other craftsmen, paying them for their respective parts in the process of manufacture, and themselves disposing of the product at home or for export. The clothiers were in this way a new class of employers, putting the master weavers or other craftsmen to work for wages. The latter still had their journeymen and apprentices, but the initiative in their industry was taken by the merchants, who provided the raw material and much of the money capital, and took charge of the sale of the completed goods. The craftsmen who were employed in this form of industry did not usually dwell in the old populous and wealthy towns. It is probable that the restrictions of the gild ordinances were disadvantageous both to the clothiers and to the small master craftsmen, and that the latter, as well as journeymen who had no chance to obtain an independent position, now that the town craft organizations were under the control of the more wealthy members, were very ready to migrate to rural villages. Thus, in so far as the weaving industry was growing up under the management of the employing clothiers, it was slipping out from under the control of the town gilds by its location in the country. The same thing occurred in other cases even without the intermediation of a new employing class. We hear of mattress makers, of rope makers, of tile makers, and other artisans establishing themselves in the country villages outside of the towns, where, as a law of 1495 says, " the wardens have no power or authority to make search." In certain parts of England, in the southwest, the west, and the northwest, independent weavers now set up for themselves in rural districts as those of the eastern counties had long done, buying their own raw materials, bringing their manufactures to completion, and then taking them to the neighboring towns and markets to sell, or hawking them through the rural districts.

These changes, along with others occurring simultaneously, led to a considerable diminution of the· prosperity of many of the large towns. They were not able to pay their usual share of taxation, the population of some of them declined, whole streets or quarters, when destroyed by fire or other catastrophe, were left unbuilt and in ruins. Many of the largest and oldest towns of England are mentioned in the statutes of the reign of Henry VIII as being more or less depleted in population. The laws and literature of the time are ringing with complaints of the " decay of the towns," where the reference is to cities, as well as where it is to rural villages. Certain new towns, it is true, were rising into greater importance, and certain rural districts were becoming populous with this body of artisans whose living was made partly by their handicraft, partly by small farming. Nevertheless the old city craft organizations were permanently weakened and impoverished by thus losing control of such a large proportion of their various industries. The occupations which were carried on in the country were pursued without supervision by the gilds. They retained control only of that part of industry which was still carried on in the towns.

40. The Influence of the Government on the Gilds. — Internal divisions and external changes in the distribution of industry were therefore alike tending to weaken the gild organization. It had to suffer also from the hostility or intrusion of the national government. Much of the policy of the government tended, it is true, as in the case of the enclosures, to check the changes in progress, and thus to protect the gild system. It has been seen that laws were passed to prohibit the exclusion of apprentices and journeymen from full membership in the crafts. As early as 1464 a law was passed to regulate the growing system of employment of craftsmen by clothiers. This was carried further in a law of 1511, and further still in 1551 and 1555. The manufacture of rope in the country parts of Dorsetshire was prohibited and restricted to the town of Bridport in 1529; the cloth manufacture which was growing up through the " hamlets, thorps, and villages " in Worcestershire was forbidden in 1553 to be carried on except in the five old towns of Worcester, Evesham, Droitwich, Kidderminster, and Bromsgrove; in 1543 it was enacted that coverlets were not to be manufactured in Yorkshire outside of the city of York, and there was still further legislation in the same direction. Numerous acts were also passed for the purpose of restoring the populousness of the towns. There is, however, little reason to believe that these laws had much more effect in preventing the narrowing of the control of the gilds and the scattering of industries from the towns to the country than the various laws against enclosures had, and the latter object was practically surrendered by the numerous exceptions to it in laws passed in 1557, 1558, and 1575. All the laws favoring the older towns were finally repealed in 1623.

Another class of laws may seem to have favored the craft organizations. These were the laws regulating the carrying on of various industries, in some of which the enforcement of the laws was intrusted to the gild authorities. The statute book during the sixteenth century is filled with laws " for the true making of pins," " for the making of friezes and cottons in Wales," " for the true currying of leather," " for the making

of iron gads," " for setting prices on wines," for the regulation
of the coopers, the tanners, the makers of woollen cloth, the
dyers, the tallow chandlers, the saddlers and girdlers, and dozens
of other occupations.   But although in many of these laws the
wardens of the appropriate crafts are given authority to carry
out the requirements of the statute, either of themselves or
along with the town officials or the justices of the peace, yet,
after all, it is the rules established by government that they
are to carry out, not their own rules, and in many of the statutes
the craft authorities are entirely ignored.   This is especially
true of the " Statute of Apprentices," passed in the fifth year
of the reign of Queen Elizabeth, 1563.   This great industrial
code, which remained on the statute book for two hundred
and fifty years, being repealed only in 1813, was primarily a re-
enactment of the statutes of laborers, which had been continued
from time to time ever since their introduction in 1349.   It made
labor compulsory and imposed on the justices of the peace the
duty of meeting in each locality once a year to establish wages
for each kind of industry.   It required a seven years' apprenticeship for every person who should engage in any trade; established a working day of twelve hours in summer and during day-
light in winter; and enacted that all engagements, except those
for piece work, should be by the year, with six months' notice of a
close of the contract by either employer or employee.   By
this statute all the relations between master and journeyman
and the rules of apprenticeship were regulated by the government instead of by the individual craft gilds.   It is evident
that the old trade organizations were being superseded in much
of their work by the national government.   Freedom of action
was also restricted by the same power in other respects also.
As early as 1436 a law had been passed, declaring that the
ordinances made by the gilds were in many cases unreasonable
and injurious, requiring them to submit their existing ordinances
to the justices at Westminster, and prohibiting them from issu-
ing any new ones until they had received the approval of these

officials. There is no indication of the enforcement of this law. In 1504, however, it was reënacted with the modification that approval might be sought from the justices on circuit. In 1530 the same requirement was again included in the law already referred to prohibiting excessive entrance fees. As the independent legislation of the gilds for their industries was already much restricted by the town governments, their remaining power to make rules for themselves must now have been very slight. Their power of jurisdiction was likewise limited by a law passed in 1504, prohibiting the companies from making any rule forbidding their members to appeal to the ordinary national courts in trade disputes.

But the heaviest blow to the gilds on the part of the government came in 1547, as a result of the Reformation. Both the organizations formed for the control of the various industries, the craft gilds, and those which have been described in Chapter III as non-industrial, social, or religious gilds, had property in their possession which had been bequeathed or given to them by members on condition that the gild would always support or help to support a priest, should see that mass was celebrated for the soul of the donor and his family, should keep a light always burning before a certain shrine, or for other religious objects. These objects were generally looked upon as superstitious by the reformers who became influential under Edward VI, and in the first year of his reign a statute was passed which confiscated to the crown, to be used for educational or other purposes, all the property of every kind of the purely religious and social gilds, and that part of the property of the craft gilds which was employed by them for religious purposes. One of the oldest forms of voluntary organization in England therefore came to an end altogether, and one of the strongest bonds which had held the members of the craft gilds together as social bodies was removed. After this time the companies had no religious functions, and were besides deprived of a considerable proportion of their wealth. This blow fell, moreover, just at a time when all the economic influences were tending toward their weakening or actual disintegration.

The trade and craft companies of London, like those of other towns, were called upon at first to pay over to the government annually the amount which they had before used for religious purposes. Three years after the confiscation they were required to pay a lump sum representing the capitalized value of this amount, estimated for the London companies at £20,000. In order to do so they were of course forced to sell or mortgage much of their land. That which they succeeded in retaining, however, or bought subsequently was relieved of all government charges, and being situated for the most part in the heart of London, ultimately became extremely valuable and is still in their possession. So far have the London companies, however, departed from their original purpose that their members have long ceased to have any connection with the occupations from which the bodies take their names.

41. General Causes and Evidences of the Decay of the Gilds. — An analogous narrowing of the interests of the crafts occurred in the form of a cessation of the mystery plays. Dramatic shows continued to be brought out yearly by the crafts in many towns well into the sixteenth century. It is to be noticed, however, that this was no longer done spontaneously. The town governments insisted that the pageants should be provided as of old, and on the approach of Corpus Christi day, or whatever festival was so celebrated in the particular town, instructions were given for their production, pecuniary help being sometimes provided to assist the companies in their expense. The profit which came to the town from the influx of visitors to see the pageants was a great inducement to the town government to insist on their continuance. On the other hand, the competition of dramas played by professional actors tended no doubt to hasten the effect of the impoverishment and loss of vitality of the gilds. In the last half of the sixteenth century the mystery plays seem to have come finally to an end.

Thus the gilds lost the unity of their membership, were weakened by the growth of industry outside of their sphere of control, superseded by the government in many of their economic functions, deprived of their administrative, legislative, and jurisdictional freedom, robbed of their religious duties and of the property which had enabled them to fulfil them, and no longer possessed even the bond of their dramatic interests. So the fraternities which had embodied so much of the life of the people of the towns during the thirteenth, fourteenth, and fifteenth centuries now came to include within their organization fewer and fewer persons and to affect a smaller and smaller part of their interests. Although the companies continued to exist into later times, yet long before the close of the period included in this chapter they had become relatively inconspicuous and insignificant.

One striking evidence of their diminished strength, and apparently a last effort to keep the gild organization in existence, is the curious combination or consolidation of the companies under the influence of the city governments. Numerous instances of the combination of several trades are to be found in the records of every town, as for instance the " company of goldsmiths and smiths and others their brethren," at Hull in 1598, which consisted of goldsmiths, smiths, pewterers, plumbers and glaziers, painters, cutlers, musicians, stationers and bookbinders, and basket-makers. A more striking instance is to be found in Ipswich in 1576, where the various occupations were all drawn up into four companies. as follows: (1) The Mercers; including the mariners, shipwrights, bookbinders, printers, fishmongers, sword setters, cooks, fletchers, arrowhead-makers, physicians, hatters, cappers, mercers, merchants, and several others. (2) The Drapers; including the joiners, carpenters, innholders, freemasons, bricklayers, tilers, carriers, casket-makers, surgeons, clothiers, and some others. (3) The Tailors; including the cutlers, smiths, barbers, chandlers, pewterers, minstrels, pedlers, plumbers, pinners, millers, millwrights, coopers, shearmen, glaziers, turners, tinkers, tailors, and others. (4) The Shoe-makers; including the curriers, collar-makers, saddlers, pointers, cobblers, skinners, tanners, butchers, carters, and laborers. Each of these four companies was to have an alderman and two wardens, and all outsiders who came to the town and wished to set up trade were to be placed by the town officials in one or the other of the four companies. The basis of union in some of these combinations was evidently the similarity of their occupations, as the various workers in leather among the " Shoemakers." In other cases there is no such simi-larity, and the only foundation that can be surmised for the particular grouping is the contiguity of the streets where the greatest number of particular artisans lived, or their propor-tionate wealth. Later, this process reached its culmination in such a case as that of Preston in 1628, where all the trades-men of the town were organized as one company or fraternity called " The Wardens and Company of Drapers, Mercers, Grocers, Salters, Ironmongers, and Haberdashers." The craft and trading gilds in their mediæval character had evidently come to an end.

42. The Growth of Native Commerce. — The most dis-tinctive characteristic of English foreign trade down to the middle of the fifteenth century consisted in the fact that it had been entirely in the hands of foreigners. The period under discussion saw it transferred with quite as great com-pleteness to the hands of Englishmen. Even before 1450 trading vessels had occasionally been sent out from the Eng-lish seaport towns on more or less extensive voyages, carrying out English goods, and bringing back those of other countries or of other parts of England. These vessels sometimes belonged to the town governments, sometimes to individual merchants. This kind of enterprise became more and more common. Individual merchants grew famous for the number and size of their ships and the extent of their trade; as for instance, William Canynges of Bristol, who in 1461 had ten vessels at sea, or Sturmys of the same town, who at about the same time sent the first English vessel to trade with the eastern Mediterranean, or John Taverner of Hull, who built in 1449 a new type of vessel modelled on the carracks of Genoa and the galleys of Venice. In the middle of the fourteenth century the longest list of merchants of any substance that could be drawn up contained only 169 names. At the beginning of the sixteenth century there were at least 3000 merchants engaged in foreign trade, and in 1601 there were about 3500 trading to the Netherlands alone. These merchants exported the old articles of English production and to a still greater extent textile goods, the manufacture of which was growing so rapidly in England. The export of wool came to an end during the reign of Queen Elizabeth, but the export of woven cloth was more than enough to take its place. There was not so much cloth now imported, but a much greater variety and quantity of food-stuffs and wines, of articles of fine manufacture, and of the special products of the countries to which English trade extended.

The entrance of English vessels into ports of towns or countries whose own vessels had been accustomed to the control of the trade with England, or where the old commercial towns of the Hanseatic League, of Flanders, or of Italy had valuable trading concessions, was not obtained without difficulty, and there was a constant succession of conflicts more or less violent, and of disputes between English and foreign sailors and merchants. The progress of English commerce was, however, facilitated by the decay in the prosperity of many of these older trading towns. The growth of strong governments in Denmark, Sweden, Norway, Poland, and Russia resulted in a withdrawal of privileges which the Hanseatic League had long possessed, and internal dissensions made the League very much weaker in the later fifteenth century than it had been during the century and a half before. The most important single occurrence showing this tendency was the capture of Novgorod by the Russian Czar and his expulsion of the merchants of the Hanse from their settlement in that commercial centre. In the same way most of the towns along the south coast of the Baltic came under the control of the kingdom of Poland.

A similar change came about in Flanders, where the semi-independent towns came under the control of the dukes of Burgundy. These sovereigns had political interests too extensive to be subordinated to the trade interests of individual towns in their dominions. Thus it was that Bruges now lost much of its prosperity, while Antwerp became one of the greatest commercial cities of Europe. Trading rights could now be obtained from centralized governments, and were not dependent on the interest or the antagonism of local merchants.

In Italy other influences were leading to much the same results. The advance of Turkish conquests was gradually increasing the difficulties of the Eastern trade, and the discovery of the route around the Cape of Good Hope in 1498 finally diverted that branch of commerce into new lines. English merchants gained access to some of this new Eastern trade through their connection with Portugal, a country advantageously situated to inherit the former trade of Italy and southern Germany. English commerce also profited by the predominance which Florence obtained over Pisa, Genoa, and other trading towns. Thus conditions on the Continent were strikingly favorable to the growing commercial enterprise of England.

43. The Merchants Adventurers. — English merchants who exported and imported goods in their own vessels were, with the exception of the staplers or exporters of wool and other staple articles, usually spoken of as " adventurers," " venturers," or " merchants adventurers." This term is used in three different senses. Sometimes it simply means merchants who entered upon adventure or risk by sending their goods outside of the country to new or unrecognized markets, as the "adventurers to Iceland," "adventurers to Spain." Again, it is applied to groups of merchants in various towns who were organized for mutual protection or other advantage, as the "fishmongers adventurers," who brought their complaints before the Royal Council in 1542; "The Master, Wardens, and Commonalty of Merchant Venturers, of Bristol," existing apparently in the fourteenth century, fully organized by 1467, and incorporated in 1552; "The Society of Merchants Adventurers of Newcastle upon Tyne," or the similar bodies at York and Exeter.

But by far the most frequent use of the term is that by which it was applied to those merchants who traded to the Netherlands and adjacent countries, especially as exporters of cloth, and who came within this period to be recognized and incorporated as the "Merchants Adventurers" in a special sense, with headquarters abroad, a coat of arms of their own, extensive privileges, great wealth, influence, and prominence. These English merchants, trading to the Netherlands in other articles than those controlled by the Staplers, apparently received privileges of trade from the duke of Brabant as early as the thirteenth century, and the right of settling their own disputes before their own "consul" in the fourteenth. But their commercial enterprises must have been quite insignificant, and it was only during the fifteenth century that they became numerous and their trade in English cloth extensive. Just at the beginning of this century, in 1407, the king of England gave a general charter to all merchants trading beyond seas to assemble in definite places and choose for themselves consuls or governors to arrange for their common trade advantage. After this time, certainly by the middle of the century, the regular series of governors of the English merchants in the Netherlands was established, one of the earliest being William Caxton, afterward the founder of printing in

England. On the basis of these concessions and of the privileges and charters granted by the home government the " Merchants Adventurers " gradually became a distinct organization, with a definite membership which was obtained by payment of a sum which gradually rose from 6s. 8d. to £20, until it was reduced by a law of Parliament in 1497 to £6 13s. 4d. They had local branches in England and on the Continent. In 1498 they were granted a coat of arms by Henry VII, and in 1503 by royal charter a distinct form of government under a governor and twenty-four assistants. In 1564 they were incorporated by a royal charter by the title of " The Merchants Adventurers of England." Long before that time they had become by far the largest and most influential company of English exporting merchants. It is said that the Merchants Adventurers furnished ten out of the sixteen London ships sent to join the fleet against the Armada.

Most of their members were London mercers, though there were also in the society members of other London companies, and traders whose homes were in other English towns than London. The meetings of the company in London were held for a long while in the Mercers' hall, and their records were kept in the same minute book as those of the Mercers until 1526. On the Continent their principal office, hall, or gathering place, the residence of their Governor and location of the " Court," or central government of the company, was at different times at Antwerp, Bruges, Calais, Hamburg, Stade, Groningen, and Middelburg; for the longest time probably at the first of these places. The larger part of the foreign trade of England during the fifteenth and most of the sixteenth century was carried on and extended as well as controlled and regulated by this great commercial company.

During the latter half of the sixteenth century, however, other companies of merchants were formed to trade with various countries, most of them receiving a government charter and patronage. Of these the Russia or Muscovy

Company obtained recognition from the government in 1554, and in 1557, when an ambassador from that country came to London, a hundred and fifty merchants trading to Russia received him in state. In 1581 the Levant or Turkey Company was formed, and its members carried their merchandise as far as the Persian Gulf. In 1585 the Barbary or Morocco Company was formed, but seems to have failed. In 1588, however, a Guinea Company began trading, and in 1600 the greatest of all, the East India Company, was chartered. The expeditions sent out by the Bristol merchants and then by the king under the Cabots, those other voyages so full of romance in search of a north-west or a northeast passage to the Orient, and the no less adventurous efforts to gain entrance to the Spanish possessions in the west, were a part of the same effort of commercial companies or interests to carry their trading into new lands.

44. Government Encouragement of Commerce. — Before the accession of Henry VII it is almost impossible to discover any deliberate or continuous policy of the government in commercial matters. From this time forward, however, through the whole period of the Tudor monarchs a tolerably consistent plan was followed of favoring English merchants and placing burdens and restrictions upon foreign traders. The merchants from the Hanse towns, with their dwellings, warehouses, and offices at the Steelyard in London, were subjected to a narrower interpretation of the privileges which they possessed by old and frequently renewed grants. In 1493 English customs officers began to intrude upon their property; in 1504 especially heavy penalties were threatened if they should send any cloth to the Netherlands during the war between the king and the duke of Burgundy. During the reign of Henry VIII the position of the Hansards was on the whole easier, but in 1551 their special privileges were taken away, and they were put in the same position as all other foreigners. There was a partial regrant of advantageous conditions in the early part of the reign of Elizabeth, but finally, in 1578, they lost their privileges forever. As a matter of fact, German traders now came more and more rarely to England, and their settlement above London Bridge was practically deserted.

The fleet from Venice also came less and less frequently. Under Henry VIII for a period of nine years no fleet came to English ports; then after an expedition had been sent out from Venice in 1517, and again in 1521, another nine years passed by. The fleet came again in 1531, 1532, and 1533, and even afterward from time to time occasional private Venetian vessels came, till a group of them suffered shipwreck on the southern coast in 1587, after which the Venetian flag disappeared entirely from those waters.

In the meantime a series of favorable commercial treaties were made in various directions by Henry VII and his successors. In 1490 he made a treaty with the king of Denmark by which English merchants obtained liberty to trade in that country, in Norway, and in Iceland. Within the same year a similar treaty was made with Florence, by which the English merchants obtained a monopoly of the sale of wool in the Florentine dominions, and the right to have an organization of their own there, which should settle trade disputes among themselves, or share in the settlement of their disputes with foreigners. In 1496 the old trading relations with the Netherlands were reëstablished on a firmer basis than ever by the treaty which has come in later times to be known as the *Intercursus Magnus*. In the same year commercial advantages were obtained from France, and in 1499 from Spain. Few opportunities were missed by the government during this period to try to secure favorable conditions for the growing English trade. Closely connected as commercial policy necessarily was with political questions, the former was always a matter of interest to the government, and in all the ups and downs of the relations of England with the continental countries during the sixteenth century the foothold gained by English merchants was always preserved or regained after a temporary loss.

The closely related question of English ship-building was also a matter of government encouragement. In 1485 a law was passed declaring that wines of the duchies of Guienne and Gascony should be imported only in vessels which were English property and manned for the most part by Englishmen. In 1489 woad, a dyestuff from southern France, was included, and it was ordered that merchandise to be exported from England or imported into England should never be shipped in foreign vessels if sufficient English vessels were in the harbor at the time. Although this policy was abandoned during the short reign of Edward VI it was renewed and made permanent under Elizabeth. By indirect means also, as by the encouragement of fisheries, English seafaring was increased.

As a result of these various forms of commercial influence, the enterprise of individual English merchants, the formation of trading companies, the assistance given by the government through commercial treaties and favoring statutes, English commerce became vastly greater than it had ever been before, reaching to Scandinavia and Russia, to Germany and the Netherlands, to France and Spain, to Italy and the eastern Mediterranean, and even occasionally to America. Moreover, it had come almost entirely into the hands of Englishmen; and the goods exported and imported were carried for the most part in ships of English build and ownership, manned by English sailors.

45. The Currency. — The changes just described were closely connected with contemporary changes in the gold and silver currency. Shillings were coined for the first time in the reign of Henry VII, a pound weight of standard silver being coined into 37 shillings and 6 pence. In 1527 Henry VIII had the same amount of metal coined into 40 shillings, and later in the year, into 45 shillings. In 1543 coin silver

L

was changed from the old standard of 11 ounces 2 pennyweights of pure silver to 18 pennyweights of alloy, so as to consist of 10 ounces of silver to 2 ounces of alloy; and this was coined into 48 shillings.   In 1545 the coin metal was made one-half silver, one-half alloy; in 1546, one-third silver, two-thirds alloy; and in 1550, one-fourth silver, three-fourths alloy. The gold coinage was correspondingly though not so excessively debased.   The lowest point of debasement for both silver and gold was reached in 1551.   In 1560 Queen Elizabeth began the work of restoring the currency to something like its old standard.   The debased money was brought to the mints, where the government paid the value of the pure silver in it.   Money of a high standard and permanently established weight was then issued in its place.   Much of the confusion and distress prevalent during the reigns of Henry VIII and Edward VI was doubtless due to this selfish and unwise monetary policy.

At about the same time a new influence on the national currency came into existence.   Strenuous but not very successful efforts had long been made to draw bullion into England and prevent English money from being taken out.   Now some of the silver and gold which was being extorted from the natives and extracted from the mines of Mexico and Peru by the Spaniards began to make its way into England, as into other countries of Europe.   These American sources of supply became productive by about 1525, but very little of this came into general European circulation or reached England till the middle of the century.   After about 1560, however, through trade, and sometimes by even more direct routes, the amount of gold and silver money in circulation in England increased enormously.   No reliable statistics exist, but there can be little doubt that the amount of money in England, as in Europe at large, was doubled, trebled, quadrupled, or perhaps increased still more largely within the next one hundred years.

This increase of money produced many effects.   One

of the most important was its effect on prices. These had begun to rise in the early part of the century, principally as a result of the debasement of the coinage. In the latter part of the century the rise was much greater, due now, no doubt, to the influx of new money. Most commodities cost quite four times as much at the end of the sixteenth century as they did at its beginning.

Another effect of the increased amount of currency appeared in the greater ease with which the use of money capital was obtained. Saving up and borrowing were both more practicable. More capital was now in existence and more persons could obtain the use of it. As a result, manufacturing, trade, and even agriculture could now be conducted on a more extensive scale, changes could be introduced, and production was apt to be profitable, as prices were increasing and returns would be greater even than those calculated upon.

46. Interest. — Any extensive and varied use of capital is closely connected with the payment of interest. In accord with a strict interpretation of certain passages in both the Old and the New Testament, the Middle Ages regarded the payment of interest for the use of money as wicked. Interest was the same as usury and was illegal. As a matter of fact, most regular occupations in the Middle Ages required very little capital, and this was usually owned by the agriculturists, handicraftsmen, or merchants themselves; so that borrowing was only necessary for personal expenses or in occasional exigencies. With the enclosures, sheep farming, consolidation of farms, and other changes in agriculture, with the beginning of manufacturing under the control of capitalist manufacturers, with the more extensive foreign trading and ship owning, and above all with the increase in the actual amount of money in existence, these circumstances were changed. It seemed natural that money which one person had in his possession, but for which he had no immediate use, should be loaned to another who could use it for his own enterprises. These enterprises might be useful to the community, advantageous to himself, and yet profitable enough to allow him to pay interest for the use of the money to the capitalist who loaned it to him. As a matter of fact much money was loaned and, legally or illegally, interest or usury was paid for it. Moreover, a change had been going on in legal opinion parallel to these economic changes, and in 1545 a law was passed practically legalizing interest if it was not at a higher rate than ten per cent. This was, however, strongly opposed by the religious opinion of the time, especially among men of Puritan tendencies. They seemed, indeed, to be partially justified by the fact that the control of capital was used by the rich men of the time in such a way as to cause great hardship. In 1552, therefore, the law of 1545 was repealed, and interest, except in the few forms in which it had always been allowed, was again prohibited. But the tide soon turned, and in 1571 interest up to ten per cent was again made lawful. From that time forward the term usury was restricted to excessive interest, and this alone was prohibited. Yet the practice of receiving interest for the loan of money was still generally condemned by writers on morals till quite the end of this period; though lawyers, merchants, and popular opinion no longer disapproved of it if the rate was moderate.

47. Paternal Government. — In many of the changes which have been described in this chapter, the share which government took was one of the most important influences. In some cases, as in the laws against enclosures, against the migration of industry from the towns to the rural districts, and against usury, the policy of king and Parliament was not successful in resisting the strong economic forces which were at work. In others, however, as in the oversight of industry, in the confiscation of the property of the gilds devoted to religious uses, in the settlement of the relations between employers and employees, in the control of foreign commerce, the policy of the government really decided what direction changes should take.

As has been seen in this chapter, after the accession of Henry VII there was a constant extension of the sphere of government till it came to pass laws upon and provide for and regulate almost all the economic interests of the nation. This was a result, in the first place, of the breaking down of those social institutions which had been most permanent and stable in earlier periods. The manor system in the country, landlord farming, the manor courts, labor dues, serfdom, were passing rapidly away; the old type of gilds, city regulations, trading at fairs, were no longer so general; it was no longer foreigners who brought foreign goods to England to be sold, or bought English goods for exportation. When these old customs were changing or passing away, the national government naturally took charge to prevent the threatened confusion of the process of disintegration. Secondly, the government itself, from the latter part of the fifteenth century onward, became abler and more vigorous, as has been pointed out in the first paragraph of this chapter. The Privy Council of the king exercised larger activities, and extended its jurisdiction into new fields. Under these circumstances, when the functions of the central government were being so widely extended, it was altogether natural that they should come to include the control of all forms of industrial life, including agriculture, manufacturing, commerce, internal trade, labor, and other social and economic relations. Thirdly, the control of economic and social matters by the government was in accordance with contemporary opinions and feelings. An enlightened absolutism seems to have commended itself to the most thoughtful men of that time. A paternalism which regulated a very wide circle of interests was unhesitatingly accepted and approved. As a result of the decay of mediæval conditions, the strengthening of national government, and the prevailing view of the proper functions of government, almost all economic conditions were regulated by the government to a degree quite unknown before. In the early part of the period this regulation was more minute, more intrusive, more evidently directed to the immediate advantage of government; but by the close of Elizabeth's reign a systematic regulation was established, which, while not controlling every detail of industrial life, yet laid down the general lines along which most of industrial life must run. Some parts of this regulation have already been analyzed. Perhaps the best instance and one of the most important parts of it is the Statute of Apprentices of 1563, already described in paragraph **40**. In the same year, 1563, a statute was passed making minute regulations for the fishing and fish-dealing trades. Foreign commerce was carried on by regulated companies; that is, companies having charters from the government, giving them a monopoly of the trade with certain countries, and laying down at least a part of the rules under which that trade should be carried on. The importation of most kinds of finished goods and the exportation of raw materials were prohibited. New industries were encouraged by patents or other government concessions. Many laws were passed, of which that of 1571, to encourage the industry of making caps, is a type. This law laid down the requirement that every person of six years old and upward should wear on every Sunday and holy day a woollen cap made in England.

The conformity of manufactures to standard was enforced either by the officers of companies which were established under the authority of the government or by government officials or patentees, and many of the methods and materials of manufacture were themselves defined by statutes or proclamation. In agriculture, while the policy was less consistent, government regulation was widely applied. There were laws, as has been noted, forbidding the possession of more than two thousand sheep by any one landholder and of more than two farms by any one tenant; laws requiring the keeping of one cow and one calf for every sixty sheep, and the raising a quarter of an acre of flax or hemp for every sixty acres devoted to other crops. The most characteristic laws for the regulation of agriculture, however, were those controlling the export of grain. In order to prevent an excessive price, grain-raisers were not allowed to export wheat or other grain when it was scarce in England. When it was cheap and plenty, they were permitted to do so, the conditions under which it was to be allowed or forbidden being decided, according to a law of 1571, by the justices of the peace of each locality, with the restriction that none should be exported when the prevailing price was more than 1s. 3d. a bushel, a limit which was raised to 2s. 6d. in 1592.

Thus, instead of industrial life being controlled and regulated by town governments, merchant and craft gilds, lords of fairs, village communities, lords of manors and their stewards, or other local bodies, it was now regulated in its main features by the all-powerful national government.

48. BIBLIOGRAPHY

Professor Ashley's second volume is of especial value for this period.

Green, Mrs. J. R.: *Town Life in England in the Fifteenth Century*, two volumes.

Cheyney, E. P.: *Social Changes in England in the Sixteenth Century*, Part I, *Rural Changes*, and *History of England from the Defeat of the Armada to the Death of Elizabeth*.

Bradley, H.: *English Enclosures*.

Gay, E. F.: *Inclosures in England in the Sixteenth Century*, *Quarterly Journal of Economics*, 1903.

A discussion of the legal character of villain tenure in the sixteenth century will be found in articles by Mr. I. S. Leadam, in *The English Historical Review*, for October, 1893, and in the *Transactions of the English Royal Historical Society* for 1892, 1893, 1894 and 1897; and by Professor Ashley in the *English Historical Review* for April, 1893, and *Annals of the American*

Academy of Political Science for January, 1891. (Reprinted in *English Economic History*, Vol. II, Chap. 4.)

Bourne, H. R. F.: *English Merchants.*

Unwin, G.: *The Guilds and Companies of London* and *Industrial Organization in the Sixteenth and Seventeenth Centuries.*

Kramer, S.: *English Craft Gilds and the Government.*

Froude, J. A.: *History of England.* Many scattered passages of great interest refer to the economic and social changes of this period, but they are frequently exaggerated, and in some cases incorrect. Almost the same remark applies to Professor Rogers' *Six Centuries of Work and Wages* and *Industrial and Commercial History of England.*

Busch, Wilhelm: *A History of England under the Tudors.* For the economic policy of Henry VII.

CHAPTER VII

THE EXPANSION OF ENGLAND

Economic Changes of the Seventeenth and Early Eighteenth Centuries

49. National Affairs from 1603 to 1760. — The last three rulers of the Tudor family had died childless. James, king of Scotland, their cousin, therefore, inherited the throne and became the first English king of the Stuart family. James reigned from 1603 to 1625. Many of the political and religious problems which had been created by the policy of the Tudor sovereigns had now to come up for solution. Parliament had long been restive under the almost autocratic government of Queen Elizabeth, but the danger of foreign invasion and internal rebellion, long-established habit, Elizabeth's personal popularity, her age, her sex, and her occasional yielding, all combined to prevent any very outspoken opposition. Under King James all these things were changed. Yet he had even higher ideas of his personal rights, powers, and duties as king than any of his predecessors. Therefore during the whole of the reign dispute and ill feeling existed between the king, his ministers, and many of the judges and other officials, on the one hand, and the majority of the House of Commons and among the middle and upper classes of the country, on the other. James would willingly have avoided calling Parliament altogether and would have carried on the government according to his own judgment and that of the ministers he selected, but it was absolutely necessary to assemble it for the passing of certain laws, and above all for the authorization of taxes to obtain the means to carry on the government. The fall in the value of gold and silver and the consequent rise of prices, and other economic changes, had reduced the income of the government just at a time when its necessary expenses were increasing, and when a spendthrift king was making profuse additional outlays. Finances were therefore a constant difficulty during his reign, as in fact they remained during the whole of the seventeenth century.

In religion James wished to maintain the middle course of the established church as it had been under Elizabeth. He was even less inclined to harsh treatment of the Roman Catholics. On the other hand, the tide of Puritan feeling appealing for greater strictness and earnestness in the church and a more democratic form of church government was rising higher and higher, and with this a desire to expel the Roman Catholics altogether. The House of Commons represented this strong Protestant feeling, so that still another cause of conflict existed between King and Parliament. Similarly, in foreign affairs and on many other questions James was at cross purposes with the main body of the English nation.

This reign was the period of foundation of England's great colonial empire. The effort to establish settlements on the North American coast were at last successful in Virginia and New England, and soon after in the West Indies. Still other districts were being settled by other European nations, ultimately to be absorbed by England. On the other side of the world the East India Company began its progress toward the subjugation of India. Nearer home, a new policy was carried out in Ireland, by which large numbers of English and Scotch immigrants were induced to settle in Ulster, the northernmost province. Thus that process was begun by which men of English race and language, living under English institutions and customs, have established centres of population, wealth, and influence in so many parts of the world.

Charles I came to the throne in 1625. Most of the characteristics of the period of James continued until the quarrels between king and Parliament became so bitter that in 1642 civil war broke out. The result of four years of fighting was the defeat and capture of the king. After fruitless attempts at a satisfactory settlement Charles was brought to trial by Parliament in 1649, declared guilty of treason, and executed.

A republican form of government was now established, known as the " Commonwealth," and kingship and the House of Lords were abolished. The army, however, had come to have a will of its own, and quarrels between its officers and the majority of Parliament were frequent. Both Parliament and army had become unpopular, taxation was heavy, and religious disputes troublesome. The majority in Parliament had carried the national church so far in the direction of Puritanism that its excesses had brought about a strong reactionary feeling. Parliament had already sat for more than ten years, hence called the " Long Parliament," and had become corrupt and despotic. Under these circumstances, one modification after another was made in the form of government until in 1653 Oliver Cromwell, the commander of the army and long the most influential man in Parliament, dissolved that body by military force and was made Lord Protector, with powers not very different from those of a king. There was now a period of good order and great military and naval success for England. Scotland and Ireland, both of which had declared against the Commonwealth, were reduced to obedience, and successful foreign wars were waged. But at home the government did not succeed in obtaining either popularity or general acceptance. Parliament after Parliament was called, but could not agree with the Protector. In 1657 Cromwell was given still higher powers, but in 1658 he died. His son, Richard Cromwell, was installed as Protector. The republican government had, however, been gradually drifting back toward the old royal form and spirit, so when the new Lord Protector proved to be unequal to the position, when the army became rebellious again, and the country threatened to fall into anarchy, Monk, an influential general, brought about the reassembling of the Long Parliament, and this body recalled the son of Charles I to take his hereditary seat as king.

This event occurred in 1660, and is known as the Restoration. Charles II reigned for twenty-five years. His reign was in one of its aspects a time of reaction in manners and morals against the overstrictness of the former Puritan control. In government, notwithstanding the independent position of the king, it was the period when some of the most important modern institutions came into existence. Permanent political parties were formed then for the first time. It was then that the custom arose by which the ministers of the government are expected to resign when there proves to be a majority in Parliament against them. It was then that a " cabinet," or group of ministers acting together and responsible for the policy of the king, was first formed. The old form of the established church came again into power, and harsh laws were enacted against Presbyterians, Baptists, Quakers, and members of the other sects which had grown up during the earlier part of the century.

It was to escape these oppressive laws that many emigrated to the colonies in America and established new settlements. Not only was the stream of emigration kept up by religious persecutions, but the prosperity and abundant opportunity for advancement furnished by the colonies attracted great numbers. The government of the Stuart kings, as well as that of the Commonwealth, constantly encouraged distant settlements for the sake of commerce, shipping, the export of English manufactured goods, and the import of raw materials. The expansion of the country through its colonial settlements therefore still continued.

The great literature which reached its climax in the reign of Elizabeth continued in equal variety and abundance throughout the reigns of James and Charles. The greatest plays of Shakespeare were written after the accession of James. Milton belonged to the Commonwealth period, and Bunyan, the famous author of *Pilgrim's Progress*, was one of those non-conformists in religion who were imprisoned under Charles II. With this reign, however, quite a new literary type arose, whose most conspicuous representative was Dryden.

In 1685 James II succeeded his brother. Instead of carrying on the government in a spirit of concession to national feeling, he adopted such an unpopular policy that in 1688 he was forced to flee from England, and his son-in-law and daughter, William and Mary, were elected to the throne. On their accession Parliament passed and the king and queen accepted a " Bill of Rights." This declared the illegality of a number of actions which recent sovereigns had claimed the right to do, and guaranteed to Englishmen a number of important individual rights, which have since been included in many other documents, especially in the constitutions of several of the American states and the first ten amendments to the Constitution of the United States. The Bill of Rights is often grouped with the Great Charter, and these two documents, along with several of the Acts of the Parliaments of Charles I accepted by the king, make the principal written elements of the English constitution. The form and powers attained by the English government have been, however, rather the result of slight changes from time to time, often without intention of influencing the constitution, than of any deliberate action. Important examples of this are certain customs of legislation which grew up under William and Mary. The Mutiny Act, by which the army is kept up, is only passed for one year at a time. The grant of taxes is also only made annually. Parliament must therefore be called every year in order to obtain money to carry on the work of government, and in order to keep up the military organization.

As a result of the Revolution of 1688, as the deposition of James II and the appointment of William and Mary are called, and of the changes which succeeded it, Parliament gradually became the most powerful part of government, and the House of Commons the strongest part of Parliament. The king's ministers came more and more to carry out the will of Parliament rather than that of the king. Somewhat later the custom grew up by which one of the ministers by presiding over the whole Cabinet, nominating its members to the king, representing it in interviews with the king, and in other ways giving unity to its action, created the position of prime minister. Thus the modern Parliamentary organization of the government was practically complete before the middle of the eighteenth century. William and Mary died childless, and Anne, Mary's sister, succeeded, and reigned till 1714. She also left no heir. In the meantime arrangements had been made to set aside the descendants of James II, who were Roman Catholics, and to give the succession to a distant line of Protestant descendants of James I. In this way George I, Elector of Hanover, of the house of Brunswick, became king, reigned till 1727, and was succeeded by George II, who reigned till 1760. The sovereigns of England have been of this family ever since.

The years following the Revolution of 1688 were a time of almost constant warfare on the Continent, in the colonies, and at sea. In many of these wars the real interests of England were but slightly concerned. In others her colonial and native dependencies were so deeply affected as to make them veritable national wars. Just at the close of the period, in 1763, the war known in Europe as the Seven Years' War and in America as the French and Indian War was brought to an end by the peace of Paris. This peace drew the outlines of the widespread empire of Great Britain, for it handed over to her Canada, the last of the French possessions in America, and guaranteed her the ultimate predominance in India.

50. The Extension of Agriculture. — During the seventeenth and the first half of the eighteenth century there are no such fundamental changes in social organization to chronicle as during the preceding century and a half. During the first hundred years of the period the whole energy of the nation seems to have been thrown into political and religious contests. Later there was development and increase of production, but they were in the main an extension or expansion of the familiar forms, not such a change of form as would cause any alteration in the position of the mass of the people.

The practice of enclosing open land had almost ceased before the death of Elizabeth. There was some enclosing under James I, but it seems to have been quite exceptional. In the main, those common pastures and open fields which had not been enclosed by the beginning of this period, probably one-half of all England, remained unenclosed till the recommencement of the process long afterward. Sheep farming gradually ceased to be so exclusively practised, and mixed agriculture became general, though few if any of those fields which had been surrounded with hedges, and come into the possession of individual farmers, were thrown open or distributed again into scattered holdings. Much new land came into cultivation or into use for pasture through the draining of marshes and fens, and the clearing of forests. This work had been begun for the extensive swampy tracts in the east of England in the latter years of Elizabeth's reign by private purchasers, assisted by an act of Parliament passed in 1601, intended to remove legal difficulties. It proceeded slowly, partly because of the expense and difficulty of putting up lasting embankments, and partly because of the opposition of the fenmen, or dwellers in the marshy districts, whose livelihood was obtained by catching the fish and water fowl that the improvements would drive away. With the seventeenth and early eighteenth centuries, however, largely through the skill of Dutch engineers and laborers, many thousands of acres of fertile land were reclaimed and devoted to grazing, and even grain-raising. Great stretches of old forest and waste land covered with rough underbrush were also reduced to cultivation.

There was much writing on agricultural subjects, and methods of farming were undoubtedly improved, especially in the eight-

eenth century. Turnips, which could be grown during the remainder of the season after a grain crop had been harvested,
and which would provide fresh food for the cattle during the
winter, were introduced from the Continent and cultivated to
some extent, as were clover and some improved grasses. But
these improvements progressed but slowly, and farming on the
whole was carried on along very much the same old lines till
quite the middle of the eighteenth century. The raising of
grain was encouraged by a system of government bounties, as
already stated in another connection. From 1689 onward a
bounty was given on all grain exported, when the prevailing
price was less than six shillings a bushel. The result was that
England exported wheat in all but famine years, that there was
a steady encouragement, even if without much result, to improve
methods of agriculture, and that landlords were able to increase
their rents. In the main, English agriculture and the organization of the agricultural classes of the population did not differ
very much at the end of this period from that at the beginning
except in the one point of quantity, the amount of produce and
the number of the population being both largely increased.

51. The Domestic System of Manufactures. — Much greater
skill in manufacturing was acquired, principally, as in earlier
periods, through the immigration of foreign artisans. In
Queen Elizabeth's time a great number of such men with their
families, who had been driven from the Netherlands by the
persecutions of the duke of Alva, came to England for refuge.
In Sandwich in 1561 some twenty families of Flemings settled
and began their manufactures of various kinds of cloth; in 1565
some thirty Dutch and Walloon families settled in Norwich
as weavers, in Maidstone a body of similar artisans who were
thread-makers settled in 1567; in 1570 a similar group carrying
on various forms of manufacture settled at Colchester; and still
others settled in some five or six other towns. After 1580 a
wave of French Huguenots, principally silk weavers, fled from
their native country and were allowed to settle in London,

Canterbury, and Coventry. The renewed persecutions of the Huguenots, culminating in the revocation of the Edict of Nantes in 1685, sent many thousands more into exile, large numbers of silk and linen weavers and manufacturers of paper, clocks, glass, and metal goods coming from Normandy and Brittany into England, and settling not only in London and its suburbs, but in many other towns of England. These foreigners, unpopular as they often were among the populace, and supported in their opportunities of carrying on their industry only by royal authority, really taught new and higher industries to the native population and eventually were absorbed into it as a more gifted and trained component.

There were also some inventions of new processes or devices for manufacture. The " stocking frame," or machine knitting was invented in the time of Queen Elizabeth, but did not get into actual use until the next century. It then became for the future an extensive industry, especially in London and Nottingham and their vicinity. The weaving of cotton goods was introduced and spread especially in the northwest, in the neighborhood of Manchester and Bolton. A machine for preparing silk thread was invented in 1719. The printing of imported white cotton goods, as calicoes and lawns, was begun, but prohibited by Parliament in the interest of woven goods manufacturers, though the printing of linens was still allowed. Stoneware was also improved. These and other new industries introduced by foreigners or developed by English inventors or enterprising artisans added to the variety and total amount of English manufacture. The old established industries, like the old coarser woollen goods and linen manufacture, increased but slowly in amount and went through no great changes of method.

These industries old and new were in some cases regulated and supervised, as to the quality of wares and methods of manufacture, by the remaining gilds or companies, with the authority which they possessed from the national government. Indeed, there were within the later sixteenth and the seventeenth cen-

M

turies some new companies organized or old ones renewed especially for this oversight, and to guard the monopoly of their members over certain industries in certain towns. In other cases rules were established for the carrying on of a special industry, and a patent or monopoly was then granted by the king by which the person or company was given the sole right to carry on the industry according to those rules, or to enforce the rules when it was carried on by other people. In still other industries a government official had the oversight and control of quality and method of manufacture. Much production, however, especially such as went on in the country, was not supervised at all, notwithstanding the intentions of the government.

Far the greater part of manufacturing industry in this period was organized according to the " domestic system," the beginnings of which have been already noticed within the previous period. That is to say, manufacturing was carried on in their own houses by small masters with a journeyman and apprentice or two. Much of it was done in the country villages or suburbs of the larger towns, and such handicraft was very generally connected with a certain amount of cultivation of the soil. A small master weaver or nail manufacturer or soap boiler or potter, would also have a little farm and divide his time between the two occupations. The implements of manufacture almost always belonged to the small master himself, though in the stocking manufacture and the silk manufacture they were often owned by employing capitalists and rented out to the small manufacturers, or even to journeymen. In some cases the raw material — wool, linen, metal, or whatever it might be — was purchased by the small manufacturer, and the goods were either manufactured for special customers or taken when completed to a neighboring town on market days, there to be sold to a local dealer, or to a merchant who would transport them to another part of the country or export them to other countries. In other cases the raw material, especially in the case of cotton, was the property of a town merchant or capitalist, who distributed it to the small domestic manufacturers in their houses in the villages, paying them for the processes of production, and himself collecting the completed product and disposing of it by sale or export. This domestic manufacture was especially common in the southwest, centre, and northwest of England, and manufacturing towns like Birmingham, Halifax, Sheffield, Leeds, Bolton, and Manchester were growing up as centres around which it gathered. Little or no organization existed among such small manufacturers, though their apprentices were of course supposed to be taken and their journeymen hired according to the provisions of the Statute of Apprentices, and their products were sometimes subjected to some governmental or other supervision.

Thus in manufacturing and artisan life as in agricultural the period was marked by an extension and increase of the amount of industry, on the same general lines as had been reached by 1600, rather than by any considerable changes.

52. Commerce under the Navigation Acts. — The same thing is true of commerce, although its vast extension was almost in the nature of a revolution. As far back as the reign of Elizabeth most of the imports into England were brought in English vessels by English importers, and the goods which were exported were sent out by English exporters. The goods which were manufactured in scattered villages or town suburbs by the domestic manufacturers were gathered by these merchants and sent abroad in ever increasing amounts. The total value of English exports in 1600 was about 10 million dollars, at the close of the century it was some 34 millions, and in 1750 about 63 millions. This trade was carried on largely by merchants who were members of those chartered trading companies which have been mentioned as existing already in the sixteenth century. Some of these were "regulated companies"; that is, they had certain requirements laid down in their charters and power to adopt further rules and regulations,

ARCTIC OCEAN

PACIFIC OCEAN

INDIAN OCEAN

AUSTRALIA

ASIA

AFRICA

EUROPE

GREENLAND

ATLANTIC OCEAN

EQUATOR

SOUTH AMERICA

NORTH AMERICA

ARCTIC OCEAN

PACIFIC OCEAN

PACIFIC OCEAN

PRINCIPAL
ENGLISH TRADE
ROUTES
ABOUT 1700

to which their members must conform. Others had similar chartered rights, but all their members invested funds in a common capital and traded as a joint stock company. In both kinds of cases each company possessed a monopoly of some certain field of trade, and was constantly engaged in the exclusion of interlopers from its trade. Of these companies the Merchants Adventurers, the oldest and one of the wealthiest, controlled the export of manufactured cloth to the Netherlands and northwestern Germany and remained prominent and active into the eighteenth century. The Levant, the Eastland, the Muscovy, the Guinea or Royal African, and, greatest of all, the East India Company, continued to exist under various forms, and carried on their distant commerce through the whole of this period. With some of the nearer parts of Europe — France, Spain, Portugal, and Italy — there was much trading by private merchants not organized as companies or only organized among themselves. The " Methuen treaty," negotiated with Portugal in 1703, gave free entry of English manufactured goods into that country in return for a decreased import duty on Portuguese wines brought into England.

The foreign lands with which these companies traded furnished at the beginning of this period the only places to which goods could be exported and from which goods could be brought ; but very soon the series of settlements of English colonists was begun, one of the principal inducements for which was that they would furnish an outlet for English goods. The " Plantation of Ulster," or introduction of English and Scotch settlers into the north of Ireland between 1610 and 1620, was the beginning of a long process of immigration into that country. But far the most important plantations as an outlet for trade, as in every respect, were those made on the coast of North America and in the West Indies. The Virginia and the Plymouth Companies played a part in the early settlement of these colonies, but they were soon superseded by the crown, single proprietaries, or the settlers themselves. Virginia, New England, Maryland, the Carolinas, and ultimately New York, Pennsylvania, and Georgia on the mainland; the islands of Bermudas, Barbadoes, and Jamaica; and ultimately Canada, came to be populous colonies inhabited by Englishmen and demanding an ever increasing supply of English manufactured goods. These colonies were controlled by the English government largely for their commercial and other forms of economic value. The production of goods needed in England but not produced there, such as sugar, tobacco, tar, and lumber, was encouraged, but the manufacture of such goods as could be exported from England was prohibited. The purchase of slaves in Africa and their exportation to the West Indies was encouraged, partly because they were paid for in Africa by English manufactured goods, partly because their use in the colonies made the supply of sugar and some other products plentiful and cheap.

Closely connected with commerce and colonies as a means of disposing of England's manufactured goods and of obtaining those things which were needed from abroad was commerce for its own sake, for the profits which it brought to those engaged in it, and for the indirect value to the nation of having a large mercantile navy.

The most important provision for this end was the passage of the " Navigation Acts." We have seen that as early as 1485 certain kinds of goods could be imported only in English vessels. But in 1651 a law was passed, and in 1660 under a more regular government reënacted in still more vigorous form, which carried this policy to its fullest extent. By these laws all importation of goods into England from any ports of Asia, Africa, or America was forbidden, except in vessels belonging to English owners, built in England and manned by English seamen; and there was the same requirement for goods exported from England to those countries. From European ports goods could be brought to England only in English vessels or in vessels the property of merchants of the country in which the port lay;

and similarly for export. These acts were directed especially against the Dutch merchants, who were fast getting control of the carrying trade. The result of the policy of the Navigation Acts was to secure to English merchants and to English ship-builders a monopoly of all the trade with the East Indies and Africa and with the American colonies, and to prevent the Dutch from competing with English merchants for the greater part of the trade with the Continent of Europe.

The characteristics of English commerce in this period, therefore, were much the same as in the last. It was, how-ever, still more completely controlled by English merchants and was vastly extended in amount. Moreover, this extension bid fair to be permanent, as it was largely brought about by the growth of populous English colonies in Ireland and America, and by the acquisition of great spheres of influence in India.

53. Finance. — The most characteristic changes of the period now being studied were in a field to which attention has been but slightly called before; that is, in finance. Capital had not existed in any large amounts in mediæval England, and even in the later centuries there had not been any consid-erable class of men whose principal interest was in the invest-ment of saved-up capital which they had in their hands. Agri-culture, manufacturing, and even commerce were carried on with very small capital and usually with such capital as each farmer, artisan, or merchant might have of his own; no use of credit to obtain money from individual men or from banks for industrial purposes being ordinarily possible. Questions connected with money, capital, borrowing, and other points of finance came into somewhat greater prominence with the six-teenth century, but they now attained an altogether new and more important position.

Taxation, which had been looked upon as abnormal and occasional during earlier times, and only justifiable when some special need for large expenditure by the government arose, such as war, a royal marriage, or the entertainment of some foreign visitor, now, after long conflicts between king and Parliament, which are of still greater constitutional than financial importance, came to be looked upon as a regular normal custom. In 1660, at the Restoration, a whole system of excise duties, taxes on imports and exports, and a hearth tax were established as a permanent means for paying the expenses of government, besides special taxes of various kinds for special demands.

Borrowing by merchants and others for ordinary purposes of business became much more usual. During most of the seventeenth century the goldsmiths were the only bankers. On account of the strong vaults of these merchants, their habitual possession of valuable material and articles, and perhaps of their reputation for probity, persons who had money beyond their immediate needs deposited it with the goldsmiths, receiving from them usually six per cent. The goldsmiths then loaned it to merchants or to the government, obtaining for it interest at the rate of eight per cent or more. This system gradually became better established and the high rates decreased. Payments came to be made by check, and promissory notes were regularly discounted by the goldsmiths.

The greatest extension in the use of credit, however, came from the establishment of the Bank of England. In 1691 the original proposition for the Bank was made to the government by William Paterson. In 1694 a charter for the Bank was finally carried through Parliament by the efforts of the ministry. The Bank consisted of a group of subscribers who agreed to loan to the government £1,200,000, the government to pay them an annual interest of eight and one-half per cent, or £100,000 in cash, guaranteed by the product of a certain tax. The subscribers were at the same time incorporated and authorized to carry on a general business of receiving deposits and lending out money at interest. The capital which was to be loaned to the government was subscribed principally by London merchants, and the Bank began its career in the old Grocers' Hall.

The regular income of £100,000 a year gave it a nucleus of strength, and enabled it to discount notes even beyond its actual deposits and to issue its own notes or paper money. Thus money could be borrowed to serve as capital for all kinds of enterprises, and there was an inducement also for persons to save money and thus create capital, since it could always bring them in a return by lending it to the Bank even if they were not in a position to put it to use themselves. Along with the normal effect of such financial inventions in developing all forms of trade and industry, there arose a remarkable series of projects and schemes of the wildest and most unstable character, and the early eighteenth century saw many losses and constant fluctuations in the realm of finance. The most famous instance of this was the " South Sea Bubble," a speculative scheme by which a regulated company, the South Sea Company, was chartered in 1719 to carry on the slave-trade to the West Indies and whale-fishing, and incidentally to loan money to the government. Its shares rose to many fold their par value and fell to almost nothing again within a few months, and the government and vast numbers of investors and speculators were involved in its failure.

The same period saw the creation of the permanent national debt. In earlier times kings and ministers had constantly borrowed money from foreign or native lenders, but it was always provided and anticipated that it would be repaid at a certain period, with the interest. With the later years of the seventeenth century, however, it became customary for the government to borrow money without any definite contract or expectation as to when it should be paid back, only making an agreement to pay a certain rate of interest upon it. This was satisfactory to all parties. The government obtained a large sum at the time, with the necessity of only paying a small sum every year for interest; investors obtained a remunerative use for their money, and if they should need the principal, some one else was always ready to pay its value to them for the

DISTRIBUTION
OF POPULATION

According to the Hearth-tax of

1750

Below 12 houses per sq. mile
Between 12 and 15 per sq. mile
Above 15 houses per sq. mile

SCALE OF MILES

0   20   40   60   80

ENGRAVED BY BORMAY & CO., N.Y.

sake of receiving the interest. The largest single element of the national debt in its early period was the loan of £1,200,000 which served as the basis for the Bank; but after that time, as for a short time before, sums were borrowed from time to time which were not repaid, but became a permanent part of the debt: the total rising to more than £75,000,000 by the middle of the century. Incidentally, this, like the deposits at the goldsmiths' and the Bank, became an opportunity for the investment of savings and an inducement to create more capital.

Fire insurance and life insurance both seem to have had their origin in the later decades of the seventeenth century. Thus in the realm of finance there was much more of novelty, of actually new development, during this period than in agriculture, manufacturing, or commerce. Yet all these forms of economic life and of the social organization which corresponded to them were alike in one respect, that they were quite minutely regulated by the national government. The fabric of paternal government which we saw rising in the time of the Tudor sovereigns remained almost intact through the whole of this period. The regulation of the conditions of labor, of trade, of importation and exportation, of finance, of agriculture, of manufacture, in more or less detail, was part of the regular work of legislation or administrative action. Either in order to reach certain ulterior ends, such as government power, a large navy, or a large body of money within the country, or simply as a part of what were looked upon at the time as the natural functions of government, laws were constantly being passed, charters granted, treaties entered into, and other action taken by government, intended to encourage one kind of industry and discourage another, to determine rates of wages and hours of labor, prescribe rules for agriculture, or individual trades or forms of business, to support some kind of industry which was threatened with decay, to restrict certain actions which were thought to be disadvantageous, to regulate the whole economic life of the nation.

It is true that much of this regulation was on the books rather than in actual existence. It would have required a much more extensive and efficient civil service, national and local, than England then possessed to enforce all or any considerable part of the provisions that were made by act of Parliament or ordered by the king and Council. Again, new industries were generally declared to be free from much of the more minute regulation, so that enterprise where it arose was not so apt to be checked as conservatism where it already existed was apt to be perpetuated. Such regulation and control, moreover, were quite in accord with the feeling and with the economic and political theories of the time, so there was but little sense of interference or tyranny felt by the governed. A regulated industrial organization slowly expanding on well-established lines was as characteristic of the theory as it was of the practice of the period.

54. BIBLIOGRAPHY

Gardiner, S. R.: *The History of England, 1603–1642,* ten volumes.

Many scattered passages in this work and in its continuations, like those in Froude's history, referred to in the last chapter, apply to the economic and social history of the period, and they are always judicious and valuable.

Hewins, W. A. S.: *English Trade and Finance, chiefly in the Seventeenth Century.*

Lingelbach, W. E.: *The Laws and Ordinances of the Merchants Adventurers.*

For this period Cunningham, Rogers, and Palgrave, in the books already referred to, are almost the only secondary authorities, except such as go into great detail on individual points. Cunningham's second volume, which includes this period, is extremely full and satisfactory.

Macpherson, D.: *Annals of Commerce* is a large collection of somewhat uncritically tested records.

CHAPTER VIII

THE PERIOD OF THE INDUSTRIAL REVOLUTION

55. National Affairs from 1760 to 1820. — The sixty years lying between these two dates were covered by the long reign of George III, the first English Hanoverian king. In the political world this period had by no means the importance that it possessed in the field of economic development. Parliament had already obtained its permanent form and powers, and when George III tried to " be a king," as his mother urged him, the effort to restore personal government was an utter failure. Between 1775 and 1783 occurred the American Revolution, by which thirteen of England's most valued colonies were lost to her and began their progress toward a greater destiny. The breach between the American colonies and the mother country was brought about largely by the obstinacy of the king and his ministers in adopting an arbitrary and unpopular policy. Other political causes no doubt contributed to the result. Yet the greater part of the alienation of feeling which underlay the Revolution was due not to political causes, but to the economic policy already described, by which American commerce and industry were bent to the interests of England.

In the American war France joined the rebellious colonies against England, and obtained advantageous terms at the peace. Within ten years the two countries had again entered upon a war, this time of vastly greater extent, and continuing almost unbroken for more than twenty years. This was a result of the outbreak of the French Revolution. In 1789 the

Estates General of France, a body corresponding in its earlier history to the English Parliament, was called for the first time for almost two hundred years. This assembly and its successors undertook to reorganize French government and society. In the course of this radical process principles were enunciated proclaiming the absolute liberty and equality of men, demanding the participation of all in government, the abolition of aristocratic privileges, and finally of royalty itself. In following out these ideas, so different from those generally accepted in Europe, France was brought into conflict with all the other European states, including Great Britain. War broke out in 1793. Fighting took place on sea and land and in various parts of the world. France in her new enthusiasm developed a strength, vigor, and capacity which enabled her to make head against the alliances of almost all the other countries of Europe, and even to gain victories and increase her territory at their expense. No peace seemed practicable. In her successive internal changes of government one of the generals of the army, Napoleon Bonaparte, obtained a more and more influential position, until in 1804 he took the title of Emperor. The wars of the French Revolution, therefore, were merged in the wars of Napoleon. Alliance after alliance was made against him, England commonly taking the initiative in the formation of them and paying large monthly subsidies to some of the continental governments to enable them to support their armies. The English navy won several brilliant victories, especially under Nelson, although her land forces played a comparatively small part until the battle of Waterloo in 1815.

The naval supremacy thus obtained made the war a matter of pecuniary profit to the English nation, notwithstanding its enormous expense; for it gave to her vessels almost a complete monopoly of the commerce and the carrying trade of the world, and to her manufactures extended markets which would otherwise have been closed to her or shared with other nations. The cutting off of continental and other sources of supply of grain and the opening of new markets greatly increased the demand for English grain and enhanced the price paid for it. This caused higher rents and further enclosure of open land. Thus the war, which had been entered upon reluctantly and with much opposition in 1793, became popular, partly because of the feeling of the English people that it had become a life and death struggle with France, but largely also because English industries were flourishing under it. The wars came to an end with the downfall of Napoleon in 1815, and an unwonted period of peace for England set in and lasted for almost forty years.

The French Revolution produced another effect in England. It awakened a certain amount of admiration for its principles of complete liberty and equality and a desire to apply them to English aristocratic society and government. In 1790 societies began to be formed, meetings held, and pamphlets issued by men who sympathized with the popular movements in France. Indeed, some of these reformers were suspected of wishing to introduce a republic in England. After the outbreak of the war the ministry determined to put down this agitation, and between 1793 and 1795 all public manifestation of sympathy with such principles was crushed out, although at the cost of considerable interference with what had been understood to be established personal rights. Much discontent continued through the whole period of the war, especially among the lower classes, though it did not take the form of organized political agitation. It was a period, as will be seen, of violent economic and social changes, which, although they enriched England as a whole and made it possible for her to support the unprecedented expenses of the long war, were very hard upon the working classes, who were used to the old ways.

After the peace of 1815, however, political agitation began again. The Whig party seemed inclined to resume the effort to carry certain moderate reforms which had been postponed on account of the war, and down below this movement there was a more radical agitation for universal suffrage and for a more democratic type of government generally. On the other hand, the Tory government, which had been in power during almost the whole war period, was determined to oppose everything in the nature of reform or change, on the ground that the outrages accompanying the French Revolution arose from just such efforts to make reforming alterations in the government. The radical agitation was supported by the discontented masses of the people who were suffering under heavy taxes, high prices, irregular employment, and many other evils they felt to be due to their interests being disregarded by government. The years intervening between 1815 and 1830 were therefore a period of constant bitterness and contention between the higher and the lower classes. Mass meetings which were called by the popular leaders were dissolved by the government, radical writers were prosecuted by the government for libel, the habeas corpus act was suspended repeatedly, and threatened rioting was met with severe measures. The actions of the ministers, while upheld by the higher classes, were bitterly attacked by others as being unconstitutional and tyrannical.

In 1800 the union of the group of British Islands under one government was completed, at least in form. Scotland had come under the same crown as England in 1603, and the two Parliaments had been united in 1707, the title Great Britain having been adopted for the combined nations. The king of England had held the title of Lord of Ireland from the time of the first conquest, and of King of Ireland since the adoption of the title by Henry VIII. The union which now took place consisted in the abolition of the separate Irish Parliament and the election of Irish members to the combined or " Imperial " Parliament of the three kingdoms sitting at Westminster. The official title of the united countries has since been " The United Kingdom of Great Britain and Ireland."

56. The Great Mechanical Inventions. — As the eighteenth century progressed one form of economic growth seems to have been pressing on the general economic organization.

This was the constant expansion of commerce, the steadily increasing demand for English manufactured goods for export. The great quantities of goods which were every year sent abroad in English ships to the colonies, to Ireland, to the Continent, to Asia and Africa, as well as those used at home, continued to be manufactured in most cases by methods, with instruments, under an organization of labor the same as that which had been in existence for centuries. The cotton and woollen goods which were sold in the West Indies and America were still carded, spun, and woven in the scattered cottages of domestic weavers and weaver-farmers in the rural districts of the west and north of England, by the hand cards, the spinning-wheel, the cumbrous, old-fashioned loom. The pieces of goods were slowly gathered from the hamlets to the towns, from the towns to the seaports, over the poorest of roads, and by the most primitive of conveyances. And these antiquated methods of manufacture and transportation were all the more at variance with the needs and possibilities of the time because there had been, as already pointed out, a steady accumulation of capital, and much of it was not remuneratively employed. The time had certainly come for some improvement in the methods of manufacture.

A closer examination into the process of production in England's principal industry, cloth-making, shows that this pressure on old methods was already felt. The raw material for such uses, as it comes from the back of the sheep, the boll of the cotton plant, or the crushed stems of the flax, is a tangled mass of fibre. The first necessary step is to straighten out the threads of this fibre, which is done in the case of wool by combing, in the others by carding, both being done at that time by hand implements. The next step is spinning, that is, drawing out the fibres, which have been made parallel by carding, into a slender cord, and at the same time twisting this sufficiently to cause the individual fibres to take hold one of another and thus make a thread of some strength. This was sometimes

N

done on the old high wheel, which was whirled around by hand and then allowed to come to rest while another section of the cotton, wool, or flax was drawn from the carded mass by hand, then whirled again, twisting this thread and winding it up on the spindle, and so on. Or it was done by the low wheel, which was kept whirling continuously by the use of a treadle worked by the foot, while the material was being drawn out all the time by the two hands, and twisted and wound continuously by the horseshoe-shaped device known as the " flyer." When the thread had been spun it was placed upon the loom; strong, firmly spun material being necessary for the " warp " of upright threads, softer and less tightly spun material for the " woof " or " weft," which was wrapped on the shuttle and thrown horizontally by hand between the two diverging lines of warp threads. After weaving, the fabric was subjected to a number of processes of finishing, fulling, shearing, dyeing, if that had not been done earlier, and others, according to the nature of the cloth or the kind of surface desired.

In these successive stages of manufacture it was the spinning that was apt to interpose the greatest obstacle, as it took the most time. From time immemorial spinning had been done, as explained, on some form of the spinning-wheel, and by women. One weaver continuously at work could easily use up the product of five or six spinners. In the domestic industry the weaving was of course carried on in the dwelling-house by the father of the family with the grown sons or journeymen, while the spinning was done for the most part by the women and younger children of the family. As it could hardly be expected that there would always be as large a proportion as six of the latter class to one of the former, outside help must be obtained and much delay often submitted to. Many a small master who had agreed to weave up the raw material sent him by the master clothier within a given time, or a cloth weaver who had planned to complete a piece by next market day, was obliged to leave his loom and search through the neighborhood for some disengaged laborer's wife or other person who would spin the weft for which he was waiting. One of the very few inventions of the early part of the century intensified this difficulty. Kay's drop box and flying shuttle, invented in 1738, made it possible for a man to sit still and by pulling two cords alternately throw the shuttle to and fro. One man could therefore weave broadcloth instead of its requiring two as before, and consequently weaving was more rapid, while no corresponding change had been introduced into the process of spinning.

Indeed, this particular difficulty was so clearly recognized that the Royal Society offered a prize for the invention of a machine that would spin several threads at the same time.

No one claimed this reward, but the spirit of invention was nevertheless awake, and experiments in more than one mechanical device were being made about the middle of the century. The first to be brought to actual completion was Hargreaves' spinning-jenny, invented in 1764. According to the traditional story James Hargreaves, a small master weaver living near Blackburn, on coming suddenly into the house caused his wife, who was spinning with the old high wheel, to spring up with a start and overset the wheel, which still continued whirling, but horizontally, and with its spindle in a vertical position. He was at once struck with the idea of using one wheel to cause a number of spindles to revolve by means of a continuous band, and by the device of substituting for the human hand a pair of bars which could be successively separated and closed, and which could be brought closer to or removed from the spindles on wheels, to spin several threads at the same time. On the basis of this idea and with the help of a neighboring mechanic he constructed a machine by which a man could spin eight threads at the same time. In honor of his wife he named it the " Spinning-jenny." The secret of this device soon came out and jennies spinning twenty or thirty or more threads at a time came into use here and there through the old spinning districts. At the same time a much more effective method was being brought to perfection by Richard Arkwright, who followed out some old experiments of Wyatt of Northampton. According to this plan the carded material was carried through successive pairs of rollers, each pair running more rapidly than the previous pair, thus stretching it out, while it was spun after leaving the last pair by flyers adapted from the old low or treadle spinning-wheel. Arkwright's first patent was taken out in 1769, and from that time forward he invented, patented, and manufactured a series of machines which made possible the spinning of a number of threads at the same time very much more rapidly than even the spinning-jenny. Great numbers of Arkwright's spinning-machines were manufactured and sold by him and his partners. He made others for use in cotton mills carried on by himself with various partners in different parts of the country. His patent was eventually set aside as having been unfairly obtained, and the machines were soon generally manufactured and used. Improvements followed. An ingenious weaver named Samuel Crompton, perceiving that the roller spinning was more rapid but that the jennies would spin the finer thread, combined the two devices into one machine, known from its hybrid origin as the " mule." This was invented in 1779, and as it was not patented it soon came into general use. These inventions in spinning reacted on the earlier processes and led to a rapid development of carding and combing machines. A carding cylinder had been invented by Paul as far back as 1748, and now came into general use, while several wool-combing machines were invented in 1792 and 1793.

So far all these inventions had been in the earlier textile processes. Use for the spun thread was found in giving fuller employment to the old hand looms, in the stocking manufacture, and for export; but no corresponding improvement had taken place in weaving. From 1784 onward a clergyman from the south of England, Dr. Edward Cartwright, was gradually

MULE-SPINNING IN 1835

(Baines: *History of Cotton Manufacture*.)

bringing to perfection a power loom which by the beginning of the nineteenth century began to come into general use. The value put upon Cartwright's invention may be judged from the fact that Parliament voted him a gift of £10,000 in 1809. Arkwright had already won a large fortune by his invention, and in 1786 was knighted in recognition of his services to the national industry.

While Cartwright was experimenting on the power loom, an invention was made far from England which was in reality an essential part of the improvement in the manufacture of cotton goods. This was the American cotton gin, for the removal of the seeds from the fibre of the boll, invented by Eli Whitney in 1792. Cotton had been introduced into the Southern states during the Revolutionary War. Its cultivation and export now became profitable, and a source of supply became available at the very time that the inventions for its manufacture were being perfected.

Spinning-jennies could be used in the household of the weaver; but the later spinning-machines were so large and cumbrous that they could not be used in a dwelling-house, and required so much power and rapidity of motion that human strength was scarcely available. Horse power was used to some extent, but water power was soon applied and special buildings came to be put up along streams where water power was available. The next stage was the application of steam power. Although the possibility of using steam for the production of force had long been familiar, and indeed used to some extent in the pumping out of mines, it did not become available for general uses until the improvements of James Watt, patented in 1769 and succeeding years. In partnership with a man named Boulton, Watt began the manufacture of steam-engines in 1781. In 1785 the first steam-engine was used for power in a cotton mill. After that time the use of steam became more and more general and by the end of the century steam power was evidently superseding water power.

57. The Factory System. — But other things were needed to make this new machinery available. It was much too expensive for the old cottage weavers to buy and use. Capital had, therefore, to be brought into manufacturing which had been previously used in trade or other employments. Capital was in reality abundant relatively to existing opportunities for investment, and the early machine spinners and weavers drew into partnership moneyed men from the towns who had previously no connection with manufacturing. Again, the new industry required bodies of laborers working regular hours under the control of their employers and in the buildings where the machines were placed and the power provided. Such groups of laborers or " mill hands " were gradually collected where the new kind of manufacturing was going on. Thus factories, in the modern sense, came into existence — a new phenomenon in the world.

These changes in manufacturing and in the organization of labor came about earliest in the manufacture of cotton goods, but the new machinery and its resulting changes were soon introduced into the woollen manufacture, then other textile lines, and ultimately into still other branches of manufacturing, such as the production of metal, wooden, and leather goods, and, indeed, into nearly all forms of production. Manufacturing since the last decades of the eighteenth century is therefore usually described as being done by the " factory system," as contrasted with the domestic system and the gild system of earlier times.

The introduction of the factory system involved many changes: the adoption of machinery and artificial power, the use of a vastly greater amount of capital, and the collection of scattered laborers into great strictly regulated establishments. It was, comparatively speaking, sudden, all its main features having been developed within the period between 1760 and 1800; and it resulted in the raising of many new and difficult social problems. For these reasons the term " Industrial Revolution," so generally applied to it, is not an exaggerated nor an unsuitable term. Almost all other forms of economic occupation have subsequently taken on the main characteristics of the factory system, in utilizing improved machinery, in the extensive scale on which they are administered, in the use of large capital, and in the organization of employees in large bodies. The Industrial Revolution may therefore be regarded as the chief characteristic distinguishing this period and the times since from all earlier ages.

58. Iron, Coal, and Transportation. — A vast increase in the production of iron and coal was going on concurrently with the rise of the factory system. The smelting of iron ore was one of the oldest industries of England, but it was a declining rather than an advancing industry. This was due to the exhaustion of the woods and forests that provided fuel, or to their retention for the future needs of ship-building and for pleasure parks. In 1760, however, Mr. Roebuck introduced at the Carron iron-works a new kind of blast furnace by which iron ore could be smelted with coal as fuel. In 1790 the steam-engine was introduced to cause the blast. Production had already begun to advance before the latter date, and it now increased by thousands of tons a year till far into the present century. Improvements were introduced in puddling, rolling, and other processes of the manufacture of iron at about the same time. The production of coal increased more than proportionately. New devices in mining were introduced, such as steam pumps, the custom of supporting the roofs of the veins with timber instead of pillars of coal, and Sir Humphry Davy's safety lamp of 1815. The smelting of iron and the use of the steam-engine made such a demand for coal that capital was applied in large quantities to its production, and more than ten million tons a year were mined before the century closed.

Some slight improvements in roads and canals had been made and others projected during the seventeenth and early eighteenth centuries; but in the last quarter of the century the work of Telford, Macadam, and other engineers, and of the private turnpike companies or public authorities who engaged them, covered England with good roads. The first canal was that from Worsley to Manchester, built by Brindley for the duke of Bridgewater in 1761. Within a few years a system of canals had been constructed which gave ready transportation for goods through all parts of the country. The continuance of this development of transportation and its fundamental modification by the introduction of railways and steamboats has been one of the most striking characteristics of the nineteenth century.

59. The Revival of Enclosures. — The changes which the latter half of the eighteenth century and the early part of the nineteenth brought were as profound in the occupation and use of the land as they were in the production and transportation of manufactured goods. An agricultural revolution was in progress as truly as was the industrial.

The improvements in the methods of farming already referred to as showing themselves earlier in the century became much more extensive. The raising of turnips and other root crops spread from experimental to ordinary farms so that a fallow year with no crop at all in the ground came to be almost unknown. Clover and artificial grasses for hay came to be raised generally, so that the supply of forage for the winter was abundant. New breeds of sheep and cattle were obtained by careful crossing and plentiful feeding, so that the average size was almost doubled, while the meat, and in some cases the wool, was improved in quality in even greater proportion. The names of such men as Jethro Tull, who introduced the "drill husbandry," Bakewell, the great improver of the breeds of cattle, and Arthur Young, the greatest agricultural observer and writer of the century, have become almost as familiar as those of Crompton, Arkwright, Watt, and other pioneers of the factory system. The general improvement in agricultural methods was due, not so much to new discoveries or inventions, as it was to the large amount of capital which was introduced into their practice. Expensive schemes of draining, marling, and other forms of fertilizing were carried out, long and careful investigations were entered upon, and managers of large farms were trained in special processes by landlords and farmers who had the command of large sums of money; and with the high prices prevalent they were abundantly remunerated for the outlay. Great numbers of " gentlemen farmers," such as Lord Townshend, the duke of Bedford, and George III himself, who wrote articles for the agricultural papers signed " Farmer George," were leaders in this agricultural progress. In 1793 a government Board of Agriculture was established, and through the whole latter part of the century numerous societies for the encouragement of scientific tillage and breeding were organized.

In the early years of the eighteenth century there had been signs of a revival of the old process of enclosures, which had been largely suspended for more than a century. This was brought about by private acts of Parliament. An act would be passed by Parliament giving legal authority to the inhabitants of some parish to throw together the scattered strips, and to redivide these and the common meadows and pastures in such a way that each person with any claim on the land should receive a proportionate share, and should have it separated from all others and entirely in his own control. It was the usual procedure for the lord of the manor, the rector of the parish, and other large landholders and persons of influence to agree on the general conditions of enclosure and draw up a bill appointing commissioners, and providing for survey, compensation, redistribution, and other requirements. They then submitted this bill to Parliament, where, unless there was some special reason to the contrary, it was passed. Its provisions were then carried out, and although legal and parliamentary fees and the expenses of survey and enclosure were large, yet as a result each inhabitant who had been able to make out a legal claim to any of the land of the parish received either some money compensation or a stretch of enclosed land. Such private enclosure acts increased slowly in number till about the middle of the century, when the increase became much more rapid. The number of enclosure acts passed by Parliament and the approximate extent of land enclosed under their provisions were as follows : —

1700–1759	. .	244 Enclosure Bills	. .	337,877 Acres	
1760–1769	. .	385 " "	. .	704,550	"
1770–1779	. .	660 " "	. .	1,207,800	"
1780–1789	. .	246 " "	. .	450,180	"
1790–1799	. .	469 " "	. .	858,270	"
1800–1809	. .	847 " "	. .	1,550,010	"
1810–1819	. .	853 " "	. .	1,560,990	"

In 1756, 1758, and 1773 general acts were passed encouraging the enclosure for common use of open pastures and arable fields, but not enclosing or dividing them permanently, and not providing for any separate ownership.

In 1801 an act was passed to make simpler and easier the passage of private bills for enclosure; and in 1836 another to make possible, with the consent of two-thirds of the persons interested, the enclosing of certain kinds of common fields even without appealing to Parliament in each particular case. Finally, in 1845, the general Enclosure Act of that year carried the policy of 1836 further and appointed a body of Enclosure Commissioners, to determine on the expediency of any proposed enclosure and to attend to carrying it out if approved. Six years afterward, however, an amendment was passed making it necessary that even after an enclosure had been approved by the Commissioners it should go to Parliament for final decision.

By measures such as these the greater part of the lands which had remained unenclosed to modern times were transformed into enclosed fields for separate cultivation or pasture. This process of enclosure was intended to make possible, and no doubt did bring about, much improved agriculture. It exerted incidentally a profound effect on the rural population. Many persons had habitually used the common pastures and open fields for pasture purposes, when they had in reality no legal claim whatever to such use. A poor man whose cow, donkey, or flock of geese had picked up a precarious livelihood on land of undistinguished ownership now found the land all enclosed and his immemorial privileges withdrawn without compensation. Naturally there was much dissatisfaction. A popular piece of doggerel declared that : —

> "The law locks up the man or woman
> Who steals the goose from off the common ;
> But leaves the greater villain loose ·
> Who steals the common from the goose."

Again, a small holder was frequently given compensation in the form of money instead of allotting to him a piece of land which was considered by the commissioners too small for effective use. The money was soon spent, whereas his former claim on the land had lasted because it could not readily be alienated.

A more important effect, however, was the introduction on these enclosed lands of a kind of agriculture which the small landholder was ill fitted to follow. Improved cultivation, a careful rotation of crops, better fertilizers, drainage, farm stock, and labor were the characteristics of the new farming, and these were ordinarily practicable only to the man who had some capital, knowledge, and enterprise. Therefore, coincidently with the enclosures began a process by which the smaller tenants began to give up their holdings to men who could pay more rent for them by consolidating them into larger farms. The freeholders also who owned small farms from time to time sold them to neighboring landowners when difficulties forced them or high prices furnished inducements.

60. Decay of Domestic Manufacture. — This process would have been a much slower one but for the contemporaneous changes that were going on in manufacturing. As has been seen, many small farmers in the rural districts made part of their livelihood by weaving or other domestic manufacture, or, as more properly described, the domestic manufacturers frequently eked out their resources by carrying on some farming. But the invention of machinery for spinning not only created a new industry, but destroyed the old. Cotton thread could be produced vastly more cheaply by machinery. In 1786 a certain quantity of a certain grade of spun yarn was worth 38 shillings; ten years later, in 1796, it was worth only 19 shillings; in 1806 it was worth but 7 shillings 2 pence, and so on down till, in 1832, it was worth but 3 shillings. Part of this reduction in price was due to the decrease in the cost of raw cotton, but far the most of it to the cheapening of spinning.

It was the same a few years later with weaving. Hand-loom weavers in Bolton, who received 25 shillings a week as wages in 1800, received only 19 shillings and 6 pence in 1810, 9 shillings in 1820, and 5 shillings 6 pence in 1830. Hand work in other lines of manufacture showed the same results. Against such reductions in wages resistance was hopeless. Hand work evidently could not compete with machine work. No amount of skill or industry or determination could enable the hand workers to make their living in the same way as of old. As a matter of fact, a long, sad, desperate struggle was kept up by a whole generation of hand laborers, especially by the hand-loom weavers, but the result was inevitable.

The rural domestic manufacturers were, as a matter of fact, devoting themselves to two inferior forms of industry. As far as they were handicraftsmen, they were competing with a vastly cheaper and better form of manufacture; as far as they were farmers, they were doing the same thing with regard to agriculture. Under these circumstances some of them gave up their holdings of land and drifted away to the towns to keep up the struggle a little longer as hand-loom weavers, and then to become laborers in the factories; others gave up their looms and devoted themselves entirely to farming for a while, but eventually sold their holdings or gave up their leases, and dropped into the class of agricultural laborers. The result was the same in either case. The small farms were consolidated, the class of yeomanry or small farmers died out, and household manufacture gave place to that of the factory. Before the end of the century the average size of English farms was computed at three hundred acres, and soon afterward domestic spinning and weaving were almost unknown.

There was considerable shifting of population. Certain parts of the country which had been quite thickly populated with small farmers or domestic manufacturers now lost the greater part of their occupants by migration to the newer manufacturing districts or to America. As in the sixteenth century, some villages disappeared entirely. Goldsmith in *The Deserted Village* described changes that really occurred, however opposed to the facts may have been his description of the earlier idyllic life whose destruction he deplored.

The existence of unenclosed commons and common fields had been accompanied by very poor farming, very thriftless and shiftless habits. The improvement of agriculture, the application of capital to that occupation, the disappearance of the domestic system of industry, and other changes made the enclosure of common land and the accompanying changes inevitable. None the less it was a relatively sudden and complete interference with the established character of rural life, and not only was the process accompanied with much suffering, but the form which took its place was marked by some serious disadvantages. This form was brought about through the rapid culmination of old familiar tendencies. The classes connected with the land came to be quite clearly distinguished into three groups: the landlords, the tenant farmers, and the farm laborers. The landlord class was a comparatively small body of nobility and gentry, a few thousand persons, who owned by far the greater portion of the land of the country. Their estates were for the most part divided up into farms, to the keeping of which in productive condition they contributed the greater part of the expense, to the administration of which trained stewards applied themselves, and in the improvement of which their owners often took a keen and enlightened interest. They received high rents, possessed unlimited local influence, and were the favored governing class of the country. The class of farmers were men of some capital, and frequently of intelligence and enterprise, though rarely of education, who held on lease from the landlords farms of some one, two, or three or more hundred acres, paying relatively large rents, and yet by the excellence of their farming making for themselves a liberal income. The farm laborers were the residuum of the changes which have been traced in the history of landholding; a large class living for the most part miserably in cottages grouped in villages, holding no land, and receiving day wages for working on the farms just described.

Notwithstanding the improvements in agriculture and the increase in the extent of cultivated land, England ceased within the eighteenth century to be a self-supporting country in food products. The form which the "corn laws" had taken in 1689 had been as follows: the raising of wheat was encouraged by prohibiting its importation and paying a bounty of about eightpence a bushel for its exportation so long as the prevailing price was less than six shillings a bushel. When it was between six shillings and six shillings eightpence a bushel its importation was forbidden, but there was no bounty paid for exportation. Between the last price and ten shillings a bushel it could be imported by paying a duty of a shilling a bushel. Above the last price it could be imported free. Nevertheless, during the latter half of the eighteenth century it became evident that there was no longer a sufficient amount of wheat raised for the needs of the English people. Between 1770 and 1790 exports and imports about balanced one another, but after the latter year the imports always exceeded the exports.

This was of course due to the great increase of population and to its employment in the field of manufactures. The population in England in 1700 was about five millions, in 1750 about six millions and a half, in 1800 about nine millions, and in 1850 about eighteen millions. That is to say, its progress was slow during the first half of the eighteenth century, more rapid during the latter half, and vastly more rapid during the first half of the nineteenth century.

61. The Laissez-faire Theory. — A scarcely less complete change than that which had occurred in manufactures, in agriculture, and in social life as based upon these, was that which was in progress at the same time in the realm of ideas, especially as applied to questions of economic and social life. The complete acceptance of the view that it was a natural and desirable part of the work of government to regulate the economic life of the people had persisted well past the middle of the eighteenth century. But very different tendencies of thought arose in the latter part of the century. One of these was the prevailing desire for greater liberty. The word liberty was defined differently by different men, but for all alike it meant a resistance to oppression, a revulsion against interference with personal freedom of action, a disinclination to be controlled any more than absolutely necessary, a belief that men had a right to be left free to do as they chose, so far as such freedom was practicable.

As applied to economic interests this liberty meant freedom for each person to make his living in the way he might see fit, and without any external restriction. Adam Smith says: "The patrimony of a poor man lies in the strength and dexterity of his hands; and to hinder him from employing this strength and dexterity in what manner he thinks proper, without injury to his neighbor, is a plain violation of this most sacred property. It is a manifest encroachment upon the just liberty both of the workman and of those who might be disposed to employ him. As it hinders the one from working at what he thinks proper, so it hinders the other from enploying whom they think proper." Government regulation, therefore, in so far as it restricted men's freedom of action in working, employing, buying, selling, etc., was an interference with their natural liberty.

A second influence in the same direction was the prevalent belief that most of the evils that existed in society were due to the mistakes of civilization, that if men could get back to a " state of nature " and start again, things might be much better. It was felt that there was too much artificiality, too much interference with natural development. Arthur Young condemned the prevailing policy of government, " because it consists of prohibiting the natural course of things. All restrictive forcible measures in domestic policy are bad." Regulation was unwise because it forced men's actions into artificial lines when it would have been much better to let them follow natural lines. Therefore it was felt not only that men had a right to carry on their economic affairs as they chose, but that it was wise to allow them to do so, because interference or regulation had been tried and found wanting. It had produced evil rather than good.

A third and by far the most important intellectual influence which tended toward the destruction of the system of regulation was the development of a consistent body of economic teaching, which claimed to have discovered natural laws showing the futility and injuriousness of any such attempts. Adam Smith's *Wealth of Nations* was published in 1776, the year of the invention of Crompton's mule, and in the decade when enclosures were more rapid than at any other time, except in the middle years of the Napoleonic wars. This was, therefore, one of the earliest, as it was far the most influential, of a series of books which represent the changes in ideas correlative to the changes in actual life already described. It has been described as having for its main object " to demonstrate that the most effectual plan for advancing a people to greatness

o

is to maintain that order of things which nature has pointed out, by allowing every man, as long as he observes the rules of justice, to pursue his own interests in his own way, and to bring both his industry and his capital into the freest competition with those of his fellow-citizens." But the most distinct influence exercised by the writings of Adam Smith and his successors was not so much in pointing out that it was unjust or unwise to interfere with men's natural liberty in the pursuit of their interests, as in showing, as it was believed, that there were natural laws which made all interference incapable of reaching the ends it aimed at. A series of works were published in the latter years of the eighteenth and the early years of the nineteenth century by Malthus, Ricardo, McCulloch, James Mill, and others, in which principles were enunciated and laws formulated which were believed to explain why all interference with free competition was useless or worse. Not only was the whole subject of economic relations clarified, much that had been regarded as wise brought into doubt, and much that had been only doubted shown to be absurd, but the attainment of many objects previously sought for was, as it was believed, shown to be impossible, and to lie outside of the realm of human control.

It was pointed out, for instance, that because of the limited amount of capital in existence at any one time, " a demand for commodities is not a demand for labor; " and therefore a law like that which required burial in a woollen shroud did not give added occupation to the people, but only diverted them from one occupation to another. Ricardo developed a law of wages to the effect that they always tend to the amount " necessary to enable the laborer to subsist, and to perpetuate his race without either increase or diminution," and that any artificial raising or lowering of wages is impossible, or else causes an increase or diminution in their number which, through competition, soon brings back the old rate. Rent was also explained by Ricardo as arising from the differences of quality between different pieces of land, and as measured by the difference in the productivity of the land under consideration and that of the poorest land under cultivation at the time; and therefore being in its amount independent of direct human control. The Malthusian law of population showed that population tended to increase in a geometrical ratio, subsistence for the population, on the other hand, only in an arithmetical ratio, and that poverty was, therefore, the natural and inevitable result in old countries of a pressure of population on subsistence. The sanction of science was thus given alike to the desires of the lovers of freedom and to the regrets of those who deplored man's departure from the state of nature.

All these intellectual tendencies and reasonings of the later eighteenth century, therefore, combined to discredit the minute regulation of economic society, which had been the traditional policy of the immediately preceding centuries. The movement of thought was definitely opposed to the continuance or extension of the supervision of the government over matters of labor, wages, hours, industry, commerce, agriculture, or other phenomena of production, distribution, exchange, or consumption. This set of opinions is known as the *laissez-faire* theory of the functions of government, the view that the duties of government should be reduced to the smallest possible number, and that it should keep out of the economic sphere altogether. Adam Smith would have restricted the functions of government to three: to protect the nation from the attacks of other nations, to protect each person in the nation from the injustice or violence of other individuals, and to carry on certain educational or similar institutions which were of general utility, but not to any one's private interest. Many of his successors would have cut off the last duty altogether.

62. Cessation of Government Regulation. These theoretical opinions came to be more and more widely held, more and more influential over the most thoughtful of English statesmen and other men of prominence, until within the first half of the nineteenth century it may be said that their acceptance was general and their influence dominant. They fell in with the actual tendencies of the times, and as a result of the natural breaking down of old conditions, the rise of new, and the general acceptance of this attitude of *laissez-faire*, a rapid and general decay of the system of government regulation took place.

The old regulation had never been so complete in reality as it was on the statute book, and much of it had died out of itself. Some of the provisions of the Statute of Apprentices were persistently disregarded, and when appeals were made for its application to farm work in the latter part of the eighteenth century Parliament refused to enforce it, as they did in the case of discharged soldiers in 1726 and of certain dyers in 1777. The assize of bread was very irregularly enforced, and that of other victuals had been given up altogether. Many commercial companies were growing up without regulation by government, and in the world of finance the hand of government was very light. The new manufactures and the new agriculture grew up to a large extent apart from government control or influence; while the forms to which the old regulation did apply were dying out. In the new factory industry practically the whole body of the employees were without the qualifications required by the Statute of Apprentices, as well as many of the hand-loom weavers who were drawn into the industry by the abundance and cheapness of machine-spun thread. In the early years of the nineteenth century a strenuous effort was made by the older weavers to have the law enforced as it stood. The whole matter was investigated by Parliament, but instead of enforcing the old law they modified it by acts passed in 1803 and 1809, so as to allow of greater liberty. The old prohibition of using fulling mills passed in 1553 was also repealed in 1809. The Statute of Apprentices after being weakened piecemeal as just mentioned, and by a further amendment removing the wages clauses in 1813, and after being referred to by Lord Mansfield as "against the natural rights and contrary to the common law rights of the land," was finally removed from the statute book in 1814. Even the "Combination Acts," which had forbidden laborers to unite to settle wages and hours, were repealed in 1824. Similar changes took place in other fields than those of the relations between employers and employees. The leading characteristic of legislation on questions of commerce, manufactures, and agriculture during the last quarter of the eighteenth century and the first half of the nineteenth consists in the fact that it almost wholly tended toward freedom from government control. The proportions in which the influence of the natural breaking down of an outgrown system, of the new conditions which were arising, and of pure theory were combined cannot of course be distinguished. All were present. Besides this there are always a large number of persons in the community who would be primarily benefited by a change, and who therefore take the initiative or exercise a special pressure in favor of it.

The Navigation Acts began to go to pieces in 1796, when the old rule restricting importations from America, Asia, and Africa to British vessels was withdrawn in favor of the United States; in 1811 the same permission to send goods to England in other than British vessels was given to Brazil, and in 1822 to the Spanish-American countries. The whole subject was investigated by a Parliamentary Commission in 1820, at the request of the London Chamber of Commerce, and a policy of withdrawal from control determined upon. In 1823 a measure was passed by which the crown was empowered to form reciprocity treaties with any other country so far as shipping was concerned, and agreements were immediately entered into with Prussia, Denmark, Hamburg, Sweden, and within the next twenty years with most other important countries. The old laws of 1660 were repealed in 1826, and a freer system substituted, while in 1849 the Navigation Acts were abolished altogether. In the meantime the monopoly of the old regulated companies was being withdrawn, the India trade being thrown open in 1813 and given up entirely by the Company in 1833. Gradually the commerce of England and of all the English colonies was opened equally to the vessels of all nations.

A beginning of removal of the import and export duties, which had been laid for the purpose of encouraging or discouraging or otherwise influencing certain lines of production or trade, was made in a commercial treaty entered into by Pitt with France in 1786, but not carried farther.

It remains to be noted in this connection that " free trade in land " was an expression often used during the same period, and consisted in an effort marked by a long series of acts of Parliament and regulations of the courts to simplify the title to land, the processes of buying and selling it, and in other ways making its use and disposal as simple and uncontrolled by external regulation as was commerce or any form of industry.

Thus the structure of regulation of industry, which had been built up in the sixteenth and seventeenth centuries, or which had survived from the Middle Ages, was now torn down ; the use of the powers of government to make men carry on their economic life in a certain way, to buy and sell, labor and hire, manufacture and cultivate, export and import, only in such ways as were thought to be best for the nation, seemed to be entirely abandoned. The *laissez-faire* view of government was to all appearances controlling all public action.

63. Individualism. — But the prevailing tendencies of thought and the economic teaching of the period were not merely negative and opposed to government regulation; they contained a positive element also. If there was to be no external control, what incentive would actuate men in their industrial existence? What force would hold economic society together? The answer was a plain one. Enlightened self-interest was the incentive, universal free competition was the force. James Anderson, in his *Political Economy*, published in 1801, says, " Private interest is the great source of public good, which, though operating unseen, never ceases one moment to act with unabating power, if it be not perverted by the futile regulations of some short-sighted politician." Again, Malthus, in his *Essay on Population*, in 1817, says: " By making the passion of self-love beyond comparison stronger than the passion of benevolence, the more ignorant are led to pursue the general happiness, an end which they would have totally failed to attain if the moving principle of their conduct had been benevolence. Benevolence, indeed, as the great and constant source of action, would require the most perfect knowledge of causes and effects, and therefore can only be the attribute of the Deity. In a being so short-sighted as man it would lead to the grossest errors, and soon transform the fair and cultivated soil of human society into a dreary scene of want and confusion."

In other words, a natural and sufficient economic force was always tending to act and to produce the best results, except in as far as it was interfered with by external regulation. If a man wishes to earn wages, to receive payment, he must observe what work another man wants done, or what goods another man desires, and offer to do that work or furnish those goods, so that the other man may be willing to remunerate him. In this way both obtain what they want, and if all others are similarly occupied all wants will be satisfied so far as practicable. But men must be entirely free to act as they think best, to choose what and when and how they will produce. The best results will be obtained where the greatest freedom exists, where men may compete with one another freed from all trammels, at liberty to pay or ask such wages, to demand or offer such prices, to accept or reject such goods, as they wish or can agree upon. If everybody else is equally free the man who offers the best to his neighbor will be preferred. Effort will thus be stimulated, self-reliance encouraged, production increased, improvement attained, and economy guaranteed. Nor should there be any special favor or encouragement given by government or by any other bodies to any special individuals or classes of persons or kinds of industry, for in this way capital and labor will be diverted from the direction which they would naturally take, and the self-reliance and energy of such favored persons diminished.

Therefore complete individualism, universal freedom of competition, was the ideal of the age, as far as there is ever any universal ideal. There certainly was a general belief among the greater number of the intelligent and influential classes, that when each person was freely seeking his own best interest he was doing the best for himself and for all. Economic society was conceived of as a number of freely competing units held in equilibrium by the force of competition, much as the material universe is held together by the attraction of gravitation. Any hindrance to this freedom of the individual to compete freely with all others, any artificial support or encouragement that gives him an advantage over others, is against his own real interest and that of society.

This ideal was necessarily as much opposed to voluntary combinations, and to restrictions imposed by custom or agreement, as it was to government regulation. Individualism is much more than a mere *laissez-faire* policy of government. It believes that every man should remain and be allowed to remain free, unrestricted, undirected, unassisted, so that he may be in a position at any time to direct his labor, ability, capital, enterprise, in any direction that may seem to him most desirable, and may be induced to put forth his best efforts to attain success. The arguments on which it was based were drawn from the domain of men's natural right to economic as to other freedom; from experience, by which it was believed that all regulation had proved to be injurious; and from economic doctrine, which was believed to have discovered natural laws that proved the necessary result of interference to be evil, or at best futile.

The changes of the time were favorable to this ideal Men had never been so free from external control by government or any other power. The completion of the process of enclosure left every agriculturist at liberty to plant and raise what he chose, and when and how he chose. In the new factories, systems of transportation, and other large establishments that were taking the places of small ones, employees were at liberty to leave their engagements at any time they chose, to go to another employer or another occupation; and the employer had the same liberty of discharging at a moment's notice. Manufacturers were at liberty to make anything they chose, and hire laborers in whatever proportion they chose. And just as early modern regulation had been given up, so the few fragments of mediæval restrictive institutions that had survived the intervening centuries were now rapidly abandoned in the stress of competitive society. Later forms of restriction, such as trade unions and trusts, had not yet grown up. Actual conditions and the theoretical statement of what was desirable approximated to one another more nearly than they usually have in the world's history.

Yet somehow the results were disappointing. More and better manufactured goods were produced and foreign goods sold, and at vastly lower prices. The same result would probably have been true in agriculture had not the corn laws long prevented this consummation, and instead distributed the surplus to paupers and the holders of government bonds through the medium of taxes. There was no doubt of English wealth and progress. England held the primacy of the world in commerce, in manufactures, in agriculture. Her rapid increase in wealth had enabled her to bear the burden, not only of her own part in the Napoleonic wars, but of much of the expense of the armament of the continental countries. Population also was increasing more rapidly than ever before. She stood before the world as the most prominent and successful modern nation in all material respects. Yet a closer examination into her internal condition shows much that was deeply unsatisfactory. The period of transition from the domestic to the factory system of industry and from the older to the new farming conditions was one of almost unrelieved misery to great masses of those who were bound to the old ways, who had neither the capital, the enterprise, nor the physical nor mental adaptability to attach themselves to the new. The hand-loom weavers kept up a hopeless struggle in the garrets and cellars of the factory towns, while their wages were sinking lower and lower till finally the whole generation died out. The small farmers who lost the support of spinning and other by-industries succumbed in the competition with the larger producers. The cottagers whose commons were lost to them by enclosures frequently failed to find a niche for themselves in their own part of the country, and became paupers or vagabonds. Many of the same sad incidents which marked the sixteenth century were characteristic of this period of analogous change, when ultimate improvement was being bought at the price of much immediate misery.

Even among those who were supposed to have reaped the advantages of the changes of the time many unpleasant phenomena appeared. The farm laborers were not worse, perhaps were better off on the average, in the matter of wages, than those of the previous generation, but they were more completely separated from the land than they had ever been before, more completely deprived of those wholesome influences which come from the use of even a small portion of land, and of the incitement to thrift that comes from the possibility of rising. Few classes of people have ever been more utterly without enjoyment or prospects than the modern English farm laborers. And one class, the yeomen, somewhat higher in position and certainly in opportunities, disappeared entirely, recruited into the class of mere laborers.

Wages were sometimes higher than under the old conditions, but they were even more irregular. Greater ups and downs occurred. Periods of very active production and of restriction of production alternated more decidedly than before, and introduced more irregularity into industry for both employers and employees. The town laborer engaged in a large establishment was, like the rural laborer on a large farm, completely separated from the land, from capital, from any active connection with the administration of industry, from any probable opportunity of rising out of the laboring class. His prospects were therefore as limited as his position was laborious and precarious.

The rapid growth of the manufacturing towns, especially in the north, drawing the scattered population of other parts of the country into their narrow limits, caused a general breakdown in the old arrangements for providing water, drainage, and fresh air, and made rents high, and consequently living in crowded rooms necessary. The factory towns in the early part of the century were filthy, crowded, and demoralizing, compared alike with their earlier and their present condition.

In the higher grades of economic society the advantages of the recent changes were more distinct, the disadvantages less so. The rise of capital and business enterprise into greater importance, and the extension of the field of competition, gave greater opportunity to employing farmers, merchants, and manufacturers, as well as to the capitalists pure and simple. But even for them the keenness of competition and the exigencies of providing for the varying conditions of distant markets made the struggle for success a harder one, and many failed in it.

In many ways, therefore, it might seem that the great material advances which had been made, the removal of artificial restrictions, the increase of liberty of action, the extension of the field of competition, the more enlightened opinions on economic and social relations, had failed to increase human happiness appreciably; indeed, for a time had made the condition of the mass of the people worse instead of better.

64. BIBLIOGRAPHY

Toynbee, Arnold: *The Industrial Revolution of the Eighteenth Century in England*, new edition, 1894.

Lecky, W. E. H.: *History of England in the Eighteenth Century*, Vol. VI, Chap. 23.

Baines, E.: *History of the Cotton Manufacture in Great Britain.*

Cooke-Taylor, R. W.: *The Modern Factory System.*

Levi, L.: *History of British Commerce and of the Economic Progress of the British Nation.*

Prothero, R. E.: *The Pioneers and Progress of English Farming.*

Rogers, J. E. T.: *Industrial and Commercial History.*

Smith, Adam: *An Inquiry into the Nature and Causes of the Wealth of Nations.*

Chapman, S. J.: *The Lancashire Cotton Industry*, Manchester, 1904.

Galloway, R. L.: *History of Coal Mining in Great Britain*, London, 1882.

Wood, H. T.: *Industrial England in the Middle of the Eighteenth Century*, London, 1913.

Gonner, E. C. K.: *Common Land and Enclosures*, 1912.

Hammond, J. L. and B.: *The Village Labourer, 1760–1832*, London, 1911.

Hammond, J. L. and B.: *The Town Labourer, 1760–1832*, London, 1917.

Hammond, J. L. and B.: *The Skilled Labourer, 1760–1832*, London, 1920.

Bowden, Witt: *The Rise of the Great Manufacturers of England*, University of Pennsylvania, Philadelphia, 1919.

Mantoux, P.: *La Révolution industrielle au XVIIIme siècle en Angleterre.*

CHAPTER IX

PREDOMINANCE OF THE INDIVIDUALIST IDEAL, 1820-1848

65. National Affairs from 1820 to 1848. — The period from 1820 to 1848 was free from any serious warfare. The British fleet intervened, it is true, to help Greece obtain her freedom from Turkey in 1827, and on the other hand, to prevent the Pasha of Egypt from becoming independent and seizing Syria and Asia Minor from Turkey in 1841. There was also a small war with China from 1839 to 1841, known as the Opium War, which resulted in England obtaining from China an indemnity and possession of the island of Hong Kong, which she made into a strong fortress and a valuable colony. There were also rather serious disputes with France, Spain, and the United States, but these were settled without war.

If external affairs were comparatively peaceful, the internal affairs of England were exceedingly stormy, and important political changes took place. The English government in the year 1820 might be described as a complete aristocracy. The king had practically no powers apart from his ministers, and they were merely the representatives of the majority in Parliament. Parliament consisted of the House of Lords and the House of Commons. The first of these houses was made up for the most part of an hereditary aristocracy. The bishops and newly created peers, the only element which did not come in by inheritance, were appointed by the king and usually from the families of those who already possessed inherited titles. The House of Commons had originally been made up of two members from each county and two from each important town. But the list of represented towns was still practically

the same as it had been in the fifteenth century, while intervening economic and other changes had, as has been seen,
made the most complete alteration in the distribution of population. Great manufacturing towns had grown up as a result
of changes in commerce and of the industrial revolution, and
these had no representation in Parliament separate from the
counties in which they lay. On the other hand, towns once of
respectable size had dwindled until they had only a few dozen
inhabitants, and in some cases had reverted to open farming
country; but these, or the landlords who owned the land on
which they had once existed, still retained their two representatives in Parliament. The county representatives were voted
for by all " forty shilling freeholders," that is, land-owners whose
farms would rent for forty shillings a year. But the whole
tendency of English landholding, as has been seen, had been
to decrease the number of land-owners in the country by increasing the size of farms, substituting renting farmers for
owners, and transforming the old yeomanry into farm laborers,
so that the actual number of voters was only a very small
proportion of the rural population.

Such great irregularities of representation had thus grown
up that the selection of more than a majority of the members of the House of Commons was in the hands of a very
small number of men, many of them already members of the
House of Lords, and all members of the aristocracy.

Just as Parliament represented only the higher classes, so
officers in the army and to a somewhat less extent the navy,
the clergy of the established church, the magistrates in the
counties, ambassadors abroad, and cabinet ministers at home,
holders of influential positions in the universities and in endowed institutions were all, as a regular thing, members
of the small class of the landed or mercantile aristocracy of
England. Perhaps one hundred thousand out of the fourteen
millions of the people of England were the veritable governing
classes. They alone had any control of national and local

government and of the most important political and social institutions.

On the other hard, among the masses of the people there was an active "radical" movement being carried on, led by a few intellectual sympathizers from the upper and middle classes. The mass meetings, processions, publications, and petitions of the agitators, demanding reforms in taxation, landholding, elections to Parliament and other abuses of the time, threw the upper classes who controlled the government into a panic. As a result the years just preceding the beginning of this period and its early part were filled with a series of prosecutions, calling out of the militia, adoption of "sedition" and other repressive laws, riots, and other forms of conflict between the governing classes and the dissatisfied masses.

The agitation for the reform of Parliament, which began again after the close of the Napoleonic wars in 1815, was carried on after 1820 with some degree of interest by the more liberal members of the Whig party in Parliament and with much more eagerness by the radical leaders of the people who had no representation in Parliament and were so deeply dissatisfied with their condition. In 1830 an opportunity to bring up a measure of parliamentary reform suddenly presented itself. George IV, who had been king since the death of his father in 1820, died in this year and his brother, William IV, became king. When a new king comes to the throne, a new election for Parliament is always held. The election held in 1830 offered a fair possibility to the Whigs who had been so long in a minority, to win a majority in Parliament. The Tory party was much divided in opinion on recent events, and in France and other countries on the Continent of Europe there had just occurred revolutionary changes which encouraged men of liberal ideas everywhere to make greater efforts to win success.

The result of the election was to give the Whigs a majority in Parliament for the first time for many years. They immediately introduced a bill for the reform of Parliament. This deprived many small and corrupt towns of their right of separate representation, transferred these representatives to the more populous towns and counties, extended the franchise to a somewhat larger number of persons, and, finally, introduced registers of voters, kept the polls open for only two days, and corrected a number of such minor abuses. There was a bitter contest in Parliament and in the country at large on the proposed change, and the measure was only carried after it had been rejected by one House of Commons, passed by a new house elected as a test of the question, then defeated by the House of Lords, and only passed by them when submitted again with the threat by the ministry of advising the king to create enough new peers to pass it if the existing members refused to do so. Its passage was thus secured in 1832. It was carried by pressure from below through all its stages. The king signed it reluctantly because it had been sent to him by Parliament, the House of Lords passed it under threats from the ministry, who based their power on the House of Commons. This body in turn had to be reconstructed by a new election before it would agree to it, and there is no doubt that the voters as well as Parliament itself were much influenced by the cry of " the Bill, the whole Bill, and nothing but the Bill," raised by mobs, associations, and meetings, consisting largely of the masses of the people who possessed no votes at all. In the last resort, therefore, it was a victory won by the masses, and, little as they profited by it immediately, it proved to be the turning point, the first step from aristocracy toward democracy. In 1837, five years after the passage of the Reform Bill, William IV died and Queen Victoria began her long reign of sixty-four years.

66. Railways. — Just as the latter part of the eighteenth and the early years of the nineteenth century were marked by a wonderful extension of manufacturing and the accompanying changes that have been described in the last chapter, so the period covered by this chapter, from 1820 to 1848, was marked by the introduction and rapid development of steam transportation. It is true that turnpikes and canals had already been introduced, but the railroads and steam navigation, which now came in, were so much more important that they have given shape to the whole period since.

For a century or more short railways, at first with wooden then with cast-iron tracks, had been laid in the coal regions and elsewhere to make it easier for horses to haul wagons or cars with heavy loads from the mines to the towns or to the river or canal side. Between 1800 and 1820, some twenty-five railways of this kind of a somewhat ambitious character, from five to ten or twenty miles long and requiring from $50,000 to $500,000 capital, were granted charters by Parliament and brought into use. On most of these horse power was used, but on some of them stationary engines drew the cars up the steeper slopes while horses were used on the level stretches. Locomotives were also being occasionally experimented with on one or two of the roads.

In 1821 a great step forward was taken. In the first place a charter was granted for a railroad to run from Stockton at the mouth of the Tees River on the east coast of England to Darlington in the coal regions. It was opened in 1825, and the cars that ran on it not only carried the coal for which it had been intended and other freight, but as many as eighty or a hundred passengers a day. The road was about twenty-five miles long. Several horse coaches ran every day at seven to nine miles an hour, and there were two stationary engines that drew the cars up inclines. So far there was nothing to distinguish it from the other railroads of the time except its greater devotion to passenger traffic. But the engineer of this road was an inventive man named George Stephenson, and on his advice the directors asked Parliament for an addition to their charter to allow them to use locomotive engines. In 1825, the year of its opening with horses and stationary engines, it put on the road six small locomotives which ran at twelve to fourteen miles an hour, drawing freight cars only. A beginning of modern railway

P

transportation had been made, so far at least as freight was concerned.

The first railroad, however, on which locomotives were regularly used for all trains was the Liverpool and Manchester Railway, opened five years later, in 1830. The trade between these two cities, one the centre of the new manufacturing industry, the other the principal port on the west coast, was very large but was entirely dependent on canal and roads. It was therefore much hampered by ice in winter, low water in summer, and by the lack of interest and enterprise of the canal and turnpike proprietors. It was said to take longer to carry goods from Manchester to Liverpool than from Liverpool to New York, and Manchester mills were often closed for lack of material when raw cotton was piled high on the Liverpool docks. In 1824 at a public meeting in Liverpool a proposal was made for the building of a railroad, subscriptions were requested, a charter applied for, and Stephenson appointed engineer. Capital was ready; it was a time of general investment and but little difficulty was found in obtaining the $2,000,000 required.

Much delay was experienced, however, in inducing Parliament to grant a charter. It had been announced that locomotives would be used on the new railway, and to these there was much opposition from land-owners, proprietors of canals and turnpike roads, and an ignorant and captious public. Magazine articles, pamphlets, and speeches in Parliament were devoted to pointing out the evil results that would follow the general use of locomotives. The directors themselves were somewhat doubtful as to the practicability and desirability of the sole use of locomotives for power. There was a widespread belief that on a smooth track the wheels of a locomotive would slip, whirling around, and not drawing the engine itself or the cars forward. There was consequently much experimentation in using cog-wheels fitting into a cogged track and with other devices, until some one made a test and found this difficulty quite imaginary. Still uncertain, the directors held an open competition at Liverpool, in October,

1829. Amid great popular interest and excitement, the "Rocket," a new type of locomotive built by Stephenson, drew twelve tons and a half twenty-nine miles an hour, gained the prize, and was accepted by the directors. The charter having been given by Parliament in the meanwhile, the road, which was thirty miles long over difficult country, was completed and opened September 15, 1830. Six trains a day began to run on it regularly

THE "ROCKET" LOCOMOTIVE, 1825
(Smiles: *Life of George Stephenson.*)

at an average speed of eighteen miles an hour and at an average passenger fare of about seven cents a mile, though this speed was soon increased and the rate of fare decreased. The company paid 8 per cent dividends in its first year, at the same time that it lessened the difficulty of transportation between the two cities enormously.

The opening of the Liverpool and Manchester Railway was

the beginning of an extremely rapid extension of railroads. The engineering success, the large amount of goods and number of passengers carried, the justification of the claims that had been made for the railroads, the failure of the evils that had been apprehended, the profitableness to stockholders, and convenience to the public all indicated the desirability of forming similar companies and building more railroads. Surveys were rapidly made all over the country for new railroads which promised to be profitable. Each year saw new applications to Parliament for charters and new construction of railway lines. In the year 1836 Parliament authorized twenty-nine new railroads, amounting all together to about 1000 miles of track. Notwithstanding a period of commercial depression which for the moment checked investment, the grant of charters and the construction of railroads soon recommenced and continued with ever increasing rapidity for some years. By 1848 some 12,000 miles of railway had been authorized and more than 5000 miles opened. Seventy-five railroads were in use and on these there were more than 25,000,000 passengers a year. All the large cities and more populous parts of the country had been connected by railways over which trains were running with comparative frequency, regularity, and rapidity. The main lines connecting London with the north, northwest, northeast, southeast, and southwest were established, and there were lines connecting the east and west coasts.

This rapid spread of the new means of transportation over the whole country had not been accomplished without the misrepresentation, dishonesty, and wild speculation that usually accompany such periods of change. The year 1845 saw what has been called the " railway mania," a great speculative excitement like the South Sea Bubble of the early eighteenth century and many other periods of speculation since. The period of commercial depression was now over, there was much capital in the country looking for investment, and every one looked on railroads as a safe and profitable form of enterprise. Men were carried away with the spectacle of their extension, usefulness, and success. Shares of new companies organized in 1844 and 1845 were sold at a constantly increasing price, even before the railroads were built. The whole country rang with the interest in railroad enterprises. Some 270 bills for chartering new railroads, aggregating between 4000 and 5000 miles, were introduced into Parliament in 1845. All classes were caught in a wild speculation, which reached to every other form of finance and industry. A frenzy seized the stock markets and thousands of men not only removed their savings from other places but bound themselves to payments far beyond any funds in their actual control. Men grew rich overnight by the rise of the price of shares they had not yet paid for in companies whose rights of way were not yet surveyed. It was said there was scarcely a family in England that was not interested directly or indirectly in the purchase and sale of railroad shares. Then the inevitable crisis came. Thursday, October 16, 1845, the Bank of England made a change in its rate of interest. Immediately dealings became slower, suspicion was aroused, and new buyers began to be alarmed. The next day settlements were demanded. In a few days failures took place, the price of shares fell, those who had subscribed but not paid were prosecuted, and those who had acted as directors of roads were in turn held responsible. Thousands of men and whole families were buried in debt. Several men committed suicide, others fled to the Continent, still others were placed in debtors' prisons.

One of the conspicuous figures of this period of speculation and crime, and one of the earliest in the long line of modern promoters was George Hudson, " the railway king," as he was called at the time. A dry-goods merchant of York, he had become wealthy, established a banking house, and was elected mayor of that city. When railroads were first introduced, he became interested and was a factor in the formation of some of the earliest small companies in the north of England, and later in their extension and combination. Under the influence of the *laissez-faire* ideas of the time the early railroads were built almost without control, regulation, or direction from the government, and they were therefore built haphazard, between any two points where the engineering difficulties were not too great and where the traffic was sufficient to promise a money profit. Within a few years a process naturally began of drawing these detached roads into some kind of system or group of systems. This was done by the purchase or lease of some of the lines by others or by amalgamation of two or more separate companies into one. This required parliamentary action in each case and gave rise to much conflict and many scandals. It was by this process and principally before 1848 that the great British railway systems of modern times, the London and Northwestern, the Great Northern, the Midland, etc., were created. It was in this process that Hudson achieved his greatest successes and committed his most dubious acts. By his ability in the organization of companies, the manipulation of finances, and the management of men, he carried out one large plan after another and accomplished the consolidation of one group after another of the detached railways. He was chairman of the boards of directors of many railroads at the same time and his advice or influence was instrumental in bringing about the investment of millions of pounds in railway operations. During the great era of speculation in 1845 Hudson was most active, presiding over boards of directors, appearing before parliamentary committees, persuading reluctant officers, outwitting rival companies, and carrying out far-reaching and often questionable plans. In two days he is said to have secured the consent of forty bodies of shareholders to arrangements involving the outlay of $50,000,000. His picture was displayed everywhere, he was elected to Parliament, and was listened to there with great respect. When the panic came he, like others, suffered losses. He now received in the newspapers as much condemnation as he had previously received adulation, and his actions were severely criticised by the parliamentary committee which investigated the railroads the next year. His downfall did not come, however, till 1849, when he was declared by a later committee to have misappropriated two and a half million dollars and to have been guilty of many illegal actions. He resigned from all his railroad connections, went abroad, and soon dropped completely out of notice.

The original expectation when railroads were built was that they would be used, as turnpikes were, by any one who was willing to run his cars and locomotives upon them, paying toll for the use of the track just as a man does in driving a wagon on a road. Those who built the railroads would make their money from the receipt of these tolls. Indeed there are a few early instances where this was tried, private carriers using the line exclusively, or along with the railway company itself. This plan was also anticipated by the government, the early railway charters all requiring that the railway should be open to the vehicles of all comers. But this plan almost immediately proved impracticable. It was necessary that only one company should use the railroad, under its own system, and that this should be the same company that owned the roadbed and other permanent equipment. A committee of Parliament which reported in 1839 declared that the original intention of Parliament to open railways to all carriers could not be carried into effect. A railway was therefore seen to be in the nature of things a monopoly.

The degree of control of the community over this monopoly was a question of dispute from the beginning, the opinion of those financially interested in the railroads being against any public regulation, whereas many private persons and successive committees of Parliament declared in favor of exercising public supervision over the conditions of railroad construction and use, the rate of their charges, and the amounts of their dividends. One parliamentary committee after another recommended some form of control. But government at that time was inefficient and unassertive ; all the tendencies of the time were against regulation. Parliament was half-hearted in the matter and contained many members whose personal interest was opposed to the proposed control; so but few and weak laws were passed to carry out the recommendations of the committees. The English railroads consequently have differed from those of the Continent of Europe in the absence or at least the slight degree of government assistance given them and control exercised over their development and management in the public interest.

Such laws as have been passed have been negative in character, directed to the prevention of serious damage to the public or unfairness to investors, rather than to the introduction of positive advantages. Acts placing the railroads to a slight degree under the control of the Board of Trade were passed in 1840 and 1842; and in 1845 a law of somewhat greater importance was passed, commonly known as the Gladstone act, since Mr. Gladstone, then a young member of the ministry of Sir Robert Peel, was chairman of the committee which recommended it, and was its principal advocate in Parliament. Its main provisions, which were far less than had been recommended by the committee, were the following. For the benefit of working people every railway line must run at least one train a day conveying third class passengers at the rate of one penny a mile. Such trains have ever since been called " parliamentary trains." Cheap rates were required for carrying mails and for the transportation of troops. All railroads to be chartered in the future should be subject to compulsory purchase by the government at any time after twenty-one years, the purchase price, if the railroad had been earning less than 10 per cent a year during the five previous years to be settled by arbitration; if earning more than 10 per cent being equal to twenty-five times its average profits. This power of purchase on the part of government has never been made use of and has long been felt to be inadequate. It has remained nevertheless a possibility and at the same time a restriction on the relations of the government to the railroads. No more effective legislation was passed until much later times, and however enterprising the roads may have been, on the whole they have been administered in the interest merely of the investors in their stocks and bonds, and primarily for the advantage neither of the public which supports them nor of the managing officials and workmen who have actually created and run them.

67. Steam Navigation. — The application of steam power to navigation over long distances belongs also in this period, and its progress was in many ways parallel to that of the railroads. Experiments in using steam power in boats had been in progress since about 1790 and steamboats had been in actual use for river and harbor traffic since 1812. From about 1820, however, there was a marked progress in the building and use of steam vessels. More were built, they were of larger size, and iron was frequently made use of as material. At that time the Clyde ship-building yards began their career of activity, and Napier's improvements in marine engines and boilers were introduced. In 1836 the first practicable screw propeller was invented by Ericsson, a Swede living in England. Shortly afterward the progress of steam ship-building in all these respects was indicated by the construction according to the plans of the famous engineer Brunel of an iron vessel driven by a screw and of 2000 tons register. By 1840 there were more than 500 steam vessels passing up and down the rivers of England and Scotland, from port to port in these countries, between England and Ireland, England and France, and along the coast of Europe to the Mediterranean, and indeed all the way to India.

The first steam vessel to cross the Atlantic seems to have been the *Savannah* in 1819, and although there were other occasional instances, no steamships regularly crossed so large a body of water until almost twenty years later. About 1832 Junius Smith, an American merchant living in London, interested himself in this project and in 1836 formed the British and American Steam Navigation Company. In 1838 that company sent the *Sirius*, a steamship of 700 tons, from Cork, and at the same time the Great Western Steamship Company, an extension of the Great Western Railway Company, sent the *Great Western* from Bristol, both bound to New York. The former reached its American port in eighteen, the latter in sixteen days. Other steamships of larger size followed and soon steam vessels were regularly plying between Great Britain and the United States and other distant parts of the world.

In 1840 the Cunard Line, one of the first of the great steamship companies, began regularly running vessels to America and later to other countries. The Peninsular and Oriental Steamship Company, whose numerous vessels have always run for the most part to the Orient, was established about the same time. The Pacific Steam Navigation Company, the Royal West India Company, and the Collins Line were all established before 1848, and the Warren, Inman, Anchor, and other lines soon afterward.

To all these British companies government subsidies were paid in the form of compensation for carrying the mails, far beyond what the government received in postage, and beyond what would have been charged for a similar amount of other freight. In fact it is doubtful whether this early distant steamship commerce carried regularly to one port would have been profitable or could have been continued, if it had not had partial government support. This policy of subsidies was in contradiction to the prevailing *laissez-faire* attitude but was justified on the ground of the national interest in the extension of steamship connection with the rest of the world.

The growth of railways and steamships made a new and vastly increased demand for iron and coal. The five thousand or more miles of track that had been laid by 1848, the locomotives, iron parts of cars and bridges, and engines and hulls of steam vessels required hundreds of thousands and eventually millions of tons of iron or steel; and steamships eventually came to require for fuel almost one-half of all the coal produced in the country. In 1829 the introduction of the hot instead of cold blast and in 1833 of raw coal instead of coke in iron smelting brought about a great economy of coal and made the production of iron cheaper and quicker. These changes increased the importance of coal and iron mining relative to manufactures, commerce, and of course to agriculture, and made England more distinctly a " workshop " than ever before. The number of one class of workingmen was greatly increased and another class was called into existence by the introduction and extension of railroads. The " navvies " or railroad laborers took their name, which is an abbreviation of " navigators," from the canals or " inland navigation," for whose construction a generation earlier this class of labor had first been drawn together. They were a nomadic body of unskilled laborers, gathered from the restless and otherwise unoccupied element among the rural population or from the towns. They were better paid than farm laborers but subjected to all the evils of constant change of location, employment under contractors, separation from families, the poorest of shelter or none at all, and the roughest of food. Their numbers rose during the period of railway building to 200,000 or more, and they were so rough and reckless that they became a source of dread to the settled communities near which they temporarily settled when some roadbed was to be levelled, embankment or cutting made, or track laid. The " truck " system or " company store," the system by which workmen were paid by allowing them to deal on credit at a store kept by the employing company or the contractors, the debt being paid by retaining its amount from their wages on pay-day, flourished under these circumstances and exercised its usual demoralizing effects. The attention of Parliament was drawn to the condition of the railway laborers and a committee made investigations and a report, but no act was passed. However, the truck system had attracted so much attention and was so widely condemned that an act of Parliament was passed in 1842 requiring all payments of wages to be made in legal money, and forbidding payment in store orders or any other form of " truck." Under changing conditions the railway laborers have remained, along with certain other classes, types of the mass of untrained, uneducated, low-paid, and unskilled labor which is one of the most serious problems of modern society.

At the other extreme of the working class the locomotive engineers and other workmen on the trains and the engineers on vessels were a new class of relatively highly paid and well-trained men, the conditions of whose employment were such as to make them strong in intelligence, organization, and influence. Along with other transport workers and the coal and iron miners whose work was so closely connected with theirs they have come to be, perhaps, the most influential of the working classes.

Among the influences of the introduction of the railroads and steamships should be included the general awakening of men's minds by breaking down isolation, creating habits of travel and intercourse, and introducing greater alertness into the older, more stationary, settled, and conservative life. The adoption of a cheap and simple system of postage in 1842 and the introduction of the electric telegraph in 1844 worked in this same direction, although the fuller effect of all these changes was to be more marked in later times than in this period of their beginnings.

68. Abolition of the Corn Laws and the Completion of Free Trade. — Closely connected with industrial progress at the time and with the relations of the various classes of the population to one another was the change of national policy with regard to imports and exports. For more than three centuries government had placed restrictions upon the importation of foreign goods and upon trade carried on with England by foreign merchants and with foreign ships. This was for the purpose of encouraging production in England, giving special advantages in English trade and shipping to Englishmen, bringing increased taxes to the government and securing a " balance of trade " advantageous to the country. The most conspicuous forms of this policy were, first, the navigation acts [1] and accompanying regulations favoring English shipping, and, secondly, protective duties upon a vast number of articles, including food and raw materials as well as manufactured articles. The customs duties on grain, the " corn laws," as they are called in England, have already been described in the last chapter.[2] They were increased in amount at the close of the Napoleonic wars in 1815, no wheat being allowed to be imported so long as the prevailing price of home-grown wheat was ten shillings a bushel or less. As there was never enough produced in England to supply the demand this kept the price usually between $2.00 and $2.50 a bushel, estimated in American money, and made the price of bread very high.

Several points of defence were made for this law. The land which had been brought into cultivation when prices were very high on account of the war could not be kept in use if the price of grain fell, while it was desirable for England to be as nearly self-supporting as possible. Taxes for the support of the poor and other local purposes fell largely upon the land-owners, who seemed to be justified, therefore, in asking high rents from the tenants of farms, which they could only pay if the price of the grain they raised remained high.

There was, however, much opposition to this high tariff on grain used for food. In 1839 an organization was formed at Manchester, which soon took the name of the Anti-Corn-Law League. It consisted largely of cotton and other manufacturers, who drew no advantage from the high price of grain and saw the burdens it placed upon the working classes, the limitation of the power of grain-raising countries to purchase manufactured goods in England, and the community of interest it gave to the land-owning aristocracy which still, even after the passage of the Reform Bill of 1832, ruled England. The principal speakers of the League were Richard Cobden, John Bright, and one or two other members of Parliament. During the

[1] See pp. 163-167.   [2] See p. 191.

years from 1839 forward a vast number of meetings were held, many pamphlets and newspapers advocating the repeal of the corn laws published, and a constant agitation kept up for that end both in the country and in Parliament. The League was well provided with funds from the wealth of the manufacturers who were especially interested in it, £12,000 having been subscribed at its very first meeting, and £60,000 at one great demonstration some years later. Much popular interest was also shown in the subject, especially as indicated by the " Corn-Law Hymns " and " Corn-Law Rhymes " of Ebenezer Elliott. These were bitter attacks on the landlords, whom he accused of starving the people by making bread dear through heavy taxation.

> Lord ! bid our palaced worms their vileness know !
> Bleach them with famine till they earn their bread !
> And, taught by pain to feel a brother's woe,
> Marvel that honest labour toils unfed !

> They never felt how vain it is to seek
> From bread-taxed trade its interdicted gain ;
> How hard to toil from dreary week to week,
> And ever labouring labour still in vain.

> *   *   *   *   *   *   *

> Then let them kneel — oh, not to us, but Thee !
> For judgment, Lord, to thee alone belongs ;
> But we are petrified with misery,
> And turned to marble by a life of wrongs.

> When shall we hear again
> Thy still small whisper, God ?
> Oh break the bondman's chain !
> Uncurse the tax-ploughed sod !

> If still thy name is love,
> Be labour's son thy care !
> And from thy earth remove
> The vermin all can spare !

The agitation continued seven or eight years. Finally, a great catastrophe brought the plan for abolishing the corn laws to a head. A blight fell upon the potato crop which formed so large a part of the food of the English, and still more of the Irish people. In 1845 and 1846 the potatoes were an almost complete failure. Much food was imported into Great Britain in ordinary years and of course a much greater amount had now to be brought from abroad. It was absurd to place heavy burdens of taxation on necessary importation of food and thus limit its amount and increase its price when it was so sorely needed. The prime minister, Sir Robert Peel, land-owner and Tory as he was, brought in a bill in 1846 for gradually decreasing the tariff on grain. This was carried, although very reluctantly, and the import duty on grain ceased in 1849.

Along with the abolition of the corn laws went the whole system of protective tariffs. Many of these were mere survivals of early attempts at minute regulation of industry and in the spirit of reform of the time were being abolished gradually by Parliament at the request of successive ministers. In the year before the abolition of the corn laws Peel had removed the duty from almost five hundred articles. Taxes on raw materials generally and even on many manufactured goods were condemned by some of the same arguments as those used against the grain duties. England was now far ahead of most other countries in the amount of her capital, the perfection of her machinery, the skill of her workingmen, and the excellence of her organization for producing manufactured goods of almost all kinds. She had become the leading industrial nation of the world. The arguments for free trade seemed therefore overwhelming. Between 1846 and 1849 the duties were taken off of two hundred more articles, and soon afterwards the few remaining duties were abolished. England had become a free-trade country. The loss of revenue to the government was made up by the adoption of an income tax.

A beginning had been made long before in giving equal advantages to foreign ships and merchants entering English harbors, as already described.[1] This process was now brought to completion, and in 1849 the last of the navigation acts were repealed. The policy of restriction on foreign trading relations had been already practically given up. In 1833 the monopoly of the East India Company, the last of the great sixteenth-century trading companies, was withdrawn and the Eastern trade thrown open to all Englishmen and foreigners.

69. Poverty of the Working Classes. — Notwithstanding the improvements in machinery, mining, agriculture, and transportation, notwithstanding the great increase in the total wealth and income of the English people, in spite of the removal of many old abuses, the abolition of the corn laws, and the reform of Parliament, the condition of the lower classes seemed to have become worse rather than better. At no time, probably, in the history of England has there been more misery among the mass of the people than in the period covered by this chapter. Its later years have come to be known as the " hungry forties." Parliamentary investigations, the reports of government boards and charitable societies, and general literature all testify to the low wages, high prices, irregular employment, crowded working and living conditions, dirt, disease, suffering, and social injustice which characterized much of the England of the first half of the nineteenth century. Bad as conditions still are in many places and in many aspects of life, the condition of the mass of the community is infinitely better than it was seventy-five years ago. It was just about this time, in 1842, that a German merchant, Friedrich Engels, living in England, wrote his " Condition of the English Working Classes," in which the deplorable state of the mass of the people is described. All other sources of information give the same impression. Wages of women at field work in the country were from 15 cents to 20 cents a day; in the mills they could earn perhaps $2.00 a week. Farm laborers earned $2.00 to $2.50 a week; unskilled

[1] See pp. 197–198.

town laborers $3 to $3.75; skilled workers, such as carpenters and masons, earned $4.50; factory laborers made sometimes as much as $5.00 a week. The prices of necessities to be bought with these wages were in many cases greater than at present. In 1840 bread cost somewhat more than it did in 1910; sugar cost twice as much, tea from twice to three times as much. The common people when regularly at work seldom had meat, and even their bread, potatoes, and turnips were of the poorest quality and insufficient in amount. But the worst evil was the irregularity of work. Beginning in 1836 and continuing to 1839 was a serious commercial depression brought about by speculation, and beginning in 1847 there was another. Mills were frequently closed, country work was hard, scarce, and irregular, and even skilled workmen were often without occupation or wages. Actual starvation was only prevented by extensive charity, and a bare and harsh subsistence was the most that could be hoped for even in the best times. With the increase of population and no public effort to provide space for it, streets and alleys were narrow, houses overcrowded, drainage bad, and the air fetid. In the large manufacturing and commercial cities like Manchester, Birmingham, and Liverpool, thousands of families lived in undrained and unventilated cellars, and in many parts of London housing conditions were quite as bad. This poverty-stricken, sordid life was not that of the poorest, most improvident, and most unfortunate of the community, but was characteristic of the great body of substantial, hard-working laboring population, only a fortunate few rising above it. It was the life of a large proportion of the fifteen million people who in 1841 made up the population of England. Moreover, the life of the working classes had to be spent without education, share in the government, or opportunity for enjoyment except of the lowest character. Among the political and industrial governing class there was at the worst much injustice and hardness; at the best, mismanagement, neglect, lack of sympathy, or a sense of utter helplessness in the presence

Q

of intolerably bad conditions. Most widespread of all was irresponsibility. The world was ruled by *laissez-faire*. It is no wonder that crime, brutality, turbulence, and deep discontent flourished among the masses. After this period slow, doubtful, frequently interrupted, and always inadequate improvements can be discovered if sought for carefully. At this time things were at their worst.

70. Reform of the Poor Law. — The sufferings and dissatisfaction of the working classes were made harder to bear by a sudden and harsh though perhaps necessary change in the system of granting public relief to the poor. Pauperism had been a serious matter in England for centuries. The enclosures in the country and gild changes in the towns in the sixteenth century had created an enormous amount of extreme poverty in addition to that which was chronic through the Middle Ages. To meet this the government of Queen Elizabeth with its usual energy enacted a series of laws for the relief of the poor, the most important of which was that of the year 1601. Under this law and its modifications overseers in each locality had taxed the property holders and provided for the support of the very poor ever since.

Poverty was at some times worse than at others. In the latter part of the eighteenth century, during the advance of the industrial revolution and the enclosure of open lands, work was irregular, wages low, and extreme poverty widespread. Under these circumstances in 1795 the magistrates of Berkshire, who had the duty under the Act of Apprentices of establishing the rate of wages in that county, at their annual meeting at the little town of Speenhamland, decided to make an increase in laborers' wages, drawing a part of it from the poor rates. Payment was to be in proportion to the price of bread and to the size of the laborer's family. Thus the workman would be provided with enough to live on, paid partly by his employer in the form of wages, partly by the poor authorities as public charity. For instance, a man with a wife and family of three children should receive nine shillings a week when bread was at its average price. Whatever his wages lacked of this amount should be paid to him by the poor authorities. This practice spread to other localities in the early nineteenth century and became so general that the original plan has often been spoken of as the "Speenhamland Act of Parliament." In fact Parliament itself increased the tendency to substitute poor relief for the payment of living wages by passing an act in 1796 allowing local authorities to give relief to poor men in their parishes without requiring them to go to the workhouse or to give proof of their incapacity.

This was an unjust and demoralizing practice to both employers and workingmen. It tempted the employing farmers in the country to cut down or keep down the wages of their laborers, knowing that these wages would be brought up to the necessary amount for subsistence by allowances from the poor rates. Wages therefore remained far below what they should be. The workingman, on the other hand, was made into a pauper with all the bad results of pauperism. He was deprived of his sense of independence, of his free voice in local affairs, and of his incitement to thrift. Knowing that he would be supported, and with wages based neither on his needs or his efforts there was no reason why he should work or save, there was no hope of improvement during his working life or of an old age elsewhere than in the poorhouse. These conditions were not so usual in the large cities or the more active manufacturing towns, though here also wages were influenced by allowances to the poor, and many other causes of poverty existed.

It was this bad system of pauperism by which England was burdened and demoralized that a group of reformers about the time of the passage of the first parliamentary reform bill undertook to correct. They were influenced partly by the prevailing ideas of *laissez-faire* and a conviction that good results could only be attained by making each man dependent on himself alone; partly by the desire to lift from the country the enormous weight of taxation for the relief of the poor; and still further by a wish to get rid of the mass of stupidity, corruption, and bad management that had grown up around the administration of the old poor laws. A commission of investigation was appointed and in 1834 made a famous report to Parliament. In the same year a new poor law was passed which has been the basis of poor relief ever since. It was carried by an unusually large majority and represented the beliefs and desires of the upper middle classes which now controlled Parliament. It introduced a sharp and sudden change in the customs of the country and brought great hardship to those whom it immediately affected, the great mass of the poor people. From these and their leaders it received the most intense disapproval and loud opposition. Nevertheless, it held its ground, was re-enacted in 1842, and its administration was placed under the supervision of the ministry in 1847.

The general plan of the new law was to leave poor relief in the hands of local authorities but to place the whole system in charge of a national board or commission who should control its policy and watch over its administration through a corps of inspectors. The country was divided into what were called " unions," or groups of parishes, in each of which there was a workhouse. No poor person could, generally speaking, be given any relief except by becoming an inmate of this workhouse. Thus the whole system of relief or partial support of the lower classes in their homes was swept away in one general regulation. There were, of course, exceptions for the old, the sick, widows and orphans for a short period after the death of the head of the family, and under the conditions of the time other exceptions were unavoidable. The whole policy of the National Board of Poor Law Commissioners, however, was that of a rigorous enforcement of the principle of the law, that there should be no relief given except in the workhouse. The workhouse itself was intentionally made unattractive to the last degree. Husbands and wives, parents and children were separated, the control exercised by the officials in charge was absolute and often oppressive, the food was poor and often inadequate, the whole atmosphere cold, repellent, and unfitted for either the comfort or the improvement of its inmates. All this was intentional; nothing was to be done to make idleness and improvidence more attractive than labor and saving. The great difficulty about the poor law was that it was only one part of a whole social system, the other parts of which gave little chance for regular or decently paid labor, or for education, health, happiness, or opportunity.

71. Chartism. — The Reform Bill of 1832 had given representation not to the masses of the people, but only to the upper middle classes. Many of the leaders of the lower classes and special sympathizers with them believed that it was due to this fact that the people were so miserable. If they had representation in Parliament they thought they could introduce reforms for the advantage of the masses and bring about the abolition of much of what seemed to them injustice. Some of the old Radicals in Parliament and outside, and some of the trade-union leaders in a lately formed workingmen's association, made up of skilled artisans of London, therefore, came together in 1837 and drew up a petition to Parliament in the form of a bill, which they called " The People's Charter " in allusion to the Great Charter. From their advocacy of this project they became known as the Chartists. It was a well-written document, calling attention to the greatness and general wealth of England, but pointing out that this was accompanied by widespread poverty, depression, and misfortune of the most active classes. The Chartists gathered up from the old agitation of the previous half century six proposed reforms, which, if adopted, they claimed would give the people a just and beneficent form of government. These six points were universal manhood suffrage, vote by ballot, division of the country into equal representative districts, a newly elected Parliament every year, abolition of the property qualification for membership in Parliament, and payment of members, so that poor men might serve.

In order to obtain popular sympathy for the movement and to bring pressure to bear on Parliament, a great series of meetings was organized in the years 1837, 1838, and 1839. These were usually held in the open air not only because the use of a hall was frequently denied but because halls were quite too small for the masses which gathered. In London and the vicinity of Manchester, Birmingham, Nottingham, Glasgow, and other northern towns monster meetings were held, torchlight processions passed through town and country, and banners with inscriptions were carried, as in earlier and later agitations. They also threatened " a solemn and sacred strike from every kind of labor," if Parliament should refuse their petition, probably the first instance of the familiar threat of a general industrial strike to reach political ends.

They had not the abundant money resources of the Anti-Corn-Law League, which was carrying on its agitation at the same time, yet branches were formed in the midlands and the north, a whole corps of speakers was trained and sent out, and several newspapers were supported. The *Northern Star*, a Chartist weekly paper published at Oldham by Feargus O'Connor, one of the leaders, attained for a while the largest circulation of any newspaper outside of London. From February to September, 1839, a convention of delegates from Chartist associations all over England met, at first in London, afterwards in Birmingham. There was much dissension in its conferences, some delegates advocating continued peaceful agitation, others preparation for a forcible uprising.

The petition was presented to the House of Commons in July, 1839, after almost two years of this agitation, by Attwood, member of Parliament from Birmingham. It was supported by a million and a quarter signatures and required twelve men to carry it into the House. Several members spoke in its favor; nevertheless it was rejected by a majority of 237 against 48. The newly reformed House of Commons was not willing even to discuss a proposal to introduce a more democratic type of government. Not only was this so, but the ministry determined to put an end to the whole agitation. In their speeches and actions both at mass meetings and in the " Convention " several of the leaders had used threats and encouraged what the government claimed was violence. The torchlight processions were prohibited, the leaders were removed from such government positions as they held, a mass meeting in Birmingham was broken up by a force of police brought from London, and several riots occurred there and in other places. Stephens, one of the Chartist speakers, was arrested and sentenced to eighteen months' imprisonment for his inflammatory addresses. Eighty men were arrested at the breaking up of the Birmingham meeting; various others were charged with having arms in their possession; Lovett and Vincent, two of the founders of the movement, were condemned to a year in prison, O'Connor to eighteen months, and four others to death, though this was commuted to imprisonment for life. Later there was an attempt in Wales to release from the jail some of those convicted, when soldiers fired on the mob, killing ten and wounding many. Seven more were condemned to death at this time, though the sentence was modified to transportation for life, and they were afterwards pardoned.

The failure of the Chartists to obtain serious consideration in Parliament, the imprisonment of some of the leaders, differences of opinion among others, absorption in trade-union activities, and the competition of interest in the Anti-Corn-Law League among the masses of the people led to a gradual decline of interest in Chartism after 1839. The continental revolution of 1848 combined with a new period of commercial depression, however, brought the old Chartist movement to life once more. A petition for the Charter, to be signed by 4,000,000 persons and carried to Parliament by 200,000 men, enough to overawe all resistance, directly from a great mass meeting, was announced by O'Connor, one of the old leaders. But the meeting, which was to be held on Kennington Common, across the Thames from London, was forbidden by the ministry, troops were called out, and a whole army of special police enrolled under the charge of the duke of Wellington. The meeting attracted but some 20,000 men, the march was stopped at the bridge, the great petition was found to contain less than half as many signatures as was claimed, and many of these fictitious, and the House of Commons refused to pay any more attention to the Charter than they had in 1839. In the meantime the repeal of the corn laws had satisfied many reformers, and the Chartist leaders and the hundreds of thousands who had hoped so much from the proposed democratic reform of Parliament gave up their agitation for the time. The whole Chartist movement belongs rather to the field of political than industrial history though its advocates were seeking industrial ends by that means.

72. Factory Legislation. — One of the greatest difficulties with which the early mill owners had to contend was the insufficient supply of labor for their factories. Since these had to be run by water power, they were placed along the rapid streams in the remote parts of Yorkshire, Lancashire, Derbyshire, and Nottinghamshire, which were sparsely populated, and where such inhabitants as there were had a strong objection to working in factories. However abundant population might be in some other parts of England, in the northwest, where the new manufacturing was growing up, and especially in the hilly rural districts, there were but few persons available to perform the work which must be done by human hands in connection with the mill machinery.

There was, however, in existence a source of supply of laborers which could furnish almost unlimited numbers and at the lowest possible cost. The parish poorhouses or workhouses of the large cities were overcrowded with children. The authorities always had difficulty in finding occupation for them when they came to an age when they could earn their own living, and any plan of putting them to work would be received with welcome.

This source of supply was early discovered and utilized by the manufacturers, and it soon became customary for them to take as apprentices large numbers of the poorhouse children. They signed contracts with the overseers of the poor by which they agreed to give board, clothing, and instruction for a certain number of years to the children who were thus bound to them. In return they put them to work in the factories. Children from seven years of age upward were engaged by hundreds from London and the other large cities, and set to work in the cotton spinning factories of the north. Since there were no other facilities for boarding them, " apprentice houses " were built for them in the vicinity of the factories, where they were placed under the care of superintendents or matrons. The conditions of life among these pauper children were, as might be expected, very hard. They were remotely situated, apart from the observation of the community, left to the burdens of unrelieved labor and the harshness of small masters or foremen. Their hours of labor were excessive. When the demands of trade were active they were often arranged in two shifts, each shift working twelve hours, one in the day and another in the night, so that it was a common saying in the north that " their beds never got cold," one set climbing into bed as the other got out. When there was no night work the day work was the longer. They were driven at their work and often abused. Their food was of the coarsest description, and they were frequently required to eat it while at their work, snatching a bite as they could while the machinery was still in motion. Much of the time which should have been devoted to rest was spent in cleaning the machinery, and there seems to have been absolutely no effort made to give them any education or opportunity for recreation.

The sad life of these little waifs, overworked, underfed, neglected, abused, in the factories and barracks in the remote glens of Yorkshire and Lancashire, came eventually to the notice of the outside world. Correspondence describing their condition began to appear in the newspapers, a Manchester

Board of Health made a presentment in 1796 calling attention to the unsanitary conditions in the cotton factories where they worked, contagious fevers were reported to be especially frequent in the apprentice houses, and in 1802 Sir Robert Peel, himself an employer of nearly a thousand such children, brought the matter to the attention of Parliament. An immediate and universal desire was expressed to abolish the abuses of the system, and as a result the " Health and Morals Act to Regulate the Labor of Bound Children in Cotton Factories " was passed in the same year. It prohibited the binding out for factory labor of children younger than nine years, restricted the hours of labor to twelve actual working hours a day, and forbade night labor. It required the walls of the factories to be properly whitewashed and the buildings to be sufficiently ventilated, insisted that the apprentices should be furnished with at least one new suit of clothes a year, and provided that they should attend religious services and be instructed in the fundamental English branches. This was the first of the " Factory Acts," for, although its application was so restricted, applying only to cotton factories, and for the most part only to bound children, the subsequent steps in the formation of the present great code of factory legislation were simply a development of the same principle, that factory labor involved conditions which it was desirable for government to regulate.

At the time of the passage of this law the introduction of steam power was already causing a transfer of the bulk of factory industry from the rural districts to which the need for water power had confined it to the towns where every other requisite for carrying on manufacturing was more easily obtainable. Here the children of families resident in the town could be obtained, and the practice of using apprentice children was largely given up. Many of the same evils, however, continued to exist here. The practice of beginning to work while extremely young, long hours, night work, unhealthy surroundings, proved to be as common among these children to whom the law did not apply as they had been among the apprentice children. These evils attracted the attention of several persons of philanthropic feeling. Robert Owen, especially, a successful manufacturer, who had introduced many reforms in his own mills, collected a large body of evidence as to the excessive labor and early age of employees in the factories even where no apprentice labor was engaged. He tried to awaken an interest in the matter by the publication of a pamphlet on the injurious consequences of the factory system, and to influence various members of Parliament to favor the passage of a law intended to improve the condition of laboring children and young people. In 1815 Sir Robert Peel again brought the matter up in Parliament. A committee was appointed to investigate the question, and a legislative agitation was thus begun which was destined to last for many years and to produce a series of laws which have gradually taken most of the conditions of employment in large establishments under the control of the government. In debates in Parliament, in testimony before government commissions of investigation, in petitions, pamphlets, and newspapers, the conditions of factory labor were described and discussed.

The bill originally introduced in 1815, after having been subjected to a series of discussions, amendments and postponements, was passed in June, 1819, being the second " Factory Act." It applied only to cotton mills, and was in the main merely an extension of the act of 1802 to the protection of children who were not pauper apprentices. It forbade the employment of any child under nine years of age, and prohibited the employment of those between nine and sixteen more than twelve hours a day, or at night. In addition to the twelve hours of actual labor, at least a half-hour must be allowed for breakfast and an hour for dinner. Other minor acts amending or extending this were passed from time to time, till in 1833 after the first parliamentary Reform Act was passed and after two successive commissions had made investigations and reports on the subject, the most important of the early laws was passed.

The law of 1833 applied practically to all textile mills, not merely to those for the spinning of cotton. The prohibition of employment of all below nine years was continued, children between nine and thirteen were to work only eight hours per day, and young persons between thirteen and eighteen only twelve hours, and none of these at night. Two whole and eight half holidays were required to be given within the year, and each child must have a surgeon's certificate of fitness for labor. There were also requirements for the education of the children and the cleanliness of the factories. But the most important clause of this statute was the provision of a corps of four factory inspectors who were sworn to their duties, salaried, and provided with extensive powers of making rules for the execution of the act, of enforcing it, and prosecuting for its violation. The earlier laws had not been efficiently carried out. Under this act numerous prosecutions and convictions took place, and factory regulation began to become a reality. The inspectors calculated during their first year of service that there were about 56,000 children between nine and thirteen, and about 108,000 young persons between thirteen and eighteen, in the factories under their supervision.

The period lying between 1840 and 1848 was one of specially great activity in social and economic agitation. Chartism, the abolition of the corn laws, the formation of trade unions, mining acts, and further extensions of the factory acts were all alike under discussion, and they all created the most intense antagonism between parties and classes. In 1844 the law commonly known as the " Children's Half-time Act " was passed. It contained a large number of general provisions for the fencing of dangerous machinery, for its stoppage while being cleaned, for the report of accidents to inspectors and district surgeons, for the public prosecution for damages of the factory owner when he should seem to be responsible for an accident, and for the enforcement of the act. Its most distinctive clause, however, was that which restricted the labor of children to a half-day, or the whole of alternate days, and required their attendance at school for the other half of their time. All women were placed by this act in the same category as young persons between thirteen and eighteen, so far as the restriction of hours of labor to twelve per day and the prohibition of night work extended.

The next statute to be passed contained the provision which had long been the most bitterly contested of any during the whole factory law agitation. This was the " Ten-hour Act " of 1847. From an early period in the century there had been a strong agitation in favor of restricting by law the hours of young persons, and from somewhat later, of women, to ten hours per day, and this proposition had been repeatedly introduced and defeated in Parliament. It was now carried. By this time the more usual length of the working day for grown men and women had been reduced to twelve hours, and in some trades to eleven. It was now made by law half-time for children, and ten hours for young persons and women, or as rearranged by another law passed three years afterward, ten and a half hours for five days of the week and a half-day on Saturday. The number of persons to whom the Ten-hour Act applied was estimated at something over 360,000. That is, including the children, at least three-fourths of all persons employed in textile industries had their hours and some other conditions of labor directly regulated by law. Moreover, the work of men employed in the same factories was so dependent on that of the women and the children, that many of these restrictions applied practically to them also.

73. Reasons for and against Factory Legislation. — The need for regulation which was claimed to exist arose from the long hours of work which were customary, from the very early age at which many children were sent to be employed in the factories, and from various incidents of manufacturing which were considered injurious, or as involving unnecessary hardship.

The actual working hours in the factories before the passage of these acts were from twelve and a half to fourteen a day. That is to say, factories usually started work in the morning at 6 o'clock and continued till 12, when a period from a half-hour to an hour was allowed for dinner, then the work began again and continued till 7.30 or 8.30 in the evening. It was customary to eat breakfast after reaching the mill, but this was done while attending the machinery, there being no general stoppage for the purpose. Some mills ran even longer hours, opening at 5 A.M. and not closing till 9 P.M. In some exceptional cases the hours were only twelve; from 6 to 12 and from 1 to 7. The inducements to long hours were very great. The profits were large, the demand for goods was constantly growing, the introduction of gas made it possible to light the factories, and the use of artificial power, either water or steam, seemed to make the labor much less severe than when the power had been provided by human muscles. Few or no holidays were regarded, except Sunday, so that work went on in an unending strain of protracted, exhausting labor, prolonged for much of the year far into the night.

To these long hours all the hands alike conformed, the children commencing and stopping work at the same time as the grown men and women. Moreover, the children often began work while extremely young. There was a great deal of work in the factories which they could do just as well, in some cases even better, than adults. They were therefore commonly sent into the mills by their parents at about the age of eight years, frequently at seven or even six. As has been before stated, more than half of the employees in many factories were below eighteen years, and of these a considerable number were mere children. Thirdly, there were certain other evils of factory labor that attracted attention and were considered by the reformers to be remediable. Many accidents occurred because the moving machinery was unprotected, the temperature in the cotton mills had to be kept high, and ventilation and cleanliness were often entirely neglected. The habit of keeping the machinery in motion while meals were being eaten was a hardship, and in many ways the employees were practically at the mercy of the proprietors of the factories so long as there was no form of oversight or of united action to prevent harshness or unfairness.

In the discussions in Parliament and outside there were of course many contradictory statements concerning the facts of the case, and much denial of general and special charges. The advocates of factory laws drew an extremely sombre picture of the evils of the factory system. The opponents of such legislation, on the other hand, declared that their statements were exaggerated or untrue, and that the condition of the factory laborer was not worse than that of other workingmen, or harder than that of the domestic worker and his family had been in earlier times.

But apart from these recriminations and contradictions, there were certain general arguments used in the debates which can be grouped into three classes on each side. For the regulating laws there was in the first place the purely sentimental argument, repulsion against the hard, unrelieved labor, the abuse, the lack of opportunity for enjoyment or recreation of the children of the factory districts; the feeling that in wealthy, humane, Christian England, it was unendurable that women and little children should work longer hours, be condemned to greater hardships, and more completely cut off from the enjoyments of life than were the slaves of tropical countries. This is the argument of Mrs. Browning's *Cry of the Children:* —

> Do ye hear the children weeping, O my brothers,
>   Ere the sorrow comes with years?
> They are leaning their young heads against their mothers,
>   And that cannot stop their tears.
> The young lambs are bleating in the meadows;
>   The young birds are chirping in the nest;
> The young fawns are playing with the shadows;
>   The young flowers are blowing toward the west;

But the young, young children, O my brothers!
  They are weeping bitterly.
They are weeping in the play-time of the others
  In the country of the free.

*   *   *   *   *   *   *

"For oh!" say the children, "we are weary,
  And we cannot run or leap:
If we cared for any meadows, it were merely
  To drop down in them and sleep."

*   *   *   *   *   *   *

They look up with their pale and sunken faces,
  And their look is dread to see,
For they mind you of their angels in high places,
  With eyes turned on Deity.
"How long," they say, "how long, O cruel nation,
  Will you stand, to move the world, on a child's heart,
Stifle down with a mailed heel its palpitation
  And tread onward to your throne amid the mart?"

Secondly, it was argued that the long hours for the children cut them off from all intellectual and moral training, that they were in no condition after such protracted labor to profit by any opportunities of education that should be supplied, that with the diminished influence of the home, and the demoralizing effects that were supposed to result from factory labor, ignorance and vice alike would continue to be its certain accompaniments, unless the age at which regular work was begun should be limited, and the number of hours of labor of young persons restricted. Thirdly, it was claimed that there was danger of the physical degeneracy of the factory population. Certain diseases, especially of the joints and limbs, were discovered to be very prevalent in the factory districts. Children who began work so early in life and were subjected to such long hours of labor did not grow so rapidly, nor reach their full stature, nor retain their vigor so late in life, as did the population outside of the factories. Therefore, for the very physical preservation of the race, it was declared to be necessary to regulate the conditions of factory labor.

On the other hand, apart from denials as to the facts of the case, there were several distinct arguments used against the adoption of factory laws. In the first place, in the interests of the manufacturers, such laws were opposed as an unjust interference with their business, an unnecessary and burdensome obstacle to their success, and a threat of ruin to a class who by giving employment to so many laborers and furnishing so much of the material for commerce were of the greatest advantage to the country. Secondly, from a somewhat broader point of view, it was declared that if such laws were adopted England would no longer be able to compete with other countries and would lose her preëminence in manufactures. The factory system was being introduced into France, Belgium, the United States, and other countries, and in none of these was there any legal restriction on the hours of labor or the age of the employees. If English manufacturers were forced to reduce the length of the day in which production was carried on, they could not produce as cheaply as these other countries, and English exports would decrease. This would reduce the national prosperity and be especially hard on the working classes themselves, as many would necessarily be thrown out of work. Thirdly, as a matter of principle it was argued that the policy of government regulation had been tried and found wanting, that after centuries of existence it had been deliberately given up, and should not be reintroduced. Laws restricting hours would interfere with the freedom of labor, with the freedom of capital, with the freedom of contract. If the employer and the employee were both satisfied with the conditions of their labor, why should the government interfere? The reason also why such regulation had failed in the past and must again, if tried now, was evident. It was an effort to alter the action of the natural laws which controlled employment, wages, profits, and other economic matters, and was bad in theory, and would therefore necessarily be injurious in practice. These and some other less general arguments were used over and over again in the various forms

R

of the discussion through almost half a century. The laws that were passed were carried because the majority in Parliament were either not convinced by adverse arguments or determined that, come what might, the evils and abuses connected with factory labor should be abolished. As a matter of fact, the factory laws were carried by the rank and file of the voting members of Parliament, not only against the protests of the manufacturers especially interested, but in spite of the warnings of those who spoke in the name of established teaching, and frequently against the opposition of the political leaders of both parties. The greatest number of those who voted for them were influenced principally by their sympathies and feelings, and yielded to the appeals of certain philanthropic advocates, the most devoted and influential of whom was Lord Ashley, afterward earl of Shaftesbury, who devoted many years to investigation and agitation on the subject both inside and out of Parliament.

As time passed on the opposition to the factory acts became less. The evil results which had been feared did not show themselves and many of their strongest opponents eventually acknowledged their necessity and benefit.

74. The First Mine Regulation Act. — By the successive acts of 1819, 1833, 1844, and 1847, a normal length of working day and regulated conditions generally had been established by government for the textile factories employing women and children. The next development was an extension of the regulation of hours and conditions of labor from factories proper to other allied fields.

A witness in one of the factory investigations had testified that " the hardest labor in the worst room in the worst conducted factory is less hard, less cruel, and less demoralizing than the labor in the best coal mine." Notwithstanding the possible exaggeration of so strong a statement, it was evident that far away from ordinary observation, unconsidered by the government, unorganized and at the mercy of their employers, subject, as was constantly reported, to the most destructive of accidents, the condition of the coal miners demanded public investigation. A commission was appointed in 1840. They made a thorough investigation of the obscure conditions of labor underground, and reported a condition of affairs which was heart-sickening. Children began their life in the coal mines at five, six, or seven years of age. Girls and women worked like boys and men; they were less than half clothed, and worked

Women's Labor in Coal Mines
(Report of Children's Employment Commission, 1842.)

alongside of men who were stark naked. There were from twelve to fourteen working hours in the twenty-four, and these were often at night. Little girls of six or eight years of age made ten to twelve trips a day up steep ladders to the surface, carrying half a hundred weight of coal in wooden buckets on their backs at each journey. Young women appeared before the commissioners when summoned from their work, dressed merely in a pair of trousers, dripping wet from the water of the mine, and already weary with the labor of a day scarcely more than begun. A common form of labor consisted of drawing on hands and knees over the inequalities of a passageway not more than two feet or twenty-eight inches high a car or tub filled with three or four hundred weight of coal, attached by a chain and hooked to a leather band around the waist. The mere recital of the testimony taken precluded all discussion as to the desirability of reform, and a law was immediately passed, in 1842, almost without dissent, which prohibited for the future all work underground by females and by boys under ten years of age. Inspectors were appointed, and by subsequent acts a whole code of regulation of mines as regards age of beginning work, hours of work, lighting, ventilation, safety, and licensing of engineers has been created.

75. **Influence of Robert Owen.** — The opinion of most men at this time, as during the period before it, was that regulation was a bad thing, that each person ought to be left free to succeed or fail according to his own efforts, without support and without interference. Especially was this true of those who, favored by fortune, the conditions of the time, or the special nature of their own abilities, were in a position to take advantage of the inventions and opportunities that were constantly presenting themselves and to utilize them to attain success and to become more wealthy or more powerful. It was widely believed both by theoretical individualists and by successful business men that self-interest should be the guiding principle in all business relations. It was unwise for the government to participate in the economic protection or to seek to increase the well-being of the community; men of enterprise had no responsibility for others connected with their enterprises, and the government had no responsibility except to secure to them opportunity.

There were, however, many who did not agree with these views, who favored restriction upon some individuals for the protection of others or for the good of all, and believed that the mass of the population would be crushed by those in a position of economic advantage unless they were protected by community action. This was as true of those parliamentary committees which proposed public control of the railroads as it was of the advocates of factory acts.

There were others who wanted to apply the idea of protection of the working classes, of general regulation, and of common action, more widely still. One of the most influential of these was Robert Owen. He was born in 1771 in Wales but grew up as a young man in Manchester, in the midst of the rising manufactures and other changes of the industrial revolution. He was poor and self-taught, but from boyhood was a wide and industrious reader and an independent thinker. He went into the spinning business in a small way but soon rose to be manager of one of the largest spinning mills in the country, which had been established in 1785 by Arkwright and a partner at New Lanark in Scotland. Here while on the one hand he made the mills a great business success, on the other he worked out various schemes for the improvement of the character of the people, the education of the children, reduction of the hours of labor, and diminution of the high cost of living. From the earliest steps of his advance as a manufacturer he declared his greater interest in what he called the " living " machinery of the business, the men, women, and children working in the mills, than in the " dead " machinery, the newly invented mechanical devices.

By 1820, the beginning of the period of this chapter, Owen was already a well-known reformer as well as a business man. He was the controlling spirit of a manufacturing community of some 3000 persons at New Lanark, which was coming to be recognized as an ideal community of workingmen and their families. It was visited by Wilberforce, Clarkson, Malthus, Bentham, and hundreds of other prominent public men, writers, members of the royal family, and others interested in Owen's scheme. His pamphlets were read by Napoleon at Elba, and taken to America by John Quincy Adams, the returning minister. Czar Alexander wanted him to come to Russia and establish another New Lanark there. He was active in the agitation that led to the adoption of the factory law of 1819, and urged in numerous speeches and pamphlets as an alternative to the proposed new poor law a scheme for the education and industrial training of the poor for self-support. He early convinced himself that the character and capacity of each human being are the product of his surroundings and that deliberate conscious effort can therefore, by improving these surroundings, relieve misery and create well-being. This one principle was at the foundation of all his actions, plans, and teachings, and he spent a lifetime and a large fortune in efforts for its dissemination, enforcement, and application.

He placed himself in bitter opposition to what he called " the puny efforts of the individual system " and advocated a " well devised rational system of organization of human society." To leave everything to self-interest and competition, as was being done in his time, was in his belief a waste of the advantages of organized society and destructive to the happiness of the individuals who compose it.

Owen was full of schemes for carrying out this theory and ultimately withdrew with his money from the Lanark mills and gave himself up to propaganda for his plans. One of the earliest of them, advocated from 1818 forward, was the establishment, through the aid of the government, of industrial villages of 200 or 300 families each, which would ultimately own and control the land, the mills, and workshops from which the inhabitants drew their living. Owen even formulated rules, made calculations, and drew plans for such a typical communistic village after which others might be modelled. Another project, somewhat less far-reaching, was for voluntary groups of people to form coöperative societies to carry on all their business and much of their social life together, with their own capital and under their own control. " Orbiston " was bought in 1826 and organized, partly at least, according to these plans, but failed and was given up in 1828. Later the " coöperators," as they came to be called, bought up two or three adjoining farms, the largest of which was named Queenwood, but was generally referred to by those interested in it as Harmony. Here they established training schools, carried on factory operations, and spent $150,000 in their equipment and early operation. In 1842 this project failed and was abandoned. Owen later visited the United States and bought an establishment in Indiana which he called New Harmony, where a mixed population gathered, and where some coöperative experiments were tried. He visited this settlement repeatedly and spoke before the two houses of Congress at their invitation on his plans.

Coöperative stores of one kind or another were established from as early a period as 1820, but most of them died out. A larger project was the establishment in London in 1832 of the " Equitable Labor Exchange." This was a store or bazaar at which any one who produced anything of saleable value could deposit it and receive for it paper money indicating the number of hours of labor taken to produce it. This was exchangeable at the store for any other article of equal labor value. The exchange roused much interest and was for a while a centre of great activity, doing business of more than £1000 a week; but, insufficiently provided with capital, administered by men of small experience, and based on a very doubtful economic principle, it did not live beyond 1834.

From 1830 forward, " Coöperative Congresses," as they were called, were held by those interested in these schemes. It was at these congresses and in the discussions connected with them that the word " Socialists " was first used to describe those interested in such schemes of complete social reform, and the fourteen latei meetings, held between 1835 and 1846, were generally known as " Socialist Congresses." But the word Socialism had at this time little more definite meaning than dissatisfaction with competition and individualism as bases of society, and it was often used interchangeably with Coöperation or even with general social reforms.

The plans of Owen ran counter to the prevailing tendencies of the period, and Owen himself, as time passed on, came into sharper and sharper personal antagonism to the most influential classes of the country. In religion he was a free thinker, and, although he did not obtrude his religious views, both those who disapproved of his religion and those who opposed his plans of social reform used this lack of orthodoxy as an occasion for condemnation of him and his opinions. He was attacked in debates in Parliament, in the newspapers, and in the churches. All the usual means of opposing reforms, the refusal of the use of halls, the publication of offensive matter, and the stirring up of riots, were used against him and those who agreed with him. He lived to be very old, used up his means, was converted to spiritualism, and more and more lost touch with the world of practical life. Therefore, notwithstanding his personal abilities, his recognized standing, and his active efforts through so many years, and notwithstanding the large numbers of those who agreed with his opinions or were led by his teachings, his influence on the actual course of events was not great. Although he was constantly active in lecturing, writing books and pamphlets, and assisting in the editing of various journals, his social projects failed and his ideas were for the time at least discredited. Apart from his influence on education, factory legislation, and later coöperation, and on the extension of ideas that were to have more effect on the future than on his own time, the work of Owen had practically died out before the end of this period, although he lived until 1858. He had little sympathy with the political proposals of the Chartists and but little belief that the reduced taxes of the corn law reformers would appreciably increase the prosperity of the people. His plans for social advance were more fundamental but less immediately practicable than theirs. Nevertheless many of the reforms which it has been found necessary to introduce later might have been brought in at this time, and much misery, loss, and conflict saved, had not self-interest been still too powerful, ignorance too widespread, and the *laissez-faire* ideas which Owen combated too strongly held.

The period was still in the main one of aristocratic conceptions of political and economic life. In the conduct of business in all its forms it was a long dead level of control by those who were in a position of advantage and without sense of social responsibility. So far as the lower classes were concerned, with the possible exceptions of the factory laws and the corn law repeal, it saw no ameliorative legislation. It was a period of great increase of total wealth of the nation, but in the distribution of this greater wealth the lower classes, overworked, underpaid, unrepresented in the government, uneducated, and without opportunity, had little share.

76. BIBLIOGRAPHY

Perris, George H.: *The Industrial History of Modern England*, London, 1914.

The best general history of this subject for the period covered by this and the remaining chapters of this book.

Slater, Gilbert: *The Making of Modern England*, London, Revised Ed., 1915.

Usher, A. P.: *Industrial History of England*, Boston, 1919.

The three text-books named above have full and valuable bibliographical lists, enabling the student to make a much more detailed study of the period than contemplated by this book.

Traill, H. D., and Mann, J. S.: *Social England*, London, 1904.

The last volume of this six-volume illustrated work deals with the art, literature, engineering, chemistry, and a great number of other phases of economic and social life from 1815 to 1885.

Walpole, Spencer: *History of England since 1815, History of Twenty-five Years*, eight volumes.

This and the two following works, although general histories of the period, give especially full accounts of some of the social movements of the 19th century.

Bright, J. F.: *History of England*, five vols.

McCarthy, J. H.: *History of Our Own Time*, and *England under Gladstone*, seven vols.

Stevens, Edward C.: *English Railways, Their Development and Their Relation to the State*, London, 1915.

Lindsay, W. S.: *History of Merchant Shipping*, 1874.

Trevelyan, George M.: *Life and Letters of John Bright.*

Engels, Friedrich: *Condition of the Working Class in England in 1844*, Translation and new ed., 1892.

Kay, J. P.: *Condition of the Working Classes in the Cotton Manufacture*, 1832.

Unwin, Mrs. Fisher: *The Land Hunger; Life under Monopoly*, 1913.

Aschrott, P. F.: *The English Poor Law System*, 1902.

Report of the Commission on the Poor Law of 1834, Reprinted 1892.

Hovel, Mark: *The Chartist Movement.*

Hutchins, B. L., and Harrison, A.: *History of Factory Legislation*, 1903.

Owen, Robert: *Autobiography*, 1857.

Jones, Lloyd: *Life, Times and Labours of Robert Owen*, London, 1905.

Podmore, F.: *Robert Owen*, 1906.

Smart, W.: *Economic Annals of the Nineteenth Century*, two volumes.

Butler, J. R. M.: *The Passing of the Great Reform Bill.*

CHAPTER X

THE SPIRIT OF COMBINED ACTION, 1848-1878

77. National Affairs from 1848 to 1878. — The long period of peace, which had lasted except for a few small conflicts since 1815, came to an end in 1854. In that year England joined with France to support Turkey and their own national interests in the eastern Mediterranean regions against what they considered the dangerous power of Russia. The war consisted for the most part of a long siege of Sebastopol, a fortified Russian city in the Crimea, the long promontory jutting out into the Black Sea, and is therefore known as the Crimean War. The losses and suffering were intense and but little was accomplished. Russia was forced to agree to respect the independence of Turkey, to promise not to keep arsenals or ships of war on the Black Sea, and to submit to the appointment of an international commission to control the navigation of the Danube. These and a number of general agreements in international affairs were made at the Peace of Paris in 1856. After this there were several wars of greater or less importance. In 1857 the Sepoys or native troops in the British service in India mutinied against their officers and led in a native uprising that seemed for a while likely to sweep all the British out of India. But here and there troops held fast, reënforcements were sent, the tide of warfare soon turned and native resistance was put down with great severity. But the government took this opportunity to abolish by act of Parliament the old political powers of the British East India Company, which had been the real government of India, and in 1858 made that country a direct dependency of the British crown. The government took more and more interest in their great Indian possession and in 1876 " Empress of India " was added to the other titles of the Queen.   During the same year as the Sepoy rebellion small wars were being carried on in Persia, China, Afghanistan, and some years later with China again, with Abyssinia, and in southern and western Africa.

These were small wars and were waged in distant parts of the world ; from the wars in Europe after the Crimea and the Civil War in America England succeeded in keeping herself free. There was, however, a bitter dispute between England and the United States, due to the sympathy of the British government with the Southern States and to its readiness to further their interests.   In 1859 England was urged to intervene in the Italian war by which the unity of that country was partially gained, in 1864 in the Danish War, in which the duchies of Schleswig and Holstein were captured by Prussia and Austria, and in 1871 when Germany defeated France and seized Alsace-Lorraine ; but her disinclination to war was so great as to prevent her from joining either side in those conflicts.   In 1870 Great Britain joined in the European treaties guaranteeing the neutrality of Belgium, in 1871 in the treaty of London she accepted the proposal of Russia to withdraw from her promise not to use the Black Sea for war purposes, and later in the same year, 1871, a new treaty was signed with the United States settling the old dispute which had come down from the Civil War.   This treaty was of especial interest and importance, not only because it reëstablished friendly relations between two naturally closely allied nations but because it gave a great impetus to the principle of settling international disputes without recourse to war.   The fisheries disputes were settled in the same way.   The boundary questions between the United States and Canada were placed for arbitration in the hands of the German Emperor, and by the treaty of 1871 the American claim for damages for losses from the Southern vessels built in English ports was referred to a tribunal of five persons to be named by Great Britain, the United States, Italy, Switzerland, and Brazil. This tribunal sat at Geneva and in 1872 gave its award, which was mainly in favor of the United States. Although this was bitterly deplored in England, the most thoughtful men in both countries placed its moral value as an enlightened form of action high above any feeling of national loss and humiliation.

An important occurrence in British and world history was the opening of the Suez Canal in 1868 and the purchase by the British government of its financial control in 1875. Irish troubles were of growing severity during this whole period. An armed uprising in favor of independence from Great Britain was tried by a small group, known as the Young Ireland party, and put down in 1848. Phœnix clubs were organized for the same purpose after 1850 and developed into the Fenian Brotherhood, made up largely of Irish Americans who had earned money and obtained political and military training in the United States during the period of the Civil War. The plots of the Fenians were met and overcome by the British government between 1865 and 1867. Attempts were made to introduce greater justice into Ireland by the disestablishment of the English Church in Ireland in 1869, the passage of a land act in 1870, and a proposal to open higher education to Catholics and Protestants alike in 1873. This last bill was defeated, and notwithstanding disestablishment and land reform dissatisfaction with their subordinate political, economic, and religious position remained widespread among the Irish. To overcome this inferiority of position by the reintroduction of their old Parliament, separate and at least partially independent from that of Great Britain, the Home Rule party was formed in 1871. Its objects were more moderate than those of the United Irishmen, the Young Ireland and the Fenian parties which had planned complete independence, and it sought to attain its ends by act of Parliament rather than by armed force. In 1877 it came under the leadership of Charles Stewart Parnell and increased rapidly in strength and influence.

The growth of the colonies and their relations to the mother country were becoming constantly more important. Canada, Australia, New Zealand, and South Africa filled up steadily with an English-speaking population, partly by immigration from the British Isles, partly by natural increase. A new constitution with self-government was conceded to Canada in 1840, similar rights were extended to the various Australian colonies between 1850 and 1860, and to the Cape of Good Hope in 1872. In 1867 the older provinces of Canada were united into a federation, and Manitoba, British Columbia, and the others, except Newfoundland, were added to it as they were more completely filled up and organized.

Just as the period covered in the last chapter saw the first parliamentary reform bill, this period saw the second. In 1867, after ten years of agitation and the defeat of several proposals, a measure quite general in character was introduced by the ministry. The proposals for parliamentary reform made by liberal members of the governing classes were as in the first reform bill strongly supported by the working classes and others outside of Parliament who as yet had no votes. Many of the influences of the time, such as the increase of education, cheap postage, the formation of trade unions, the victory of the more democratic side in the American Civil War, were favorable to an extension of the right of representation more widely among the people. The Reform Bill of 1867 was therefore amended extensively while it was in Parliament, until when it was passed it gave the right of voting to the working classes who lived in the towns which already sent members to Parliament, and equalized the right of representation somewhat further by increasing the number of members from the larger towns and decreasing the number from the smaller towns. It gave votes to more than a million men who had not had them before. It may be fairly said that after the passage of the Reform Bill of 1867 the mass of the people of England, for the first time in its history, were directly represented in its government.

One of the effects of this popular influence on government both before and after the actual adoption of the new reform bill was the passage of several liberal measures. Those which were of an economic or social nature, such as the acts legalizing trade unions in 1871 and 1875 will be more fully described in later paragraphs of this chapter. Others of a more general character were the admission of the Jews into Parliament and abolition of the property requirement for membership in 1858, the establishment in 1861 of the Post Office Savings Bank, the introduction of voting by ballot, instead of orally, in 1872, the reform laws in Ireland already mentioned, an act establishing elementary education in 1870, a civil service reform act in 1870, a reorganization of the army in 1870 and 1871, and of the law courts in 1873, and a bill opening the universities of Oxford and Cambridge to the members of all religious bodies alike. Victoria was queen during this whole period and a long series of active ministers carried on the government and did their part in securing the adoption of these laws. The most prominent on the Liberal side were Lord John Russell, Lord Palmerston, and Mr. Gladstone; on the Conservative side, Lord Derby and Mr. Disraeli. These statesmen for the most part alternated with one another as prime minister, no party having retained its majority in Parliament and no prime minister having retained his office for more than five or six years continuously.

78. General Industrial and Commercial Progress. — In the thirty years that fall within the period of this chapter many new devices were introduced in manufacturing, mining, transportation, and agriculture. " Ring " spinning, a device by which spindles could be driven at vastly greater speed, sometimes as rapidly as 13,000 revolutions a minute, which had been invented in 1830, now came into general use, as well as improved looms, combing, and other textile machinery. In 1856 the Bessemer process of transforming iron into steel much more cheaply than before led to a vast increase in the use of steel instead of wrought iron. The Siemens or " open hearth " process was invented in 1866, and phosphorus ores were for the first time satisfactorily smelted by the " basic " process in 1879. The discovery of many new chemical processes, including the manufacture of aniline dyes, also occurred at this time. It was certain of these chemical discoveries, especially that of the bromogelatine plate, about 1870, that made possible the great advance of photography in its manifold forms that has been so characteristic of modern times. In the same general field of discovery was the invention of artificial means of refrigeration or the making of ice about 1860. Cold storage of food products and the importation of frozen meat from New Zealand and other distant parts of the earth followed and transformed the problems of the supply and cost of food.

There was an immense advance in every kind of production. Factories, machinery, docks, harbors, steamships, railroads, locomotives, cars, and other instruments of transportation multiplied enormously and in turn increased the supply of the things they made or transported. One of England's greatest industries became the production of machines for further production.

The production of coal increased during this period from about 40 million tons a year to about 120 million tons. The yearly production of iron was also tripled. Until some time after the end of this period Great Britain was far ahead of the United States, Germany, or any other country in the production of iron and steel, and practically controlled those markets as well as her own. The amount of ship-building rose from a little more than 100,000 tons a year to about 400,000, and these ships, due to greater speed, dock facilities, and organization, did a great deal more work ton for ton at the end than at the beginning of the period. The export of goods manufactured or mined in England or brought into England from abroad for purposes of export, and the importation of food, raw materials, and other goods all increased as rapidly as other forms of economic activity. The increase of trade with West Africa and with India, China,

Australia, and New Zealand, the effect of the opening of the Suez Canal, was very marked during this period. The value of annual exports from Great Britain was somewhat more than three times as great in 1878 as in 1848. England was not only the " workshop of the world," as Carlyle called her, she was also the greatest commercial country of the world.

Notwithstanding these inventions and this increase, if a careful examination is made of the industrial activity of the time, it will be observed that changes of organization were even more important. There was a marked increase in the size of business establishments. There were not so many more business concerns, but each was usually much larger. If an average cotton mill, for instance, could have been found at the beginning of the period it would have contained about 10,000 spindles; at the end of the period, about 15,000; an average weaving mill would have contained 150 looms in 1848, 200 in 1878. In 1878 there were cotton mills that ran more than 150,000 spindles and there were weaving mills with as many as 4000 looms. Manufacturing concerns of such extent were entirely unknown at an earlier period. This increase in the size of establishments rather than their number was true of transportation, mining, and banking as well as of manufacture, and has continued ever since. All this industrial development led to the formation of a large number of large fortunes, and to the creation of a more numerous well-to-do middle class. Whether the economic position of the great mass of the people was even yet appreciably improved is doubtful.

79. Agricultural Development. — The gradual advance in methods of agriculture which had begun in the eighteenth century had continued during the first half of the nineteenth until by the beginning of this period most of the discoveries which are now utilized in modern agriculture had been made. The use of them was, however, still restricted to a comparatively few advanced farmers. The characteristic of this period was the spread of these improved methods almost universally

s

through English agriculture. This spread was attained partly through writings on the subject, partly through the influence of local agricultural societies and of the Royal Agricultural Society, founded under the patronage of the queen in 1838, and partly through the continuous application of new capital and scientific knowledge to agriculture. The abolition of the corn laws in 1846 for a while frightened farmers into a panic, but there were so many favorable influences in existence that any injurious effect this may have had was soon overcome.

The principal forms of improvement in agriculture that were thus spread widely in English farming were the extension of drainage, the discovery and use of artificial fertilizers like guano, bone meal, and phosphates, the introduction of improved farm machinery, and the importation of cattle food. Guano was imported by the millions of tons from Peru, bones were collected and brought to England from the deserts of Africa and the Pampas of South America, to be ground and used on the farms; beans, linseed, and Indian corn were introduced for the feeding of cattle from Asia, Russia, and the United States. Improved agricultural implements, such as ploughs, harrows, drills, mowing, reaping, and threshing machines, came into general use, and after 1850 steam power was introduced for many uses on the farm. Many improved forms of agricultural machinery were introduced in the first place from America, but their manufacture soon became one of the largest of English industries.

Before 1878 the average yield of land, economy in the production of crops, and excellence of the breeds of farm and stock animals reached as high a level as has been attained since in England, and higher than has been reached in any other country or in any earlier period. There were several defects in the English agricultural system, as will be pointed out later, but so far as excellence of scientific farming goes England stood by this time at the head of all countries in the world. The ten years from 1852 to 1862, in the middle of this period, has been chosen by students of agricultural history as on the whole the most prosperous period of British agriculture.

80. Preservation of Remaining Open Lands. — In the course of agricultural improvement, as has been seen, the old open fields of the Middle Ages were at successive periods very generally enclosed into modern fenced or hedged farms. This process had been brought practically to completion by the beginning of this period. There had been in the later eighteenth and early nineteenth centuries some 4000 private acts of Parliament passed for the purpose, and by these, by voluntary agreement, and by the action of the Enclosure Commissioners already described more than seven million acres had been enclosed, and so far as farming lands were concerned England was an enclosed country.

But now a reaction set in. Along with the open-field farming lands it was perceived that open commons, village greens, gentlemen's parks, and the old national forest lands were being enclosed, and frequently for building or railroad, not for agricultural uses, to the serious detriment of the health and of the enjoyment of the people, and to the destruction of the beauty of the country. The dread of interference by the government with matters that might be left to private settlement was also passing away. In 1865 the House of Commons appointed a commission to investigate the question of open spaces near the city of London, and the next year on their recommendation Parliament passed a law by which the Enclosure Commissioners were empowered to make regulations for the use of all commons within fifteen miles of London as public parks, except so far as the legal rights of the lords of the manors in which the commons lay should prevent. A contest had already arisen between several of these lords of manors having the control of open commons, whose interest it was to enclose and sell them, and other persons having vague rights of pasturage and other use of them, whose interest it was to preserve them as open spaces. To aid the latter in their legal resistance to proposed enclosures, a " Commons Preservation Society " was formed in 1865. As a result a number of contests were decided in the year 1866 in favor of those who opposed enclosures.

The first case to attract attention was that of Wimbledon Common, just west of London. Earl Spencer, the lord of the manor of Wimbledon, had offered to give up his rights on the common to the inhabitants of the vicinity in return for a nominal rent and certain privileges; and had proposed that a third of the common should be sold, and the money obtained for it used to fence, drain, beautify, and keep up the remainder. The neighboring inhabitants, however, preferred the spacious common as it stood, and when a bill to carry out Lord Spencer's proposal had been introduced into Parliament, they contended that they had legal rights on the common which he could not disregard, and that they objected to its enclosure. The parliamentary committee practically decided in their favor, and the proposition was dropped. An important decision in a similar case was made by the courts in 1870. Berkhamstead Common, an open stretch some three miles long and half a mile wide, lying near the town of Berkhamstead, twenty-five miles north of London, had been used for pasturing animals, cutting turf, digging gravel, gathering furze, and as a place of general recreation and enjoyment by the people of the two manors in which it lay, from time immemorial. In 1866 Lord Brownlow, the lord of these two manors, began making enclosures upon it, erecting two iron fences across it so as to enclose 434 acres and to separate the remainder into two entirely distinct parts. The legal advisers of Lord Brownlow declared that the inhabitants had no rights which would prevent him from enclosing parts of the common, although to satisfy them he offered to give to them the entire control over one part of it. The Commons Preservation Society, however, advised the inhabitants differently, and encouraged them to make a legal contest. One of their number, Augustus Smith, a wealthy and obstinate man, a member of Parliament, and a possessor of rights on the common both as a freeholder and a copyholder, was induced to take action in his own name and as a representative of other claimants of common rights. He engaged in London a force of one hundred and twenty laborers, sent them down at night by train, and before morning had broken down Lord Brownlow's two miles of iron fences, on which he had spent some £5000, and piled their sections neatly up on another part of the common. Two lawsuits followed: one by Lord Brownlow against Mr. Smith for trespass, the other a cross suit in the Chancery Court by Mr. Smith to ascertain the commoners' rights, and prevent the enclosure of the common. After a long trial the decision was given in Mr. Smith's favor, and not only was Berkhamstead Common thus preserved as an open space, but a precedent set for the future decision of other similar cases. Within the years between 1866 and 1874 dispute after dispute analogous to this arose, and decision after decision was given declaring the illegality of enclosures by a lord of a manor where there were claims of commoners which they still asserted and valued and which could be used as an obstacle to enclosure. Hampstead Heath, Ashdown Forest, Malvern Hills, Plumstead, Tooting, Wandsworth, Coulston, Dartford, and a great many other commons, village greens, roadside wastes, and other open spaces were saved from enclosure, and some places were partly opened up again, as a result either of lawsuits, of parliamentary action, or of voluntary agreements and purchase.

Perhaps the most conspicuous instance was that of Epping Forest. This common consisted of an open tract about thirteen miles long and one mile wide, containing in 1870 about three thousand acres of open common land. Enclosure was being actively carried on by some nineteen lords of manors, and some three thousand acres had been enclosed by rather high-handed means within the preceding twenty years. Among the various land-owners who claimed rights of common upon a part of the Forest was, however, the City of London, and in 1871 the City began suit against the various lords of manors, under the claim that it possessed pasture rights, not only in the manor of Ilford, in which its property of two hundred acres was situated, but, since the district was a royal forest, over the whole of it. The City asked that the lords of manors should be prevented from enclosing any more of it, and required to throw open again what they had enclosed during the last twenty years. After a long and expensive legal battle and a concurrent investigation by a committee of Parliament, both extending over three years, a decision was given in favor of the City of London and other commoners, and the lords of manors were forced to give back about three thousand acres. The whole was made permanently into a public park. The old forest rights of the crown proved to be favorable to the commoners, and thus obtained at least one tardy justification to set against their long and dark record in the past.

In 1871, in one of the cases which had been appealed, the Lord Chancellor laid down a principle indicating a reaction in the judicial attitude on the subject, when he declared that no enclosure should be made except when there was a manifest advantage in it; as contrasted with the former policy of enclosing unless there was some strong reason against it. In 1876 Parliament passed a law amending the acts of 1801 and 1845, and directing the Enclosure Commissioners to reverse their former rule of action. That is to say, they were not to approve any enclosure unless it could be shown to be to the manifest advantage of the neighborhood, as well as to the interest of the parties directly concerned. Later by the Commons Law Amendment Act, it was required that every proposed enclosure of any kind should first be advertised and opportunity given for objection, then submitted to the Board of Agriculture for its approval, and this approval should only be given when such an enclosure was for the general benefit of the public. No desire of a lord of a manor to enclose ground for his private park or game preserve, or to use it for building ground, would now be allowed to succeed. The interest of the community at large was placed above the private advantage and even liberty of action of landholders. The authorities do not merely see that justice is done between lord and commoners on the manor, but that both alike shall be restrained from doing what is not to the public advantage. Indeed, Parliament at a later time went one step further, and by an order set a precedent for taking a common entirely out of the hands of the lord of the manor, and putting it in the hands of a board to keep it for public uses. Thus not only did the enclosing movement decrease for lack of open farming land to enclose, but public opinion and law interposed to preserve such remaining open land as had not been already divided. Whatever land remained that was not in individual ownership and occupancy was to be retained under the control of the community at large, and to be used for the benefit of all.

81. The Introduction of Coöperation. — Numerous coöperative societies, with varying objects and methods, formed part of the agitation, experimentation, and discussion characteristic of the early years of the nineteenth century which has been described in connection with the life of Robert Owen.[1] Many plans were, however, at that time spoken of indiscriminately as " coöperative." The coöperative movement as a definite, continuous development dates from the organization of the " Rochdale Equitable Pioneers " in 1844. This society was composed of twenty-eight working weavers of that town, who saved up one pound each, and thus created a capital of twenty-eight pounds, which they invested in flour, oatmeal, butter, sugar, and some other groceries. They opened a store in the house of one of their number in Toad Lane, Rochdale, for the sale of these articles to their own members under a plan previously agreed upon. The principal points of their scheme, afterward known as the " Rochdale Plan," were as follows : sale of goods at regular market prices, division of profits to members at quarterly intervals in proportion to purchases, subscription to capital in instalments by members, and payment of five per

[1] See pp. 246–8.

cent interest on this capital.   There were also various provisions
of minor importance, such as absolute purity and honesty of
goods, insistence on cash payments, devoting a part of their
earnings to education or other self-improvement, settling all
questions by equal vote, no matter how many shares the
member might hold.   These arrangements sprang naturally
from the fact that they proposed carrying on their store for
their own benefit, alike as managers, shareholders, and purchasers of their goods.

The source of the profits they would have to divide among
their members was the same as in the case of any ordinary store.
The difference between the wholesale price, at which they would
buy, and the retail market price, at which they would sell,
would be the gross profits.   From this would have to be paid,
normally, rent for their store, wages for their salesmen, and
interest on their capital.   But after these were paid there should
still remain a certain amount of net profit, and this it was which
they proposed to divide among themselves as purchasers, instead of leaving it to be taken by an ordinary store proprietor.
The capital they themselves furnished, and consequently paid
themselves the interest.   The first two items, rent and wages,
also amounted to nothing at first, though naturally they must
be accounted for if their store rose to any success.   As a matter
of fact, their success was immediate and striking.   They admitted new members freely, and at the end of the first year of
their existence had increased in numbers to seventy-four, with
£187 capital.   During the year they had done a business of
£710, and distributed profits of £22.   A table of the increase
of this first successful coöperative establishment during its
next thirty years will give an idea of its growth.

DATE	MEMBERS	CAPITAL	BUSINESS	PROFITS
1855	1,400	£ 11,032	£ 44,902	£ 3,109
1865	5,326	78,778	196,234	25,156
1875	8,415	225,682	305,657	48,212

They soon extended their business in variety as well as in total amount. In 1847 they added the sale of linen and woollen goods, in 1850 of meat, in 1867 they began baking and selling bread to their customers. They opened eventually a dozen or more branch stores in Rochdale, the original Toad Lane house being superseded by a great distributing building or central store, with a library and reading room. They came to own much property in the town, and spread their activity into many lines. The example of the Rochdale society was followed by many others, especially in the north of England and south of Scotland. A few years after its foundation two large and successful societies were started in Oldham, having between them by 1860 more than 3000 members, and doing a business of some £80,000 a year. In Liverpool, Manchester, Birmingham, and other cities similar societies grew up at the same period. In 1863 there were some 454 coöperative societies of this kind in existence, 381 of them together having 108,000 members and doing an annual business of about £2,600,000. One hundred and seventeen of the total number of societies were in Lancashire and 96 in Yorkshire. Many of these eventually came to have a varied and extensive activity. The Leeds Coöperative Society, for instance, somewhat later had a grist mill, 69 grocery and provision stores, 20 dry goods and millinery shops, 9 boot and shoe shops, and 40 butcher shops. It had 12 coal depots, a furnishing store, a bakery, a tailoring establishment, a boot and shoe factory, a brush factory, and acted as a builder of houses and cottages. The work done by these coöperative stores so far as they are concerns selling to their members is known as " distributive coöperation," or " coöperation in distribution." They combine the seller and the buyer into one group. From one point of view the society is a store-keeping body, buying goods at wholesale and selling them at retail. From another point of view, exactly the same group of persons, the members of the society, are the customers of the store, the purchasers and consumers of the goods. Whenever any body of men form an association to carry on an establishment which sells them the goods they need, dividing the profits of the buying and selling among the members of the association, it is a society for distributive coöperation.

A variation from the Rochdale plan is that used in three or perhaps more societies organized in London between 1856 and 1875 by officials and employees of the government. These are the Civil Service Supply Association, the Civil Service Coöperative Society, and the Army and Navy Stores. In these, instead of buying at wholesale and selling at retail rates, sharing the profits at the end of a given term, they sell as well as buy at wholesale rates, except for the slight increase necessary to pay the expenses of carrying on the store. In other words, the members obtain their goods for use at cheap rates instead of dividing up a business profit.

But these and still other variations have had only a slight connection with the working-class coöperative movement just described. A more direct development of it was the formation, in 1864, of the Wholesale Coöperative Society, at Manchester, a body holding much the same relation to the coöperative societies that each of them does to its individual members. The shareholders are the retail coöperative societies, which supply the capital and control its actions. During its first year the Wholesale Society possessed a capital of £2456 and did a business of £51,858. In 1865 its capital was something over £7000 and business over £120,000. Ten years later, in 1875, its capital was £360,527 and yearly business £2,103,226. Its purchasing agents were widely distributed in various parts of the world. In 1873 it purchased and began running a cracker factory, shortly afterward a boot and shoe factory, the next year a soap factory. Subsequently it took up a woollen goods factory, cocoa works, and the manufacture of ready-made clothing. Somewhat later it employed something over 5000 persons, had large branches in London, Newcastle, and Leicester, agencies and depots in various countries, and ran six steamships. In 1872 it established a banking department, which within a year had more than a million dollars on deposit and has since conducted the financial business of more than a thousand coöperative societies besides many trade unions and individual accounts. Coöperative stores, belonging to wholesale and retail distributive coöperative societies, are thus a well-established and steadily, if somewhat slowly, extending element in modern industrial society.

82. Coöperation in Production. — But the greatest problems in the relations of modern industrial classes to one another are not connected with buying and selling, but with employment and wages. The competition between employer and employee is more intense than that between buyer and seller and has more influence on the constitution of society. This opposition of employer and employee is especially prominent in manufacturing, and the form of coöperation which is based on a combination or union of these two classes is therefore commonly called "coöperation in production," as distinguished from coöperation in distribution. Societies have been formed on a coöperative basis to produce one or another kind of goods from the earliest years of the century, but their real development dates from a period somewhat later than that of the coöperative stores, that is, from about 1850. In this year there were in existence in England bodies of workmen who were carrying on, with more or less outside advice, assistance, or control, a coöperative tailoring establishment, a bakery, a printing shop, two building establishments, a piano factory, a shoe factory, and several flour mills. These companies were all formed on the same general plan. The workmen were generally the members of the company. They paid themselves the prevailing rate of wages, then divided among themselves either equally or in proportion to their wages the net profits of the business, when there were any, having first reserved a sufficient amount to pay interest on capital. As a matter of fact, the capital and much of the direction was contributed from outside by persons philanthropically interested in the plans, but the ideal recognized and desired was that capital should be subscribed, interest received, and all administration carried on by the workmen-coöperators themselves. In this way, in a coöperative productive establishment, there would not be two classes, employer and employee. The same individuals would be acting in both capacities, either themselves or through their elected managers. All of these early companies failed or dissolved sooner or later, but in the meantime others had been established. By 1862 some 113 productive societies had been formed, including 28 textile manufacturing companies, 8 boot and shoe factories, 7 societies of iron workers, 4 of brush makers, and organizations in various other trades. Among the most conspicuous of these were three which were much discussed during their period of prosperity. They were the Liverpool Working Tailors' Association, which lasted from 1850 to 1860; the Manchester Working Tailors' Association, which flourished from 1850 to 1872; and the Manchester Working Hatters' Association, 1851–1873. These companies had at different times from 6 to 30 members each. After the great strike of the Amalgamated Society of Engineers, in 1852, a series of iron workers' coöperative associations were formed. In the next twenty years, between 1862 and 1882, some 163 productive societies were formed, and somewhat later there were in existence 143 societies solely for coöperative production, with some 25,000 members. Coöperative production has been distinctly less prosperous than coöperative distribution. Most purely coöperative productive societies have had a short and troubled existence, though their dissolution has in many cases been the result of contention rather than ordinary failure and has not always involved pecuniary loss. In addition to the usual difficulties of all business, insufficiency of capital, incompetency of buying and selling agents and of managers, dishonesty of trusted officials or of debtors, commercial panics, and other adversities, to which coöperative, quite as much as or even more than individual companies have been subject, there are peculiar dangers often fatal to their coöperative principles. For instance, more than one such association, after going through a period of struggle and sacrifice, and emerging into a period of prosperity, has yielded to the temptation to hire additional employees just as any other employer might, at regular wages, without admitting them to any share in the profits, interest, or control of the business. Such a concern is little more than an ordinary joint-stock company with an unusually large number of shareholders. As a matter of fact, plain, clear-cut coöperative production makes up but a small part of that which is currently reported and known as such. A fairer statement would be that there is a large element of coöperation in a great many productive establishments. Nevertheless, productive societies more or less consistent to coöperative principles exist in considerable numbers and have even shown a distinct increase of growth in recent years.

Very much the same statements are true of another branch of coöperative effort, — coöperation in farming. Experiments were made very early, they have been numerous, mostly short-lived, and yet show a tendency to increase within the last decade. Sixty or more societies have engaged in coöperative farming, but only half a dozen are now in existence. The practicability and desirability of the application of coöperative ideals to agriculture is nevertheless a subject of constant discussion among those interested in coöperation, and new schemes are being tried from time to time.

83. Legal and Social Encouragement of Coöperation. — The growth of coöperation, like that of other schemes, has been dependent on successive modifications of the law; though it was rather its defects than its opposition that caused the difficulty in this case. When coöperative organizations were first formed it was found that by the Common Law they could not legally deal as societies with non-members; that they could not hold land for investment, or for any other purpose than the transaction of their own business, or more than one acre even for this purpose; that they could not loan money to other societies; that they could not sue on the embezzlement or misuse of their funds by their officers; and that each member was responsible for the debts of the whole society. Eight or ten statutes have been passed to cure the legal defects from which coöperative associations suffered. The most important of these were the " Frugal Investment Clause " in the Friendly Societies Act of 1846, by which such associations were allowed to be formed and permitted to hold personal property for the purposes of a society for savings; the Industrial and Provident Societies Act of 1852, by which coöperative societies were definitely authorized and obtained the right to sue as if they were corporations; the Act of 1862, which repealed the former acts, gave them the right of incorporation, made each member liable for debt only to the extent of his own investment, and allowed them greater latitude for investments; the third Industrial and Provident Societies Act of 1876, which again repealed previous acts, and established a veritable code for their regulation and extension. All the needs of the coöperative movement, so far as they have been discovered and agreed upon by those interested in its propagation, have thus been provided for, so far as the law can do so.

Coöperation has always contained an element of philanthropy, or at least of enthusiastic belief on the part of those especially interested in it, that it was destined to be of great service to humanity, and to solve many of the problems of modern social organization. Advocates of coöperation have not therefore been content simply to organize societies which would conduce to their own profit, but have kept up a constant propaganda for their extension. There was a period, already referred to, of about twenty years, from 1820 to 1840, before coöperation was placed on a solid footing, when it was advocated and tried in numerous experiments as a part of the agitation begun by Robert Owen for the establishment of socialistic communities. In 1850 a group of philanthropic and enthusiastic young men, including such able and prominent men as Thomas Hughes, Frederick D. Maurice, and others who have since been connected through long lives with coöperative effort, formed themselves into a " Society for promoting Working Men's Associations," which sent out lecturers, published tracts and a newspaper, loaned money, promoted legislation, and took other action for the encouragement of coöperation. Its members were commonly known as the " Christian Socialists." They had but scant success, and in 1851 dissolved the Association and founded instead a " Working Men's College " in London, which long remained a centre of coöperative and reforming agitation.

So far, this effort to extend and regulate the movement came rather from outside sympathizers than from coöperators themselves. With 1869, however, began a series of annual Coöperative Congresses which, like the annual Trade Union Congresses, have sprung from the initiative of workingmen themselves and which are still continued. Papers are read, addresses made, experiences compared, and most important of all a Central Board and a Parliamentary Committee elected for the ensuing year. At the first Congress, in 1869, a Coöperative Union was formed which aims to include all the coöperative societies of the country, and as a matter of fact does include about three-fourths of them. The Central Coöperative Board represents this Union. It is divided into seven sections, each having charge of the affairs of one of the seven districts into which the country is divided for coöperative work. The Board issues a journal, prints pamphlets, keeps up correspondence, holds public examinations on auditing, book-keeping, and the principles of coöperation, and acts as a statistical, propagandist, and regulative body. There is also a " Coöperative Guild " and a " Women's Coöperative Guild." Long afterward the coöperators decided to go into politics and formed a separate parliamentary party.

84. Coöperation in Credit. — In England building societies are not usually recognized as a form of coöperation, but they are in reality coöperative in the field of credit in the same way as the associations already discussed are in distribution, in production, or in agriculture. Building societies are defined in one of the statutes as bodies formed " for the purpose of raising by the subscription of the members a stock or fund for making advances to members out of the funds of the society." The general plan of one of these societies is as follows : A number of persons become members, each taking one or more shares. Each shareholder is required to pay into the treasury a certain sum each month. There is thus created each month a new capital sum which can be loaned to some member who may wish to borrow it and be able and willing to give security and to pay interest. The borrower will afterward have to pay not only his monthly dues, but the interest on his loan. The proportionate amount of the interest received is credited to each member, borrower and non-borrower alike, so that after a certain number of months, by the receipts from dues and interest, the borrower will have repaid his loan, whilst the members who have not borrowed will receive a corresponding sum in cash. Borrowers and lenders are thus the same group of persons, just as sellers and consumers are in distributive, and employers and employees in productive coöperation. The members of such societies are enabled to obtain loans when otherwise they might not be able to ; the periodical dues create a succession of small amounts to be loaned, when otherwise this class of persons could hardly save up a sufficient sum to be used as capital ; and finally by paying the interest to their collective group, so that a proportionate part of it is returned to the borrower, and by the continuance of the payment of dues, the repayment of the loan is less of a burden than in ordinary loans obtained from a bank or a capitalist. Loans to their members have been usually restricted to money to be used for the building of a dwelling-house or store or the purchase of land; whence their name of " building societies." Their formation dates from 1815, their extension, from about 1834. Laws authorizing and regulating their operations were passed in 1836 and 1874.

The one feature common to all forms of coöperation is the union of previously competing economic classes. In a co-operative store, competition between buyer and seller does not exist; and the same is true for borrower and lender in a building and loan association and for employer and em-ployee in a coöperative factory. Coöperation is therefore in line with many other recent movements in being a reaction from the competition which was so strenuously praised earlier in the nineteenth century.

85. Profit Sharing. — There is a device which has been introduced into many establishments which stands midway between simple competitive relations and full coöperation. It diminishes, though it does not remove, the opposition between employer and employee. This is " profit sharing." In the year 1865 Henry Briggs, Son and Co., operators of collieries in Yorkshire, after long and disastrous conflicts with the miners' trade unions, offered as a measure of conciliation to their em-ployees or opposition to the trade union that whenever the net profit of the business should be more than ten per cent on their investment, one-half of all such surplus profit should be divided among the workmen in proportion to the wages they had earned in the previous year. The expectation was that the increased regularity of work and interest, effort and devotion put into the work by the men would be such as to make the total earnings of the employers as great, notwithstanding their sacrifice to the men of the half of the profits above ten per cent. This antici-pation was justified. After a short period of suspicion on the part of the men, and doubt on the part of the employers, both parties seemed to be converted to the advantages of profit

T

sharing, a sanguine report of their experience was made by a member of the firm to the Social Science Association in 1868, sums between one and six thousand pounds were divided yearly among the employees, while the percentage of profits to the owners rose to as much as eighteen per cent.

This experiment split on the rock of dissension in 1875, but in the meantime others, either in imitation of their plan or independently, had introduced the same or other forms of profit sharing. Another colliery, two iron works, a textile factory, a millinery firm, a printing shop, and some others admitted their employees to a share in the profits within the years 1865 and 1866. The same plan was then introduced into certain retail stores, and into a considerable variety of occupations, including several large farms where a share of all profits was offered to the laborers as a " bonus " in addition to their wages. The results were very various, ranging all the way from the most extraordinary success to complete and discouraging failure.

Sometimes the payment of a share in the profits of the business is made, in the case of joint-stock companies, in the form of the grant of a proportionate number of the shares of the company. In this way the employees have become interested in the business, not only in the capacity of profit sharing workmen, but of dividend receiving stockholders. This form of profit sharing has been distinguished by calling it " labor co-partnership," and is said to have been especially successful. At a period somewhat after the close of this chapter, in 1894, there were reported to be in England 101 profit sharing businesses with over 28,000 employees. In 1912 there were 133 such establishments with 106,000 employees.

A great many other employers, corporate or individual, provide laborers' dwellings at favorable rents, furnish meals at cost price, subsidize insurance funds, offer easy terms to those wishing to become shareholders in the business, support reading rooms, music halls, and gymnasiums, or take other means of admitting their employees to advantages other than the simple receipt of competitive wages. Yet the entire control of capital and management, in the case of firms which share profits with their employees, remains in the hands of the employers, so that there is in these cases rather an enlightened view of the position of the employing class than a combination of two classes in one, as in coöperation.

86. Continuance of Factory Legislation. — The factory inspectors provided for in the factory act of 1833 became propagandists for further factory legislation. In their annual and special reports they continually called attention to the inadequacy of the laws already passed and to other fields where regulation was needed. The voluntary " short time committees " which had been formed in the early period of the discussion of the subject, and the " Factory Acts Reform Association," which was formed later, also pressed for further laws. As time passed on many of those who had on principle opposed early legislation most bitterly, Graham, Roebuck, and even Cobden, converted by its results, withdrew their opposition and announced that they were willing to see it carried further. In many cases it was found that the output of factories had increased rather than decreased as a result of cutting down excessive hours of labor. Thus in all later discussions a considerable number of factory owners were themselves on the side of regulation. A letter from a manufacturer in a Birmingham paper states, with regard to one of the later acts, that " nineteen-twentieths of the earthenware manufacturers were opposed to the act when it was first introduced, myself among the number. I consider that nineteen-twentieths now would be unwilling to part with it." More legislation in the same line was bound to come. Some of the later laws were simply to correct defects in those already passed. For instance, in 1850 and 1853 a " normal working day " for women, young persons, and children was established in order successfully to accomplish the objects intended by the law. All work must be between six o'clock in the morning and six in the evening, or between seven in the morning and seven in the evening. This was to prevent what was known as the "relay system," in use in many mills, by which women, young persons, and children, although not actually working more than the ten hours or the half-time permitted by law, were shifted about and their time so broken that they were in reality kept about the mills the whole fifteen hours considered to be day time, and the inspectors prevented from seeing that they were worked overtime.

The most important new laws were those that extended control into new industries. All factory legislation so far described, with slight exceptions, had applied to textile mills only. This was not so much because working conditions there were worse, but because the cotton mills especially were larger, more conspicuous, and newer, and therefore both were more likely to attract attention and were easier to be controlled by law. The reformers in advocating the earlier laws had declared that they would not be satisfied until all women, young persons, and children were protected from overwork and dangerous conditions and given more opportunity. The reports of the Children's Employment Commission of 1843 and the similar commission which made a series of reports from 1863 to 1868 gradually familiarized the country with the universality as well as the reality of the evils they described. The fact that women and children in lacemaking were often kept at work during busy seasons till nine, ten, and even twelve o'clock at night; that the girls in dye-houses who carried wet goods on their backs into drying rooms at as high a temperature as 110, and then out on to the grass fields, were often summoned to work at four or five o'clock in the morning; that there were more than 2000 children under ten years of age at work in the Birmingham hardware industry, one-fourth of them under eight; and that weak sight, blindness, and lead poisoning were prevalent in the potteries and other industries, which were carried on under shockingly unsanitary conditions — these facts, becoming gradually familiar, made the community ready to look upon factory regulation as a desirable general system, not merely a plan for getting rid of evils in the cotton mills.

As a result of these influences occasional new acts were passed such as that for calico printing in 1846. A large number of statutes were passed between 1867 and 1874 to extend the provisions of earlier acts to dye-works, lacemaking, potteries, match making, straw braiding, hosiery and clothing manufacturing; and by the "Factory Acts Extension Act" of 1867 to a large number of metal, paper, and other trades. In 1867 a factory was defined as any establishment where more than fifty persons were engaged, and all such institutions were brought under the factory acts. In the same year a "workshop regulation" act was passed making provision for hours and conditions of labor for women, young persons, and children, and for sanitation and other requirements, in all establishments where less than fifty persons were employed. In this way practically all establishments which were in any way connected with manufacturing were brought under a certain amount of regulation.

Some of these acts changed the provisions of the early acts in various ways, mostly in the direction of greater severity, but in some cases in the way of exceptions and modifications that deprived them of much of their value and introduced almost hopeless variety and confusion. To meet these difficulties in 1876 a commission of investigation was appointed and in accordance with their report in 1878 the "Factory and Workshop Consolidation Act" repealed almost all the former special laws and substituted for them a veritable factory code containing a vast number of provisions for the regulation of industrial establishments. This law covered more than fifty printed pages of the statute book. Its principal general provisions were as follows: the limit of prohibited labor was raised from nine to ten years, "children" in the terms of the statute being those between ten and fourteen, and "young persons" those between fourteen and eighteen years of age. For all such the day's work must begin either at six or seven, and close at the same hour in the evening, two hours being allowed for meal times. All Saturdays and eight other days in the year must be half-holidays, while the whole of Christmas Day and Good Friday, or two alternative days, must be allowed as holidays. Children could work for only one-half of each day or on the whole of alternate days, and must attend school on the days or parts of days on which they did not work. There were minute provisions governing sanitary conditions, safety from machinery, and in dangerous occupations, meal-times, medical certificates of fitness for employment, and reports of accidents. Finally it included the necessary body of provisions for administration, enforcement, penalties, and exceptions. The law of 1878 is the codification of all the factory laws passed up to that time and the basis of all that have been passed since.

87. Rise of Trade Unions. — From the period covered by this chapter onward to the present time, organizations of workingmen for self-defence or self-advancement in matters of wages, hours, and other working conditions have become increasingly more prominent. Their beginnings lie in still earlier times, and to trace them it will be necessary to go back not only to the period covered by the chapter preceding this but to the period of the industrial revolution. Among tailors, hatmakers, shoemakers, and other artisans there were numerous journeymen's associations in the nature of trade unions in the eighteenth and early nineteenth century. But the conditions became much more favorable for the extension of workingmen's organizations as time passed on. Under the old gild conditions, when most men rose successively from apprentice to journeyman, and from journeyman to employer, when the relations between the employing master and his journeymen and apprentices were very close, and the advantages of the gild were participated in to a certain degree by all grades of the producing body, organizations of the employed against the employers could hardly exist. It has been seen that the growth of separate combinations was one of the indications of a breaking down of the gild system. Even in later times, when establishments were still small and scattered, when the law required that engagements should be made for long periods, and that none should work in an industry except those who had been apprenticed to it, and when rates of wages and hours of labor were settled by law, the opposition between the interests of employers and employees was not so strongly marked. The occasion or opportunity for union amongst the workmen in most trades still hardly existed. Where workmen did organize themselves it was in trades where the employers made up a well-to-do class and where the prospect of the ordinary workman ever reaching the position of an employer was slight.

The changes of the industrial revolution, however, made a profound difference. With the growth of factories and the increase in the size of business establishments, railway companies, and large scale mining, the employer and employee came to be farther apart, while at the same time the employees in any one establishment or trade were thrown more closely together. When a large number of laborers were gathered together in one establishment, all in a similar position one to the other and with common interests as to wages, hours of labor, and other conditions of their work, the fact that they were one homogeneous class could hardly escape their recognition. Since these common interests were in so many respects opposed to those of their employers, the advantage of combination to obtain added strength in the settlement of disputed questions was equally evident. As the Statute of Apprentices was no longer in force, and freedom of contract had taken its place, a dispute between an employer and a single employee would result in the discharge of the latter. If the dispute was between the employer and his whole body of employees, each one of the latter would be in a vastly stronger position, and there would be something like equality on the two sides of the contest. Under these circumstances of homogeneity of the interests of the laborers, of opposition of their interests to those of the employer, and of the absence of any external control over either, combinations among workmen, or trade unions, naturally sprang up.

88. The Combination Acts. Opposition of Public Opinion. — Their growth, however, was slow and interrupted. The poverty, ignorance, and lack of training of the laborers interposed a serious obstacle to the formation of permanent unions; and a still more tangible difficulty lay in the opposition of the law and of public opinion. A trade union may be defined as an organized body of workmen, the object of which is to obtain more favorable conditions of labor for its members. In order to exist a certain amount of intelligence, a certain degree of training in working together, and some regularity of money contributions on the part of its members are necessary, and these powers and habits were but slightly developed in the early years of last century.

In order to obtain the objects of the union a " strike," or concerted refusal to work except on certain conditions, is the natural means to be employed. But such action, in fact the existence of a combination contemplating such action, was at that time against the law. A long series of statutes known as the " Combination Acts " had been passed from time to time since the sixteenth century, the object of which was to prevent artisans or tradesmen, either employers or employees, from combining to change the rate of wages or other conditions of labor and service which had been legally established by the government or had become customary. The last of the combination acts was passed in the year 1800 in response to many petitions of manufacturers to Parliament complaining that combinations of workmen were being formed. It was clearly an exercise of the power of the employing class to use their representation in Parliament to legislate in their own interest. It provided that all combinations whatever between journeymen or other workmen for obtaining an advance in wages for themselves or other workmen, or for decreasing the number of hours of labor, or for endeavoring to prevent any employer from engaging any one whom he might choose, or for persuading any other workmen not to work, or for refusing to work with any other men, should be illegal. Attendance at any meeting called for such a purpose or subscribing to funds or inviting others to attend such a meeting was likewise illegal. Any justice of the peace was empowered to convict by summary process and to sentence to three months' imprisonment any workman who entered into such a combination. Employers were likewise prohibited from entering into combinations to reduce the wages of workmen or alter the hours of work, under penalty of £20 fine, though it could hardly have been expected that this provision would be carried out, and no prosecution, as a matter of fact, was ever brought under it. There was an interesting provision for compulsory arbitration of wages and hours, but this also remained unobserved.

The combination laws did not remain a dead letter. In the almost incredible partiality of the law at that period, while employers who combined were in no single case prosecuted, there were a vast number of cases of fine and imprisonment of trade unionists under the law of 1800. In 1818 two officers of a weavers' union at Bolton were sentenced to one year's imprisonment, and in the next year a number of cotton spinners at Manchester were sentenced to various terms of imprisonment. In 1817 ten delegates sent by journeymen calico printers to a meeting to form an organization were seized with all their papers by the constables and sentenced for three months, though no dispute was in progress. The general panic of the upper classes in the early part of the century, in fear of democratic movements on the part of the people, helped to cause an extremely harsh application of the combination acts. The magistrates often confused trade disputes with seditious agitation.

Quite apart from the combination laws, the ordinary action of trade unions was held by the judges to be illegal by the Common Law, under the doctrine that combined attempts to influence wages, hours, prices, or apprenticeship were conspiracies in restraint of trade. Such conspiracies were repeatedly declared to be illegal. Five journeymen printers were tried, convicted, and sentenced to two years' imprisonment each at London in 1798 for a combination to demand more wages on threat of strike. Five leaders in a strike of weavers were sentenced under the Common Law to terms of imprisonment extending from four to eighteen months in 1812; and there are many other instances.

In addition to their illegality, trade unions in their early days were extremely unpopular with the most influential classes of English society. The employers, against whose power they were organized, naturally antagonized them for fear they would raise wages and in other ways give the workmen the upper hand; they were opposed by the aristocratic feeling of the country, because they brought about an increase in the power of the lower classes; the clergy deprecated their growth as a manifestation of discontent, whereas contentment was the virtue then most regularly inculcated upon the lower classes; philanthropists, who had more faith in what should be done for than by the workingmen, distrusted their self-interested and vaguely directed efforts. Those who were interested in foreign trade feared they would increase prices, and thus render England incapable of competing with other nations. Those who were influenced by the teachings of political economy opposed them as being harmful, or at best futile efforts to interfere with the free action of those natural forces which, in the long run, must, as they thought, govern the laborer's wages. If the average rate of wages at any particular time was merely the quotient obtained by dividing the number of laborers into the wages fund, an organized effort to change the rate of wages would necessarily be a failure, or could at most only result in driving some other laborers out of employment or reducing their wages. Finally, there was a widespread feeling that trade unions were unscrupulous bodies whose officers over-awed or deceived the great majority of their fellow-workmen, and then by their help tyrannized over the employers and threw trade into recurring conditions of confusion. That same great body of uninstructed public opinion, which, on the whole, favored the factory laws, was quite clearly opposed to trade unions. With the incompetency of their own class, the power of the employing class, the strength of the law, and the force of public opinion opposed to their existence and actions, it is not a matter of wonder that the development of these working-class organizations was only very gradual. Nevertheless these obstacles were one by one removed.

89. Legalization of Trade Unions. — During the early years of the century combinations of workmen, more or less long-lived, actually existed in many trades, sometimes secretly because of their illegality, sometimes openly, until it became of sufficient interest to some one to prosecute them or their officers, sometimes making the misleading claim of being benefit societies. Yet the numerous prosecutions and punishments alluded to above embittered the working classes and led to frequent threats and much mutual suspicion of employer and employee. The combination acts were looked upon by many as an interference with the perfect freedom which ought theoretically to be allowed to each person to employ his labor like his capital in the manner he might deem most advantageous. Their inconsistency with the general movement of abolition of restrictions then in progress could hardly escape observation. The philosophic tendencies of the time therefore combined with the aspirations of the leaders of the working classes to rouse an agitation in favor of the repeal of the combination laws. A liberal tradesman of London, Francis Place, took up the unwisdom and injustice of the combination acts as a matter of special interest and spent a vast amount of labor and thought in creating an interest in their repeal. The matter was brought up in Parliament and two successive committees were appointed to investigate the questions involved. As a result, a thoroughgoing repeal law was passed in 1824. A bitter attack upon this repeal was, however, begun immediately; many strikes occurred, some of them accompanied with violence, the whole question was brought up anew, and after a long and stirring series of parliamentary hearings the law of 1824 was repealed and another and less liberal law substituted for it in 1825. This law, as finally adopted, repealed all the combination acts which stood upon the statute book, and relieved from punishment men who met for the sole purpose of agreeing on the rate of wages or the number of hours they would work, so long as this agreement referred to the wages or hours of those only who were present at the meeting. At the same time it declared the illegality of any violence, threats, intimidation, molestation, or obstruction used to induce any other workmen to strike or to join their association or to take any action in regard to hours or wages. Any attempt to bring pressure to bear upon an employer to make any change in his business was also forbidden, and most important of all the Common Law opposition was left unrepealed.

The effect of the legislation of 1825 was to enable trade unions to exist if their activity was restricted to an agreement upon their own wages or hours. " Collective bargaining," as it came to be called, was clearly acknowledged to be legal. Any effort, however, to establish wages and hours for other persons than those taking part in their meetings, or any strike on questions of piecework or number of apprentices or machinery or non-union workmen, was still illegal, both by this statute and by Common Law. Their legality was therefore still incomplete. A group of Lancashire miners in 1832 were punished under the Common Law for illegal combination, on the ground of interference, because they had written to their employers declaring their intention of striking, and in 1834 some workmen in a pottery were imprisoned on the charge of "intimidation," which consisted in their visiting their employers as representatives of the remainder of the workmen. The vague words, "molestation," "obstruction," and "intimidation," used in the law were capable of being construed, as they actually were, in such a way as to prevent any considerable activity on the part of trade unions. The best known case is of six farm laborers in Dorsetshire who were tried and given the harsh sentence of transportation to Australia for seven years because in their initiation of members into a union they had used secret oaths, which were forbidden by an old and half-forgotten law of the time of the French Revolution. In this case the authorities had gone too far; a great protest was raised in Parliament, pamphlets were published, and the first of the labor demonstrations in the streets of London which have later become so familiar took place, some 30,000 men being in line. The ministry were forced to bow to the storm and pardon the men.

A great stimulus was given by the law passed in 1825 to the formation of organizations among workingmen, and the period of their legal growth and development began from that date, notwithstanding the narrow field of activity allowed them by the law as it then stood. In 1859 a further change in the law was made, by which it became lawful to combine to demand a change of wages or hours, even if the action involved other persons than those taking part in the agreement, and to exercise peaceful persuasion upon others to join the strikers in their action.

Within the bounds of the limited legal powers granted by the laws of 1825 and 1859, large numbers of trade unions were formed, much agitation carried on, strikes won and lost, pressure exerted upon Parliament, and the most active and capable of the working classes gradually brought to take an interest in the movement. This growth was unfortunately accompanied by a considerable amount of disorder. During times of industrial struggle non-strikers were sometimes beaten, employers were assaulted, property was destroyed, and in certain industrial communities confusion and outrage occurred every few years. The complicity of the trade unions as such in these disorders was constantly asserted by their opponents and as constantly denied by their supporters; but there seems little doubt that while by far the greatest amount of disorder was due to individual strikers or their sympathizers, and would have occurred, perhaps in even more intense form, if there had been no trade unions, yet there were many cases where the organized unions were themselves responsible.

In 1867, as the result of a series of prolonged strikes and accompanying outrages in Sheffield, Nottingham, and Manchester, a committee appointed by the government and consisting of able and influential men made a full investigation and report on the conditions of the trade unions of the time, and recommended, somewhat to the public surprise, that further laws for the protection and at the same time for the regulation of trade unions be passed. As a result two laws were passed in the year 1871, the Trade Union Act and the Criminal Law Amendment Act. By the first of these it was declared that trade unions were no longer to be considered illegal either by Statute or Common Law simply because they were " in restraint of trade," and that they might be registered as benefit societies, and thereby become quasi-corporations, to the extent at least of having their funds protected by law and being able to hold property for the proper uses of their organization. This practically legalized the unions completely, or at least was considered at the time to have done so. At the same time the Liberal majority in Parliament, who had passed this far-reaching law only under pressure and were but half-hearted in their approval of trade unions, by the second law of the same year made more clear and vigorous the prohibition of " molesting," " obstructing," " threatening," " persistently following," " watching," or " besetting " any workman who had

not voluntarily joined the trade union. As these terms were still
undefined, the law might be, and it was, still sufficiently elastic
to allow magistrates or judges who disapproved of trade unionism to punish men for some of the ordinary forms of persuasion
or pressure used in industrial conflicts. The trade unionists
and their sympathizers were therefore still dissatisfied.
An agitation was immediately begun for the repeal or modification of this later law. This was accomplished finally by
the trade union acts of 1875 and 1876, by which it was declared that no action committed by a group of workmen was
punishable unless the same act was criminal if committed by
a single individual. " Picketing " or peaceful persuasion of
non-union workmen was expressly permitted, some of the elastic
words of disapproval used in previous laws were omitted altogether, offences especially likely to occur in such disputes
were relegated to the ordinary criminal law, and the whole
question of the illegality of conspiracy, as it was believed, was
cleared up in such a way as not to treat trade unions in any
different way from other bodies, or to interfere with their
existence or normal actions.

Thus, by the four steps taken in 1825, 1859, 1871, and 1875,
all trace of illegality was supposed to have been taken away from
trade unions and their ordinary actions. They were now
considered to have the same legal right to exist, to hold property,
and to carry out the objects of their organization that a banking
or manufacturing company or a social or literary club had.

90. Public Acceptance of Trade Unions. — The passing
away of the popular disapproval of trade unions was more
gradual and indefinite, but not less real. The employers,
after many hard-fought battles in their own trades, in the
newspapers, and in Parliament, came in a great number of
cases to prefer that there should be a well-organized trade
union in their industry rather than a chaotic body of restless
and unorganized laborers. The aristocratic dread of lower-
class organizations and activity became less strong and less

important as political violence ceased to threaten and as English society as a whole became more democratic. The Reform Bill of 1867 was a voluntary concession by the higher and middle classes to the lower, showing that political dread of the working classes and their trade unions had disappeared. The older type of clergymen of the established church, who had all the sympathies and prejudices of the aristocracy, were largely superseded by men who, like Kingsley and Maurice, took the deepest interest in working-class movements and who taught struggle and effort rather than acceptance and contentment.

The formation of trade unions, even while it led to higher wages, shorter hours, and a more independent and self-assertive body of laborers, made labor so much more efficient that, taken in connection with other elements of English economic activity, it led to no resulting loss of her industrial supremacy. As to the economic arguments against trade unions, they became less influential with the discrediting of much of the theoretical teaching on which they were based. In 1867 a book by W. T. Thornton, *On Labor, its Wrongful Claims and Rightful Dues*, successfully attacked the wages-fund theory; since which time the belief that the rate of wages was absolutely determined by the amount of that fund and the number of laborers has gradually been given up. The belief in the possibility of voluntary limitation of the effect of the so-called " natural laws " of the economic teachers of the early and middle parts of the century has grown stronger and spread more widely. Finally, the general popular feeling of suspicion and dislike of trade unions decreased as their lawfulness was acknowledged, and as their own policy became more distinctly orderly and moderate.

Probably the best proof of this general acceptance of trade unions was the spread of " conciliation," as it was called, for the settlement of questions of rates of wages and other trade questions. This meant the appointment of conciliation boards, consisting of equal numbers of representatives of the employers and the organized employees, through whose action matters of dispute were gradually brought to a solution. From about 1860 onward such boards were formed in one industry after another, beginning with the Nottingham hosiery trade. In 1867 a " Conciliation Act " was passed through Parliament for the encouragement of such boards, which would have had power to enforce their awards, but very little use was made of this act. On the other hand, by the close of the period of this chapter two or three hundred voluntary conciliation boards had been formed, all recognizing the existence of trade unions as the normal form of organization of the working classes and the method of collective bargaining as the best way of settling the relations of employers and employees. For many years they exerted a considerable influence until new questions had come up that made them less satisfactory.

91. Growth of Trade Unions. — The actual growth of trade unionism was irregular and interrupted, and has spread from many scattered centres. Hundreds of unions were formed, lived for a time, and went out of existence; some dwindled into insignificance and then revived in some special need; others have survived from the very beginning of the century to the present. The workmen in some parts of the country and in certain trades were early and strongly organized, in others they have scarcely even yet become interested or made the effort to form unions. There were unions among the hatters, compositors, shipwrights, and others in London and elsewhere even before the legalizing statute of 1825, and many of the "friendly societies " in the trades made agreements concerning wages and hours and thus served as trade unions during the same early period. Immediately after 1824, as already stated, a great many new unions were formed; but bad times ensued, there was much conflict and failure, and a period of decay of unions followed.

Beginning again, just before the period of the beginning of this chapter, about 1842, a more steady growth and extension

U

of unions began which continued almost without a break. Especially in the period from 1870 to 1878, the period of their full legalization and a time of great commercial progress, the unions grew rapidly. By that time the cotton spinners, miners, printers, glass makers, iron workers, bricklayers, carpenters, and scores of other crafts scattered through the English industrial districts were well organized into unions, with constitutions, officers, and executive boards, regular meetings, established practices and ideals. In many cases monthly or weekly trade journals were published as organs of the unions. Many strikes occurred, sometimes successful, sometimes failures, and unions were sometimes formed for the special object of carrying on a strike in trades not organized at other times. But far more important were the permanent unions which exerted a steady pressure in the interest of their own body through long periods of time; and, basing their action on a body of " trade-union principles," enforced scales of wages, rates for overtime, and other standards, without conflict or with very infrequent strikes. In some thirty-five general lines of industry the number of members of organized unions at the close of the period was something over 300,000. These were, generally speaking, the most intelligent, highly paid, regularly employed, and conservative workmen in these industries, and the industries represented were the most solid. In some occupations practically every operative was a member of a trade union.

The unions had also established an extensive system of union funds or money " benefits " of various kinds, created by payments from their members and payable to their members under certain conditions. The most important classes of benefits were sick pay, superannuation allowances, funeral benefits, out-of-work support, accident payments, strike pay, and help in the replacement of lost tools. At a period somewhat later than this it was calculated that fourteen of the leading unions in the engineering, building, and printing trades had paid out, up to that date, some $38,000,000 in benefits of this kind. Of this sum only about $2,000,000 had been paid out for strike purposes. These large funds held for various insurance purposes were one of the most marked characteristics of the older English trade unions as compared with those formed at a later date and with those in other countries.

92. Extension and Federation of Trade Unions. — From the earliest days of trade-union organization there have been efforts to extend the unions beyond the boundaries of the single occupation or the single locality. The earliest form of union was a body made up of the workmen of some one industry in some one locality, as the gold beaters of London, or the cutlers of Sheffield, or the cotton spinners of Manchester. Three forms of extension soon took place: first, the formation of national societies composed of men of the same trade through the whole country; secondly, the formation of " trades councils," — bodies representing all the different trades in any one locality; and, thirdly, the formation of a great national organization of workingmen or trade unionists.

The first of these forms of extension dates from the earliest years of the century, though such bodies had often only a transitory existence. The Manchester cotton spinners took the initiative in organizing a national body in that industry in 1829; in 1831 a National Potters' union is heard of, and others in the same decade. The largest and most permanent national bodies, however, such as the compositors, the flint-glass makers, miners, and others were formed after 1842, the miners in 1844 numbering 70,000 voting members. The increasing ease of travel and cheapness of postage and the improved education and intelligence of the workingmen made the formation of national societies more practicable, and before 1878 most of the important trade unions had become national bodies with local branches.

The second form of extension, the trades council, dates from a somewhat later period. Such a body arose usually when some matter of common interest happened in the labor world, and delegates from the various unions in each locality were called upon to organize, and to subscribe funds, prepare a petition to Parliament, or take other common action. In this temporary form they existed from an early date. The first permanent local board, made up of representatives of the various unions in the locality of Liverpool, was formed in 1848 to protect trade unionists from prosecutions for illegal conspiracy. In 1857 a permanent body was formed in Sheffield, and in the years immediately following in Glasgow, London, Bristol, and other cities. They have since come into existence in most of the larger industrial towns, but their influence has been variable and limited.

The formation of a general body of organized workingmen of all industries and from all parts of the country was an old plan. Such efforts were largely the product of the ideas and agitation of Robert Owen. Various such societies were early formed, only to play a more or less conspicuous rôle for a few years and then drop out of existence. In 1830 a " National Association for the Protection of Labor " was formed, in 1834 a " Grand National Consolidated Trades Union," in 1845 a " National Association of United Trades for the Protection of Labor," and in 1874 a " Federation of Organized Trade Societies," each of which had a short popularity and influence, and then died.

A more practicable if less ambitious plan of unification of interests was discovered in the form of an " Annual Trade Union Congress." This institution grew out of the trades councils. In 1864 the Glasgow trades council called a meeting of delegates from all trade unions to take action on the state of the law of employment, and in 1867 the Sheffield trades council called a similar meeting to agree upon measures of opposition to lockouts. The next year, 1868, the Manchester trades council issued a call for " a Congress of the Representatives of Trades Councils, Federations of Trades, and Trade Societies in general." Its plan was based on the annual meetings of the Social Science Association, and it was contemplated that it should meet each year in a different city and sit for five or six days. This first general Congress was attended by 34 delegates, who claimed to represent some 118,000 trade unionists. The next meeting, at Birmingham, in 1869, was attended by 48 delegates, representing 40 separate unions, with some 250,000 members. With the exception of the next year, 1870, the Congress has met annually since, the meetings taking place at Nottingham, Leeds, Sheffield, and other cities, with an attendance varying between one and two hundred delegates, representing, it was claimed, at the close of this period, about a million trade uinonists. It elects each year a Parliamentary Committee consisting of ten members and a secretary, whose duty it is to attend in London during the sittings of Parliament and exert what influence they can on legislation or appointments in the interests of the trade unionists whom they represent. In fact, most of the activity of the Congress was for a number of years represented by the Parliamentary Committee, the meetings themselves being devoted largely to commonplace discussions, points of conflict between the unions being intentionally ruled out. There were later some heated contests in the Congress on questions of general policy, but on the whole it and its Parliamentary Committee are a somewhat loose representation of the unity and solidarity of feeling of the great army of trade unionists.

A less definite but scarcely less important form of trade-union extension is the constant assistance given, usually in the shape of subscription of funds, by the richer trade unions to the poorer, by those in a prosperous position at the time to those engaged in a strike, or by the older unions to the new. From the very earliest days of trade unionism this has been a familiar practice and probably millions of dollars have thus been subscribed by workingmen for the help of others in the winning of strikes, the establishment of trade-union regulations, or the spread of trade-union principles.

The trade-union movement had resulted by 1878 in the

formation of a powerful group of federated organizations, with periodicals, funds, and a representative body, including far the most important and influential part of the working classes, whose existence and practice of " collective bargaining " were acknowledged by the law, more or less fully approved by public opinion, and exercising a considerable influence in national affairs.

93. Employers' Organizations. — Employers' associations were formed from time to time to take common action in resistance to trade unions or for common negotiations with them. As early as 1814 the master cutlers formed the " Sheffield Mercantile and Manufacturing Union," for the purpose of keeping down piece-work wages to their existing rate. It was one of the grievances of the workmen at the time that these employers' combinations were not prosecuted under the law of conspiracy, although theirs were. In 1851 the " Central Association of Employers of Operative Engineers " was formed to resist the strong union of the " Amalgamated Engineers." In 1858 the " Central Association of Master Builders " was formed to resist the efforts of the workmen in the building trades to reduce the working hours to nine. They have also had their national bodies, such as the " Iron Trade Employers' Association," active in 1878, and their general federations, such as the " National Federation of Associated Employers of Labor," which was formed in 1873 to meet the rapid growth of trade unions at the period, and included prominent ship-builders, textile manufacturers, engineers, iron manufacturers, and builders. The " lock-out " was adopted by these federations of employers to bring their employees to terms in a dispute or, in many cases, to anticipate a strike. By this plan every shop or factory of the employers in the organization was closed over a large area and the income of the men was cut off until they should yield in the dispute.

Many of these organizations, especially the national or district organizations of the employers in single trades, existed primarily for other and more general purposes, but incidentally the representatives of the masters in their associations regularly arranged wages and other labor conditions with the representatives of the workingmen's associations, or, when relations were less satisfactory, united in the efforts and expenses of a struggle with them. They, like the trade unions, have also exerted an influence on legislation in matters connected with the relations between employers and employees.

94. BIBLIOGRAPHY

Byrn, Edward W.: *Progress of Invention in the Nineteenth Century*, N. Y., 1900.

Jeans, J. S.: *Steel, its History, Manufacture, etc.*, 1880.

Potter, Beatrice (Mrs. Sidney Webb): *The Coöperative Movement in Great Britain*, 1892. A small book.

Holyoake, G. T.: *History of Coöperation in England*, 2 volumes, 1877. A long and loosely arranged but interesting book by a participant in this and many other social movements of the time.

Redfern, Percy: *The Story of the Coöperative Wholesale Society*, 1913.

Williams, Aneurin: *Co-partnership and Profit Sharing*, London, 1913.

Report on Profit Sharing and Labor Co-Partnership in the United Kingdom, published by the Labor Department of the British Board of Trade, 1912.

Webb, Sidney and Beatrice: *History of Trade Unionism*, London, new ed., 1911.

Hasbach, W. (Translated by Ruth Kenyon): *A History of the English Agricultural Labourer*, London, 1908.

Slater, Gilbert: *The English Peasantry and the Enclosure of the Common Fields*, London, 1907.

Hutchins, B. L., and Harrison, A.: *History of Factory Legislation*, Westminster, 1903.

Shaw-Lefevre, G.: *English Commons and Forests*.

Wallas, G.: *Life of Francis Place*.

CHAPTER XI

LIBERAL INFLUENCES ON INDUSTRIAL LIFE, 1878-1906

95. National Affairs from 1878 to 1906. — The reign of Queen Victoria continued to 1901. The fiftieth anniversary of the queen's accession was celebrated in 1887 as her " golden jubilee " and the sixtieth in 1897 as her " diamond jubilee." On both these occasions there were great expressions of appreciation and personal loyalty to the aged queen, and still more conspicuous recognition that the British Empire had become during her long reign a much more extensive and complex group of countries, of which England was only the centre. Both in the empire and in England itself many new questions had arisen. After the queen's death, in 1901, the Prince of Wales, already sixty years old, became king as Edward VII. Neither the queen during the latter years of her life nor the king exerted a very serious influence on the affairs of government. These were carried on, as during the previous period, by an alternation of ministries supported by corresponding majorities in Parliament. The old Liberal party was broken up by a split on the Irish question in 1886, and the Conservatives, strengthened by this, held office more than three-quarters of the time, and were continuously in power for the last ten years of the period.

One of the only large pieces of legislation accomplished by the Liberal party in the short period it held office was the third parliamentary reform bill, carrying further the principles of the two bills of 1832 and 1867. This bill was introduced by Mr. Gladstone in the spring of 1884. The principal class of persons not before having votes, which were given them by this bill, were the agricultural laborers, a very large, very poor, and very ignorant class. There was much opposition to enfranchising them, but Mr. Gladstone and the Liberal majority pressed the measure through the House of Commons. It was defeated in the House of Lords, but after a summer of extensive agitation by the masses of the people, of threats on the part of the leaders, and efforts to avoid conflict between the two houses of Parliament by the queen, a compromise was reached, and the measure passed both houses late in 1884. Something like two million votes were added to the electorate, so that almost every grown man in England now had a vote. Afterward, in 1885, a bill was passed making three important changes in the arrangement of representation: first, all towns below 15,000 inhabitants ceased to have representation separately from the counties in which they lay; second, all towns between 15,000 and 50,000 were given one representative each; and, third, all larger towns and counties were divided into single-member districts, each with as near 50,000 inhabitants as possible. Thus the old Chartist ideals of equal electoral districts and manhood suffrage were nearly attained; vote by ballot and abolition of property qualifications for membership had already been granted. At about the same time, in 1883, the " corrupt practices " act was passed regulating elections more strictly, and making them less expensive by restricting to a definite sum the amount that could be spent by any candidate for election expenses. England was fast approaching a democracy. Yet men were still allowed to give more than one vote when they had property in several places, women were not allowed to vote, members of Parliament were not paid, and there were many other exceptions to equality.

The principal occurrence in the relations between England and Ireland was the approach toward success of the home rule movement in 1886. Mr. Gladstone at last became converted to the desirability of giving Ireland home rule and carried a large part of the Liberal party with him. When, however, the bill providing for a separate Irish parliament for Irish affairs

DISTRIBUTION OF POPULATION
IN
ENGLAND and WALES
1891

SCALE OF ENGLISH MILES

20   40   60   80   100

EXPLANATION

Under 100
From 100 to 200
" 200 to 300
" 300 to 500
" 500 to 1000
Over 1000
Cities having population of more than
100,000 are indicated by
black dots

ENGRAVED BY BORMAY & CO., N.Y.

was introduced into Parliament several of the Liberal party broke with their leader and voted against the bill. It was therefore defeated and when new elections were held the home rule part of the Liberal party lost its majority. The Liberals who had opposed home rule took the name of Liberal-Unionists, acted with the Conservatives, and soon became united with them into one party, commonly known as the Unionist party. Mr. Gladstone with the old Liberals when he was defeated went out of office. When he became prime minister again in 1892 he introduced another home rule bill, of a somewhat different character from that of 1886, and this time succeeded in carrying it through the House of Commons, but it was defeated in the House of Lords and the feeling of the country was not enough in its favor to overcome that opposition. In 1898 acts giving greater power to local governments and greater encouragement to agriculture and industry in Ireland were passed by the Unionists, but notwithstanding the increased prosperity and local self-government these laws introduced they did not satisfy the Irish people.

In foreign affairs, England followed its usual practice of refraining from intervention unless its own commercial interests were involved. The victory of the Russians over the Turks in 1877–1878, however, seemed to threaten these, and the government in 1878 joined with some of the other countries to call an international congress which met at Berlin in July, 1878. British influence here was strong enough to secure such a rearrangement of the boundaries of the Balkan countries lying between Russia and Turkey as would, it was expected, restrain the government of the former from aggression and prevent Turkey from being too seriously weakened. England also agreed to protect the Asiatic territories of Turkey from further attack. In return British dominion was extended by the grant to her by Turkey of the island of Cyprus, with a promise that the Turkish government would introduce reform in the treatment of its Christian subjects. These results were considered at the time to be a great triumph for Great Britain, but most of the territorial arrangements were soon overthrown, the reforms were neglected, and the problem of the Near East left probably in worse condition than before.

Egypt from the middle of the nineteenth century had come into closer and closer connection with European countries, especially England and France, whose capitalists loaned her government vast sums of money. The purchase of the controlling interest in the Suez Canal by England in 1875 has already been mentioned. In 1876 the English and French governments, in order to protect the investments of their citizens, forced the Egyptian government to accept their control of its finances and through them of its general policy. This, along with other causes, led to an uprising of the native Egyptian party in 1881. The next year Great Britain sent a fleet to Alexandria which bombarded the city, landed an army, and defeated the Egyptian party. The British government, although it held troops in Egypt and controlled its administration through one of its own officials, Lord Cromer, announced that its occupation of the country was only temporary and that the control would eventually be withdrawn. No suitable time or circumstances were ever found, however, and long afterward Great Britain's temporary occupation was altered by proclamation into a permanent protectorate.

At the other end of Africa, the differences of interest and feeling between the Boers, who were descendants of the early Dutch settlers, and the English government brought on at the close of the nineteenth century the most serious war in which England had been engaged since the Crimean War. The British government claimed control not only over the inhabitants, British, Dutch, and native, in the group of colonies of which Cape Colony was the chief, but over the Dutch or Boer emigrants who had left those colonies and established themselves in the Orange Free State and the Transvaal Republic in the interior of the country. A long series of disputes, made more intense by the discovery in 1885 of gold mines and diamond diggings in their territory, brought about hostilities in 1899. Great Britain found it necessary to add more and more troops to her forces in South Africa at the beginning of the contest until she had an army there of 250,000 men. The last Boers did not lay down their arms until 1902. Great Britain annexed the two Boer colonies, adopted a liberal attitude toward them in 1906, gave them the same self-government that had been already conceded to the other South African colonies, and in 1910 organized them all as the Union of South Africa, a confederation of self-governing colonies, somewhat similar to the Dominion of Canada and the Commonwealth of Australia.

96. The Decline of Agriculture. — Although agriculture had diminished, ever since the industrial revolution, in relative importance to other forms of national industry, this did not mean that agriculture itself was necessarily less prosperous; it only meant that a larger part of the population of England gained their living from manufactures, commerce, mining, transportation, and other forms of industry. Indeed, as has been seen in earlier chapters, agriculture had by the introduction of improved machinery, fertilizers, and methods of cultivation, and by an increased amount of capital risen to high prosperity. From about 1874 onward, however, this condition of prosperity began conspicuously to decline and the three classes connected with agriculture, the land-owners, the tenant farmers, and the farm laborers, were all faced with serious problems and suffered a period of relative adversity.

The causes of this change are difficult to determine, various, and the subject of much difference of opinion. The facts themselves are not so doubtful. The price of grain and most other farm products began almost steadily to decline. Whereas wheat had for many years seldom sold at less than $1.50 a bushel, and frequently brought $2 a bushel or more, in the year 1875 its average price was $1.40 a bushel and from that time with but few advances it fell to $1 in 1885 to $.72 in 1895, and did not rise again to an average of $1 a bushel during the period of this

chapter, or indeed until the eve of the Great War. The price
of other farm products nearly corresponded to that of wheat.
There were other difficulties besides low prices. There were
many bad seasons, in successive years the bleak springs and
rainy summers to which England is subject made crops short and
cattle diseases frequent. Two periods, one from 1875 to 1884,
the other from 1891 to 1899, were really calamitous. The low
prices forced farmers to ask for low rents from the land-owners,
and discouraged them from putting capital into their farming
and from keeping the land hardest to cultivate in use.   Landlords either resisted the demand for lower rent or when they had
to grant it were forced to cut off much of their expenditure.
The farm laborers had their wages reduced, or entered into a
struggle with the farmers to keep their wages up, or went into
the cities to seek other kinds of work.   All interests and occupations connected with country life suffered.

A government commission, known as the Duke of Richmond's
Commission, sat from 1879 to 1882 to investigate the depression
in agriculture, and another commission made inquiries in 1893.
The reports of these commissions proved the distress but were
not very helpful in pointing out either causes or remedies.
In them it was shown that the rental value of farming lands had
in five years been reduced by some $25,000,000, and the yearly
income of landlords, farmers, and laborers together had been reduced by some $200,000,000. The amount of land being used
for grain-raising was reduced by about a third, from something
over eight million to five and a half million acres.   Cattle-raising
and dairying were somewhat more profitable and the land used
for pasture was during the same period increased, although
there were bitter complaints even from dairy farmers. The
total amount of food produced in England was being very much
reduced, land was going out of cultivation, and cost of production was little if at all diminished. As a result of the recommendations of the two investigating commissions a Department of
Agriculture was established in the government, a Minister of

Agriculture appointed, and a number of changes favorable to agriculture made in the laws. The principal cause of the trouble was in all probability foreign competition. The increased cheapness and ease of freight service both by land and sea brought American, Canadian, Russian, and other distant supplies of wheat directly to English markets. The same was true of meats brought in refrigerator vessels from New Zealand and Argentina. Improvements in production, some of them even of English origin, were adopted in the agriculture of distant countries. Grain raised and cattle grown on a large scale on new soils in a favorable climate, and transported by cheap freight, could be sold in England far cheaper than they could be produced in the difficult English climate and partially outworn soil under a system where large rents were paid to a landlord class, and where the actual laborers had so little interest in the soil and drew so little of their own sustenance from it. Even if the agriculture of the country were of a highly developed character, it was under a handicap as against foreign-grown products. Prices everywhere were also falling, probably in response to far-reaching currency changes which affected all countries alike.

Nevertheless the farming class of England adapted themselves more or less to the changed conditions. More varied agriculture was introduced, greater attention was given to fruit-raising, gardening, and poultry farming, and many forms of economy were adopted in the effort to make farming pay even under the difficulties of the time. The weight of rents was also gradually lifted to some degree from the two lower of the classes which drew their support from the land.

97. Small Holdings and Allotments. — The special interest in questions connected with the land extended also to questions of possible improvement in the position of the tenant farmers and farm laborers. In 1875, 1883, and 1900 three successive "Agricultural Holdings" acts were passed. One of the provisions of these laws was that when improvements were made by the tenant during the period in which he held the land compensation for them must be made by the landlord to the tenant when the latter gave up his holding. This is the same principle that was carried to much greater lengths in the Irish Land bills and the Scotch Crofter's acts.

By the Small Holdings Act of 1892 it was provided that tenants who wished to rent small farms and could not secure them otherwise might obtain them from the local authorities, who were empowered to buy land for that purpose and rent it out in small holdings of not more than fifteen acres to actual cultivators.

A still further and more important development in the same direction is the effort to introduce "peasant proprietorship," or the ownership of small amounts of farming land by persons who would otherwise necessarily be either tenants or mere laborers on other men's land. There has been an old dispute as to the relative advantages of a system of large farms rented by men who have considerable capital, knowledge, and enterprise, as in England; and of a system of small farms, owned and worked by men who are mere peasants, as in France. The older economists generally advocated the former system as better in itself, and also pointed out that a policy of withdrawal by government from any regulation was tending to make it universal. Others have been more impressed with the good effects of the ownership of land on the mental and moral character of the population, and with the desirability of the existence of a series of steps by which a thrifty and ambitious farm laborer could rise to a higher position. There has been for some time as a result of this belief an agitation in favor of the creation of smaller farms, of giving assistance in their purchase, and of thus introducing a more mixed system of rural land occupancy, and bringing back something of the earlier English yeoman farming.

This movement also obtained recognition by Parliament in the Small Holdings Act of 1892. This law made it the duty of each county council, when there seemed to be any sufficient demand for small farms, from one to fifty acres in size, to acquire in any way possible short of compulsory purchase, suitable land, to adapt it for farming purposes by fencing, making roads, and, if necessary, erecting suitable buildings; and then to dispose of it by sale, or, as a matter of exception, as before stated, on lease, to such men as should themselves cultivate it. The terms of sale were to be advantageous to the purchaser. He must pay at least as much as a fifth of the price down, but one-quarter of it might be left on perpetual ground rent, and the remainder, slightly more than one-half, might be repaid in half-yearly instalments during any period less than fifty years. The county council was also given power to loan money to tenants of small holdings to buy them from their landlords, where they could arrange terms of purchase but had not the necessary means.

Still another movement for getting more of the land into the hands of the people has been the establishment and wide spread of what are called "allotments." These are pieces of land, usually from one-eighth of an acre to an acre in size, rented out to poor or working class families, not with the idea that they can obtain a living from them, but that they can cultivate them at spare times so as to obtain a certain amount of food and enjoyment and decrease the expenses of living. Early in the century this was done as a part of the poor law legislation, but in 1885 an "Allotments and Small Holdings Association" was formed to encourage this as a general practice. Laws which were passed in 1882 and 1887 made it the duty of the authorities of parishes, when there seemed to be a demand for allotments, to provide all the land that was needed for the purpose, giving them, if needed, and under certain restrictions, the right of compulsory purchase of any particular piece of land which they should feel to be desirable. This was to be divided up and rented out in allotments from one-quarter of an acre to an acre in size. By laws passed in 1890 and 1894 this plan of making it

x

the bounden duty of the local government to provide sufficient allotments for the demand and giving them power to purchase land even without the consent of its owners was carried still further and put in the hands of the parish council. The growth in numbers of such allotments was very rapid and has not yet ceased. The approximate numbers at several periods were as follows:

1873	246,398
1888	357,795
1890	455,005
1895	579,133

In addition to those formed and granted out by the public local authorities many large land-owners, railroad companies, and others have made allotments to their tenants and employees. Large tracts of land subdivided into such small patches are now a common sight in England, simulating in appearance the old open fields of the Middle Ages and early modern times.

98. The Increasing Predominance of Finance. — In the fields of manufacturing, transportation, mining, and general trade there has been no such general depression as in the field of agriculture. The progress of invention, the continually widening sphere of the application of electricity, the development of quick and varied forms of communication, acting through long distances through the telegraph, telephone, and wireless, have gone far to transform all industrial life and have made possible enormous production and ready distribution. Yet the most influential changes of this period were, as has been said of the preceding period, in the direction of organization rather than invention, and in the sphere of finance rather than of more purely industrial life.

Several important changes in the financial sphere began or became conspicuous in this period: the transformation of individual concerns and partnerships into joint-stock companies, the concentration of separate companies into " trusts " or other combinations, the purchase of industrial undertakings by financial interests, and the continued and extended investments of British capital abroad. A few words may be said about each of these. The first process is one of long standing. Many undertakings such as the great commercial companies, railroads, banks, and others were joint-stock companies from the beginning, though often with a preponderance of the stock in the hands of some one man or family. But as time went on the necessity for more capital and new ability, the appearance of some new opportunity, or, in some cases, the desire to avoid bankruptcy, led even individuals and private partnerships to seek incorporation as stock companies, often retaining the old name and sometimes retaining a majority of the stock and thereby a control of the business. In this way stock companies became almost universal in many fields of industry, and much more usual in all. Such businesses are owned by the group of stockholders and usually managed by the board of directors, officers, and managers elected by them, though in recent times some enlightened companies have admitted representatives of the employees to membership on the boards of directors and others even to a share in the management. This, however, was for the most part after the close of the period covered by this chapter.

About 1890 a movement began and long continued to gain force for the combination of competing concerns in the same general line of trade in a non-competing body. Such combinations have taken many forms, but they are all alike directed to the increase of profit or the avoidance of loss resulting from intense competition. Some of them are associations of all or most of the companies in one general line to control conditions of sale, prices, and rates for shipping. An agreement was made among them all to charge the same price, to give the same length of credit, and to pay the same shipping rates. In the drug trade, for instance, in 1902, an association was formed among 2000 retail druggists to control the price of 370 articles. Other combinations are associations to restrict the output so as to avoid overstocking the market, such as the Tinplate

Manufacturers' Association, in Wales, and the Cloth Spinners', in Lancashire, which lasted for two years. Still others divided the sphere of possible sales among them, agreeing to leave a certain territory to each. A conspicuous example of still another form of combination, the sales association, was the J. and P. Coats, Limited. This old firm of thread manufacturers entered into successive combinations with wider and wider groups of companies in the same line, retaining the old name but becoming practically a union of all the thread manufacturers of England, selling their goods through their own office under the name of the Central Thread Agency.

Still other combinations have been of the manufacturers with the producers of the raw materials of their manufacture and of other industries connected with it, as the Coleman Mustard manufacturers, who also make tin because it is used in their work. In some cases practically every process from the obtaining of the raw material to the delivery of the finished product is under the same firm or company. This is often spoken of as a " vertical " as distinct from " horizontal " combination. Such substitution of monopoly for competition is forbidden by law in the United States, but in England it has progressed to great lengths, limited only by the extent to which it has been found practicable or profitable. Various amalgamations have united from two or three to fifty or more formerly independent businesses, and they have control all the way from fifty or sixty per cent to an entire monopoly of their respective trades or groups of trades.

While these changes have been in progress, there have been many instances of purchase outright of manufacturing and transportation concerns or amalgamations by banks or groups of capitalists who had money to invest but had no previous connection with the industry concerned. The procedure was a financial one only, the result simply of a search for profitable investment by possessors of capital. The former proprietors withdrew from the business, keeping a minority of the stock or investing the proceeds of the sale otherwise. In such cases the managers, the employees, and the public became dependent, in a certain sense, on banking or other capital-owning bodies, and these owners of the capital had practically no connection with the business except the receipt of dividends or interest on their invested or loaned capital. A large part of the spinning industry in Lancashire, the first fruits of the industrial revolution, has gone through these successive changes, many of the largest groups of mills having been lately sold to financial syndicates formed for the purpose of purchasing them, but having no connection with the industry except its ownership. The same thing is true in many other lines of industry.

The formation of joint-stock companies, the union of these into great combinations, and the sale of the stock of these organizations to purely financial interests, have given a predominance in industrial life to the element of pure capital, apart from personality and public service, which it has not had at any earlier period. It is the most complete development yet reached of " capitalism," the form of industry in which all production and economic policy are directed toward the largest and most certain reward for the use of the capital invested in it.

Another form of capitalism dates from a somewhat earlier period. So much wealth was amassed in England that it was often difficult to find in England itself investments for it that offered good returns. About the middle of the nineteenth century, therefore, the process began of the investment of English money in the British colonies and foreign countries. Some of these investments were in the form of loans to colonial and foreign governments; English investors loaned money on government bonds in Egypt, Turkey, Mexico, European and South American states, and many other countries and municipalities. Investments were also made in the stocks and bonds of English companies which obtained concessions to build railroads, establish banks, open up mines, develop oil wells, and exploit the other natural resources of foreign countries, especially of the more backward countries of Asia, Africa, Central and South America. Still other British capital was invested in trade between Great Britain and these distant countries, carried on in close connection with the companies engaged in their internal development. Much of this capital, like that used in the later developments in England itself, was provided by banks or syndicates of large investors. So a great network of investments outside of England was created which has had a deep influence on British political and economic policy both in respect to internal and to external affairs. Great Britain became a great creditor nation to which much of the rest of the world paid tribute.

The profits on these loans were found not only in the actual use of British capital in distant regions, but in the profits obtained through speculation in those investments, in floating new companies, in manipulating the securities of old companies, and in provision of loans for the wars and other expeditions carried out in the interest of those investments. This phase of capitalism led on to what has often been called " economic imperialism," that is to say, the acquisition of control of regions outside of Great Britain and her self-governing colonies, largely for the sake of providing profitable investments for the wealth of British capitalists or financial concerns. By a careful estimate the amount of British capital invested abroad in government loans, in railways, banks, and mines, at the beginning of the period covered by this chapter, 1878, was some $3\frac{3}{4}$ billion dollars. Twenty years later, in the middle of the period, it was more than 10 billion dollars. At its close, it was probably 15 billions, though no exact statistics are available for that date. The annual income to English investors from these foreign sources was estimated about the close of the nineteenth century at $500,000,000 a year.

This income, like all incomes from investments, was distributed among a comparatively few persons of very large wealth, and a very large number, — there is no practicable means of finding how large a number, — of persons whose inherited means or whose savings were invested in that way.

99. Entrance of Government into the Economic Field. — Established custom in England and the individualist teachings of the first three-quarters of the nineteenth century were alike opposed to the government taking part in economic affairs. A certain amount of regulation had of course been imposed upon manufacturing, transportation, and landholding in the interest either of the public or of employees, and the government had given some encouragement to various forms of enterprises, such as the establishment of steamship lines, but these were not actual government operations. The government had taken up certain activities in the support of health and education, but these were not industrial in their character. Yet there were certain lines of economic usefulness that seemed so natural that they were entered upon by the government without any intention of deliberately following a new policy.

The post-office is such an old and well-established branch of the government's activity as not in itself to be included among newly adopted functions; but from a period somewhat earlier than the beginning of this chapter other duties have been placed upon it which amount to the government entering through the post-office into a much more widely extended industrial field. In 1861, the post-office savings-bank was established and it has grown and extended itself widely since. Any sum from one shilling upward is now accepted from any depositor until his desposits rise to £50 in any one year or a total of £200 in all. It presents great attractions from its security and its convenience. The government through the post-office pays two and one-half per cent interest on deposits. In 1870 approximately £14,000,000 was deposited in the post-office savings-banks, in 1880 £31,000,000, and ten years later £62,000,000. In 1880 arrangements were made by which government bonds and annuities could be bought through the post-office. In 1890 some £4,600,000 was invested in government stock in this way.

The parcels post was established in 1883. This branch of the post-office does a large part of the work that would otherwise be done by private express companies. It takes charge of packages up to eleven pounds in weight and under certain circumstances up to twenty-one pounds, presented at any branch post-office, and on prepayment of regular charges delivers them to their consignees.

In the meantime another form of communication had begun to compete with the transmission of letters. This was the telegraph. The telegraph system of England was built up in the main and in its early stages by private persons and companies. After more than twenty-five years of competitive development, however, there was widespread public dissatisfaction with the service. Messages were expensive and telegraphing inconvenient. Many towns with populations from three thousand to six thousand were without telegraphic facilities nearer than five or ten miles, while the offices of competing companies were numerous in busy centres. In 1870, therefore, all private telegraph companies were bought up by the government at an expense of something over ten million pounds. A strict telegraphic monopoly in the hands of the government was established, and the telegraph was made an integral part of the post-office system.

In 1878 the telephone began to compete with the telegraph, and its relation to the government telegraphic monopoly became a matter of question. At first the government adopted the policy of collecting a ten per cent royalty on all telephone messages, but allowed telephone systems to be established by private companies. In the meantime the various companies were being bought up successively by the National Telephone Company, which was thus securing a virtual monopoly. In 1892 Parliament authorized the Postmaster General to spend £1,000,000, subsequently raised to £1,300,000, in the purchase of telephone lines, and prohibited any private construction of new lines. As a result, by 1897, the government had bought up all the main or trunk telephone lines and wires, leaving to the National Telephone Company its monopoly of all telephone communication inside of the towns. This monopoly was supposed to be in its legal possession until 1904, when it was anticipated that the government would buy out its property at a valuation. In 1898, however, there was an inquiry into the validity of the company's claims by Parliament. The monopoly of the National Company was discredited, a new act was passed in 1899, and the government began to enter into competition with it within the towns and to authorize local governments and private companies under certain circumstances to do the same. It was provided that every extension of an old company and every new company must obtain a government license and that on the expiring of this license, as in the case of the railroads, the plant could be bought by the government. In the meantime the post-office authorities had power to restrict rates. An appropriation of £2,000,000 was later put in the hands of the Postmaster General to extend the government telephone system. It seems quite certain that by 1925, at latest, all telephones will be in the hands of the government.

Many activities of the community as a whole are in England carried out not by the national government but by city, borough, and county governments under authority given them by Parliament. The general theory in England is that local governments cannot do anything that they are not specially authorized to do by the central government. In 1870 an act was passed giving local authorities the right to purchase and run, or themselves establish " tramway " or street-car lines. This power was made use of and a number of the towns gradually took over and ran their own street-car systems.

In 1880 local authorities were permitted to float bonds for the purpose of carrying on these and certain other municipal enterprises, and much capital was borrowed and utilized in that way. In 1896 a " Light Railways " act was passed for the encouragement of publicly owned passenger and light freight lines over longer distances than simply within the towns.

In 1884 an important government investigation of the problem of the crowded dwelling sections in the towns was carried out and, as a result of their report, in 1890 the " Housing of the Working Classes Act " was passed. According to its provisions, when it is brought to the attention of the local authorities that any district or street or alley is in such a condition that the houses in it are unfit for human habitation, or that the narrowness, want of light or air, or bad drainage makes the district dangerous to the health of the inhabitants or their neighbors, and that these conditions cannot be readily remedied except by an entire rearrangement of the district, then it becomes the duty of the local authorities to take the matter in hand. They are bound to draw up and, on approval by the proper superior authorities, to carry out a plan for widening the streets and approaches to them, providing proper sanitary arrangements, tearing down the old houses, and building new ones in sufficient number and suitable character to provide dwelling accommodation for as many persons of the working class as were displaced by the changes. Private rights or claims are not allowed to stand in the way of any such public action in favor of the general health and well-being, as the local authorities are clothed by the law with the right of purchase of the land and buildings of the locality at a valuation, even against the wishes of the owners, though they must obtain parliamentary confirmation of such a compulsory purchase. Several acts have been passed to provide for the public acquisition or building of workingmen's dwellings. In 1899 the " Small Dwellings Acquisition Act " gave power to any local authority to loan four-fifths of the cost of purchase of a small house, to be repaid by the borrower by instalments within thirty years.

There were many other forms of what is called in England " Municipal Trading " or " Municipal Ownership," such as gas and water works, steamboats, markets, bath-houses, wash-houses, slaughter-houses, and restaurants. These are real instances of government ownership and industry, although carried out by local not by the central government.

100. Employers' Liability and Workmen's Compensation. — With the increasing use of machinery and of steam power for manufacturing and transportation, and in the absence of precaution and regulations, accidents to workmen became much more numerous. Satisfactory statistics do not exist for early periods, but it was well known that in every large industry scores of deaths and hundreds of less serious accidents were constantly occurring. Each of these brought not only its physical suffering but loss of power of the workman for a longer or shorter time to support himself and his family; and at the same time reduced the productiveness of industry. In the four years from 1872 to 1876, for instance, there were 261 explosions of factory boilers, by which 308 persons were killed and 535 injured. As machinery was speeded up, the frequency of accidents became constantly greater. The life of a workman in a factory, shop, or mine, or on a railroad, was comparable in danger to that of a soldier or sailor. In 1899 serious or petty accidents to the number of 70,760 were reported from industrial establishments.

By Common Law, as defined in a decision given in 1837, damages for accident could be sued for in the case of negligence, and obtained by a workman, just as by any other person, except in two cases. If the accident was the result of his own contributory negligence or the negligence of a fellow-employee, no compensation for injuries would be allowed by the courts. The theory in the first case was that in the implied contract between employer and employee, the employee agreed to accept the ordinary risks of the business. If he made these risks greater by his own carelessness, he must suffer for it. In the second case it was construed that he accepted the risks of the business including those that arose from the carelessness of his fellow-employees. In the large establishments of modern times, however, vast numbers of men were fellow-employees in the eyes of the law, and the doctrine of " common employment," as it was called, prevented the recovery of damages in so many cases as to attract widespread attention. For instance, in the case of a railroad accident due to the carelessness of a flagman, the passengers could obtain damages but the engineer and brakeman could not, for the flagman was their fellow-employee. From 1865 forward this provision of the law was frequently complained of by factory inspectors, leaders of the workingmen, and others, but as constantly upheld by the courts.

In 1876 a committee of the House of Commons on the relations of master and servant took evidence on this matter and recommended in its report that the common law be amended in this respect. Accordingly in 1880 the " Employers' Liability Act " was passed which abolished the doctrine of " common employment " as to much of its application, made the employer liable for all accidents due to defective machinery or negligence, and made it possible for the employee, on bringing suit, to obtain compensation for accidental injury in the great majority of cases. This arrangement was, however, cumbrous, expensive, and unsatisfactory, involving a special lawsuit in each case.

In 1893 a bill was introduced in Parliament by the ministry of the time to make the employer responsible for damages in all cases, except that of contributory negligence on the part of the workmen, but it was not passed. In 1897, however, the " Workmen's Compensation Act " was passed, changing the basis of the law entirely. By this act it was provided in a large number of employments that, in case of accident to a workman causing death or incapacitating him for a period of more than two weeks, compensation in proportion to the wages he formerly earned should be paid by the employer, as a matter of course, unless " serious and wilful misconduct " on the part of the workman could be shown to have existed. The liability of employers became, therefore, a matter of insurance of workmen against accidents arising out of their employment, imposed by the law upon employers. It was no longer damages for negligence but a form of compulsory insurance. In other words, after 1897, a legal, if only an implied part of the contract between employer and employee in all forms of modern industry in which accidents are likely to occur was that the employer should insure the employee against the dangers of his work. A new form of insurance grew up about this requirement and became almost universal. The cost of the insurance was necessarily added to the general cost of production.

101. Developments in Trade Unionism. — By the close of the last period trade unions had gained full legal and economic recognition, though they did not of course exist in all industries or include by any means the whole body of the working classes. These older unions had a well-marked character. They existed usually only in the skilled trades; unskilled workmen, general laborers, and women were not organized. They admitted only members who had gone through a full apprenticeship, and they were therefore somewhat exclusive. They had usually considerable funds for insurance purposes, requiring comparatively large payments of dues, often a shilling a week. Their financial interests were often of as great interest to them as their immediate trade interests or even greater. These characteristics, as well as the fact that some of them had been long in existence, and the older and more staid men had come into positions of almost complete ascendancy, brought it about that the old trade unions were conservative and almost aristocratic in their character and policy. They were opposed to any combined political action, believing that they could best reach their ends by trade negotiations merely, or where legislation was necessary obtaining it through one or other of the great political parties. Again they were in almost all cases " craft unions," that is to say, each craft or branch of trade had its own union. The workmen in any one establishment were therefore apt to be members of several different trade unions. The locomotive engineers, the firemen, the conductors, the switchmen, and other employees of the railroads had each their separate organization. The bricklayers, carpenters, stone masons, iron workers, and other crafts concerned with building had each its union. These unions extended through the whole country, but in any one building operation each of them was apt to be represented. The body of workmen as a whole in one industrial concern, whether it was a house, a railroad, a mine, or a factory, were not organized or recognized as a single body. The organization of workmen by whole industries, instead of by separate crafts in those industries, is known as " industrial unionism " as distinct from " craft unionism."

Most of the concessions to workingmen so far mentioned were obtained by the influence of the trade unions as they then existed; largely through the parliamentary committee of the annual trades-union congress. The Employers' Liability and Workmen's Compensation acts described in the last paragraph were adopted largely in response to the trade-union demands expressed in their annual congresses from 1872 onward. Workingmen were appointed not infrequently to positions as factory inspectors, and trade-union leaders were from time to time added to the list of local magistrates in industrial neighborhoods. From 1884 onward, first the national government, then city and county governments, were induced to pay all their industrial employees and require from all their contractors the payment of " fair wages," which were interpreted to mean trade-union rates. Certain labor leaders were elected to Parliament on the Liberal ticket and appointed to various parliamentary or royal commissions. But it was not the successes of the old form of unionism but the changes in it that were most conspicuous and important in this period.

The masses of untrained common laborers, especially in London, their poverty and their frequent unemployment, were coming to attract more and more attention. They had no part nor lot in the trade-union movement as it existed. Along with them were a vast number of skilled but irregularly employed workmen, largely included in the trade unions but apparently unable to rise above the merest necessities of comfort and decency, and in times of bad trade apt to fall into the same pit of unemployment and poverty as the unskilled laborers. A series of parliamentary and other investigations and reports made from 1880 onward threw light on the sad conditions of a great part of the laboring population of England even after the great advances and reforms since 1848.

In 1886 and 1887 a series of processions followed by meetings of "the unemployed" took place in London, especially at Trafalgar Square, the traditional place for speeches terminating political processions. On several of these occasions there was rioting. The police authorities finally prohibited these meetings, new demonstrations against what were considered attacks on the freedom of speech took place, new riots followed, and a number of speakers, including some members of Parliament, were prosecuted and imprisoned. These events and the activity of the socialist discussions then in progress, which will be described in the next paragraph, aroused the interest of the community and seem to have given courage to an entirely new group of workmen and women to form unions and insist on better conditions of life. In July, 1888, the women who dipped matches, a quite unskilled and very much underpaid trade, ventured to strike, public subscriptions for their assistance were made, and they won their strike. The next summer the stokers and general workmen in the London gas works formed a union and struck for a reduction of their hours from twelve to eight and, rather unexpectedly, gained their terms.

About the docks in the east end of London several thousand poor, irregularly employed and unorganized laborers gathered daily to pick up casual labor in loading and unloading vessels at whatever time these arrived or were ready to depart. Efforts had been made for some time by leaders among themselves to form them into one or more unions. Rather suddenly in August, 1889, a strike broke out, the men flocked to membership in the unions, some ten thousand men left their work, skilful leadership was developed, and the general public contributed funds and protested against bringing in strike breakers. Money was subscribed not only from the older trade unions from all parts of England but from America and Australia. More than £50,000 was put at the service of the managers of the strike and in this case the newspapers were generally sympathetic. Finally the men won most of their demands, and a group of permanent trade unions among the laborers was formed not only at the docks but on the railroads, among sailors and firemen, and in other occupations and in other parts of the country. These new unions usually required small payments, collected no benefit funds, and admitted practically everybody who wanted to enter. They also brought to the surface a new group of leaders of much ability and influence, especially John Burns, Tom Mann, and Ben Tillet. An entirely new element was thus introduced into the trade-union body. This sudden addition and awakening of interest also reacted on the older unions and led to a rapid increase in their numbers, so that by the close of the period covered by this chapter there were all together some 1200 recognized unions in Great Britain with more than 2,000,000 members. The accumulated funds in the possession of these unions amounted to about $28,000,000 and their expenditure to about $10,000,000 a year, most of it collected by regular dues. There were by this time in various localities 265 trade councils with about a million members. These were of course already members of national or local unions and should not be counted twice.

An " amalgamation " or " confederation " usually means in England a combination of a number of local unions of the same craft into a national union; but from 1880 onward there were a number of instances of combinations of several different but allied crafts into one association, thus bringing about a substitution of industrial for craft unions. Instances of this are the Association of Locomotive Engineers and Firemen, formed in 1880; an association of spinners, weavers, and carding room workers, formed in 1886; the union of all the railwaymen except engineers and firemen; and many of the unskilled laborers' unions formed in 1889 and subsequently.

As a result of the changes of this period, of the teachings of socialism, and the rise of a new type of leaders of more radical opinions than the old, there grew up a general division on points of policy among trade unionists into two loosely distinguished groups commonly spoken of as the "right" and the "left" wing. Some unions belonged practically entirely to one side or the other, in other unions there was a division, with a tendency only in one direction or the other. These differences appeared in the annual trade-union congresses which continued to be held during this whole period, the main course of trade-union activity being conservative or progressive according to the victory of the "right" or the "left" in these meetings. The most characteristic developments of the period remained, however, first, the formation of the new more popular and radical unskilled workmen's unions, secondly, a great increase in the numbers and accumulated wealth of the unions, thirdly, the beginning of industrial unionism, and, lastly, a threatened breach in the general trade-union body between the more conservative and the more progressive or radical elements.

102. Entrance of Trade Unions into Politics. — The trade unions were slow to go into politics. Their leaders believed that they could best reach their ends by negotiating directly with their employers in the matters that interested them, and until after the passage of the parliamentary reform bills of 1867 and 1884, they could take no part as voters in the larger political affairs of the country. After they had the franchise, they voted for the most part for the candidates of the Conservative or Liberal parties who announced views favorable to

Y

labor interests. The Trade-Union Congress of 1869 created a "Labor Representation Committee" to encourage representation of labor in Parliament and occasionally independent candidates, mostly trade-union officers, offered themselves as candidates and appealed for workingmen's votes. In a few cases trade unions voted money to help pay the expenses of campaigns. In 1874 two miners' officials in northern constituencies, Alexander Macdonald and Thomas Burt, were elected and became the first "labor members" of Parliament. At the election of 1880 three labor men were elected.

The period following 1885, as already indicated, was one of great agitation and excitement among the trade unions and as a result in 1892 sixteen labor men were elected. But there was still no separate labor party, the members acting independently, or more usually with the Liberal party. They were often spoken of as the "Liberal-Labor Members."

In 1893, however, at a conference held in the manufacturing town of Bradford, a separate political party was organized, known as the Independent Labor party, hoping to draw effective support from workingmen on the basis of a group of the socialistic principles which will be described in the next section. But although it elected several hundred members of town, county, and other local bodies, in parliamentary elections it had little success. It was not until 1900 that it elected its first representative in Parliament. In 1906 seven of its candidates were elected.

In the meantime, however, in the Trade-Union Congress of 1899, the general body of unionists abandoned their traditional policy of keeping out of politics. By a vote representing about 500,000 members against 400,000 they instructed the Labor Representation Committee to devise and carry out some plan for securing direct representation of organized labor in Parliament and in local governing bodies. This body proceeded to establish a new party, independent of either the Conservative or Liberal parties and of the Independent Labor and other socialist parties.   It asked, however, for the support of all trade unions, coöperative, socialist, and other working class organizations, and offered to work with the Liberals for general reforming ends.   It held its organization meeting in London early in 1900.   The new party could not, of course, demand the votes of all the members of the unions which supported it, but from among the 41 unions with about 300,000 members which declared their adherence to it in 1900, the 158 unions with 900,000 members which declared for it in 1903, — and two socialist bodies with some 20,000 members, — it recruited a considerable body of voters.   In 1906, at the first parliamentary election held after its formation, it adopted the official title of the Labor party and elected twenty-nine of its candidates. There were, besides these, twenty-five representatives of the Independent Labor party, Liberal-Labor and private members, so that all together there were by the close of this period fifty-four " labor " members in Parliament.

A marked characteristic of the Labor and socialistic parties has been the close control which they have exercised over the parliamentary action of those who have been elected as their representatives.   Instead of the merely general expectation of the older Liberal and Unionist parties that members will vote in accordance with the principles and program of their parties, representatives of these newer parties agree to be guided in their actions by the requirements of their party as shown by the votes of its annual conferences or interpreted by the executive committee of the party elected at these conferences.

103. Socialism. — The first group of men in England who called themselves socialists and to whom the name was applied by others were, as has been stated in Chapter IX, the followers of Robert Owen, who from about 1830 used that name to indicate their opposition to the purely competitive and individualist ideal of business and society then generally accepted, and their belief that some sort of social reorganization was desirable and practicable.[1] About 1850 Charles Kingsley, Frederick D. Maurice, and some others established the newspaper called the *Christian Socialist*, in which they advocated social reforms, such as coöperation. Socialism in the first half of the century meant social reform. It was based on the belief that there was much injustice and misery in English society that ought not to be " let alone," but should and could be gotten rid of by the adoption of some such devices as coöperation or the establishment of self-governing and self-supporting communities, from which competition should be excluded and in which private property would play but a small part. Much criticism of the prevailing individualist or " let alone " policy of the time appears in the writings of Shelley, Carlyle, Ruskin, Hood, Dickens, and other poets, essayists, and novelists.

From 1848 onward " socialism " was given a new meaning by the writings of certain German and French economists and historians who developed what is often called " scientific socialism." This can be understood at least in part from one of its earliest productions, the *Communist Manifesto*. This was written in 1847 by Karl Marx and Friedrich Engels, members of a group of Germans living in England in exile on account of their part in the political agitations in favor of greater liberty in their own country. It was published in 1848 in London, in German, and was later translated into English, French, and many other languages. It introduced into common discussion the idea that all society is in modern times divided into two classes, employers and workingmen, capital and labor, bourgeoisie and proletariat; and that there is necessarily a struggle between these two classes. According to the *Manifesto* the laborers are the real producers, and the owners of land and capital are, under present circumstances, " exploiting " them, that is to say, withholding from them part of the product of their labor. The interests of workingmen in all countries are the same and in all countries they are opposed to those of their

[1] See pp. 247–8.

employers. They should therefore be united in a close international bond. These socialists or communists, — the names were at that time used interchangeably, though the " communism " of that time is more nearly what is meant by socialism in modern times, while " communism " has taken on a new meaning — looked forward to a revolution by which the workingman would get control of the government and use it to introduce different laws of property and a different and, as they believed, a more equal, more prosperous, and happy form of society. Whether this revolution should be a violent one or merely a matter of voting was not clearly expressed. Since the authors believed that the old form of competitive society would break down of itself, the question of whether any violence would be needed would have to be left to the future to decide.

The *Manifesto* and similar writings expressing these views which were published on the Continent during the following years were known more or less in England, but for a long time had very little effect on men's thinking. When the " International Workingmen's Association " was established in 1864, when Marx' great work " Capital " began its publication in 1867, and while socialism was gaining the adherence of hundreds of thousands in Germany, France, Italy, and elsewhere on the Continent, in England but little was heard of it. This was due no doubt partly to the habits of thought and action of the English people, who are not attracted by general theories, and prefer changes to come gradually; partly to the predominant interest of the most intelligent English workingmen in cooperation, trade unions, factory laws, education, and other reform movements; partly to their free institutions, by which, as most men believed, changes could be obtained through act of Parliament whenever the pressure became strong enough, without the necessity for either a violent revolution or even a complete transformation such as the socialists anticipated.

It was not until after 1880 that socialist organizations were formed in Great Britain. The later seventies and early eighties were a period of severe commercial, industrial, and agricultural depression which caused great loss and suffering and aroused much discussion and criticism of accepted practices. Unrestricted competition began to lose its hold on general thought. The final reaction against *laissez-faire* showed itself in many ways, some of which have been already described. Changes in the conduct of trade itself occurred; such laws as the workmen's compensation act were passed; factory legislation was carried further, and the trade unions organized themselves more strongly. There was also much effort on the part of many conscientious and thoughtful persons to correct some of the evils of competitive society by personal effort. The Salvation Army was founded by William Booth in 1878 and during this period established its shelters and workshops. Toynbee Hall, the first and best known of the social settlement houses, was established in 1885. It was named after Arnold Toynbee, a gifted young Oxford man much interested in social problems. Several other such settlements followed. Henry George's book, *Progress and Poverty*, an attack on the system of private landholding, first printed in San Francisco in 1879, was republished in England soon afterwards and sold in hundreds of thousands of copies. George himself, as well as Thomas Davidson, another American reformer, lectured there with much success and popular interest in 1883 and 1884.

In the midst of these many forms of agitation for special reforms, it is not strange that some men organized for an entire reorganization of society. In 1877 the successors of the old Christian Socialists reorganized themselves as the Guild of St. Matthew, a religious association with a socialistic program. In 1884 the Social Democratic Federation was formed. Its most prominent organizer was H. M. Hyndman, but among its members were the artist William Morris and a number of other well-to-do and educated men and women. It was based on the teachings of Karl Marx and the other scientific socialists and early adopted a program of ultimate possession of land and capital by the government and immediate introduction of free education for everybody, a minimum wage and similar proposals. They established a weekly newspaper *Justice*, and a monthly *The Social Democrat*. They made some efforts, though unsuccessful, to elect representatives to Parliament and kept up an organization and propaganda. They still exist under the name of the Social Democratic party.

In 1884 the Fabian Society was organized, having as its aim " the reorganization of society by the emancipation of land and industrial capital from individual and class ownership, and the vesting of them in the community for the common benefit." The members of this society were mainly journalists, artists, literary men and women, teachers, and social workers. They differed from the Social Democratic Federation by seeking their end not by an immediate and direct effort to bring about changes, by legislation or otherwise, but by the permeation of all the thinking and writing of the time with socialistic teaching. Their name was taken from the Roman general Quintus Fabius Cunctator, because like him they expected to obtain conquest by delay until their opponents had become weakened and those who agreed with them had become vastly more numerous and stronger. From 1885 forward they issued a series of "Fabian Tracts " applying socialistic principles to various problems of the day ; in 1889 a volume of " Fabian Essays " was published. It is said that three-quarters of a million copies of these small publications were circulated within less than ten years. They formed also almost a hundred branches for discussion and agitation. In speeches and articles delivered and written by thousands yearly and in the course of the conversation of their members they did much to weaken belief in the sufficiency of competition and to spread socialistic thought.

All of these societies were under the leadership of men of the middle or upper, well-educated and comparatively comfortable classes, and drew their membership principally from the same classes. In 1893 a distinctly socialist organization was formed among the workingmen. This was the Independent Labor party, already referred to, organized under the influence of an active working class leader, Keir Hardy. He was devoted to socialist principles and had frequently been a delegate to the annual Trade-Union Congress and tried without success to induce that body to adopt a complete socialist program. At the meeting of the Trade-Union Congress at Glasgow in 1892, although no official action was taken, a group of socialist members got together and agreed to call a meeting to form a socialist party. At this meeting, held at Bradford, a considerable number of delegates agreed to form this new body, without at the same time separating themselves from their trade unions, with the object of extending their doctrines among workingmen and of electing members to Parliament pledged to their thorough-going reforms. The Independent Labor party became a vigorous and aggressive body especially strong in leadership among the working classes. In 1906 the " Church Socialist League " was organized.

Yet, notwithstanding the formation and activity of these organizations, socialism as an organized movement did not flourish. This was due principally to a continuance of the causes that have been previously stated. Most Englishmen believed that the ends which the socialist had at heart could be reached in other ways than by such a sudden and complete change. Therefore, although there were many socialists, there was but little formal and deliberately planned socialism. In the trade unions there were many members who called themselves and really were socialists, and much of the policy advocated at the Trade Union Congresses after about 1890 was essentially socialistic. In that year a resolution was passed declaring for regulation of the hours of labor in all trades by Parliament, and a number of measures were adopted favoring interference by the government in what would formerly have been considered matters of private agreement.

Moreover, many of the laws being passed by Parliament were more than half socialistic and the extended functions of the national government and many local governments were of the same character. At the close of the period of this chapter, therefore, the year 1906, the organizations which called themselves socialistic were not growing appreciably, but socialism itself, broadly considered, was growing rapidly in men's minds, in the policy of many organizations, in legislation, and in daily practice.

104. BIBLIOGRAPHY

Haggard, H. Rider: *Rural England*, 1906.

Heath, F. G.: *British Rural Life and Labour*, London, 1911.

Jebb, L.: *The Small Holdings of England, a Survey of Various Existing Conditions.*

Ashley, W. J.: (Editor) *British Industries*, 2d ed., London, 1907.

Hobson, J. A.: *The Evolution of Modern Capitalism*, London, 1894.

Macrosty, H. W.: *The Trust Movement in British Industry*, London, 1907.

Macgregor, D. H.: *Industrial Combination*, London, 1906.

Hyndman, H. M.: *Commercial Crises of the Nineteenth Century*, London, 1892.

Bowley, H. L.: *Wages in the United Kingdom in the Nineteenth Century*, 1900.

Aronson, V. R.: *The Workmen's Compensation Act of 1906.*

Birrell, Augustine: *Law of Employers' Liability.*

Orth, Samuel P.: *Socialism and Democracy in Europe*, New York, 1913.

Smith, H. W., and Nash, Vaughan: *The Story of the Dockers' Strike*, London, 1889.

Noel, Conrad: *The Labour Party*, London, 1906.

Humphrey, A. W.: *A History of Labour Representation*, London, 1912.

George, Henry: *Progress and Poverty.*
Fabian Essays in Socialism, London, 1890.
Ensor, R. C.: *Modern Socialism,* London, 1907.
Foster, H. V. Arnold: *English Socialism of To-day,* London, 1908.
Macdonald, J. Ramsay: *The Socialist Movement,* London, 1911.   (A small book in the Home University Library.)
Beer, M.: *A History of English Socialism.*

CHAPTER XII

DEMOCRATIC INFLUENCES ON INDUSTRIAL LIFE, 1906-1920

105. National Affairs from 1906 to 1920. — By the end of 1905 the Conservative or Unionist party, which had so long held control of the government, had lost the confidence of the people, and at the elections held in January, 1906, a combination of parties opposed to it, the Liberals, Irish Nationalists, and Labor party, obtained a large majority in Parliament and formed a new ministry. It was this combined party that carried through the series of economic and social reforms to which so much of this chapter is devoted.

In addition a number of changes of a more political nature were made. In 1911 a bill known as the Parliament Act was passed giving to the House of Commons much greater power. In case of a dispute between the House of Commons and the House of Lords on any proposed bill, it would become law when the House of Commons passed it, if it were a bill concerned with taxation or appropriations, immediately, whether the House of Lords approved it or not. Any other bill, if passed by the House of Commons three times in successive sessions would become law, even if the House of Lords defeated it each time. At the same time it was provided that Parliament should not sit longer than five years without a new election. Members of Parliament, who had before served without salary, were now to be paid, so that a more democratic element might serve as representatives of the people.

The occurrence of this period of the most overwhelming importance was, of course, the Great War, begun August 4, 1914, and closed by the armistice of November 11, 1918, followed by

the Peace of Versailles, signed June 28, 1919. Its most remarkable feature in a military way was the creation of an army
of 7,500,000 men and the transportation of most of them to
France or to other fields of warfare. The small standing army
in existence at the beginning of the war was rapidly increased
in 1914 and 1915 by voluntary enlistments; in 1916 compulsory military service was adopted, and the various colonies
sent vast contributions of troops for the united British army.
The troops were supplied with munitions by the government
by establishing enormous manufactories for war material, by
employing immense numbers of men and women, and controlling all the sources of supply needed for them.

During the course of the war not only were the losses and
sufferings enormous, but much of the form of government and
of the organization of society was for the time transformed.
A coalition ministry was formed composed of the Liberals, the
parties which had worked with them before the war and a large
number of Conservatives. In 1916 Mr. Asquith, the prime
minister, resigned and Lloyd George took his place. A "war
cabinet" of five men was also appointed to provide for carrying
on the war more effectively. After the war a new reform bill was
introduced and carried in February, 1918. It is known as the
Representation of the People Act. By it what was practically
universal suffrage was introduced for both men and women.
With a few exceptions one vote only was allowed to each voter,
and the representative districts were made almost exactly
equal in number of inhabitants. The old programme of the
Chartists for parliamentary reform, universal suffrage, vote by
ballot, abolition of property qualification for membership,
payment of members, equal electoral districts, and annual
Parliaments was by the act of 1918 completed, except for the
last point, and in some respects, as in women's suffrage, and
in the supremacy of the House of Commons over the House of
Lords, democracy was carried further than the Chartists had
ever planned.

As soon as the war was over, Lloyd George, the prime minister, appealed to the country for the continued support of the Coalition ministry, dissolved Parliament, which had already by special arrangement sat longer than the law permitted, and in December, 1918, the first election under the new reform bill was held. The Irish members, dissatisfied with the treatment of Ireland, and the Labor representatives, dissatisfied with the treatment of labor questions, refused to support the ministry any longer. The elections nevertheless went strongly in favor of the Coalition ministry, which was thus given a continued lease of life as a combination of part of the old Liberals with the Unionists.

During the war Ireland was more disturbed even than usual. A home rule bill was carried in 1914, against the serious opposition of Ulster, but as the war began almost immediately its enforcement was suspended until the end of the war and it became practically obsolete. Although there were many voluntary enlistments from Ireland in the early part of the war, many Irishmen felt that they had no interest in it, and indeed that it might properly be used as an opportunity to force Great Britain to grant them more complete self-government. As a result of this feeling and of the failure of the government to arouse a spirit of devotion to the British cause among the Irish people, the society known as Sinn Fein, whose object was the complete separation of Ireland from Great Britain, spread widely. In April, 1916, they rose in revolt in Dublin but were soon put down and the leaders executed. Some of the Irish leaders plotted with the Germans, and Sir Roger Casement was captured as he landed from a German submarine on the Irish coast, tried for treason, and hanged. When conscription was adopted for Great Britain it was not applied to Ireland for fear of an uprising, and when later Ireland was included in the law, the opposition was so great that it was not actually enforced. Nevertheless the Sinn Fein or republican party steadily grew in numbers, and when the new elections for

Parliament took place in December, 1918, they carried almost every division in Ireland, leaving the Home Rulers but 7 seats and the Unionists of Ulster their usual group of 25 representatives. The 73 who had been elected from the Sinn Fein party thereupon refused to attend the United Parliament, organized a separate parliament of their own at Dublin, declared the independence of the Irish republic, and sought the recognition of other countries.

Neither the British ministry nor other governments, however, gave any recognition to this proposed separation from Great Britain. A well-known military commander, General French, himself an Irishman, was appointed lord lieutenant and tried with a strong hand to prevent resistance to the government, but there was much disorder and many assassinations occurred, including an attempt in 1919 against General French himself. These attacks for the most part went untried and unpunished because of the alienation of the mass of people from the government, and the consequent failure of jury trials.

In February, 1920, a new effort at settlement was made by the introduction into Parliament of a bill providing for the establishment of two " home rule " parliaments in Ireland, one for the main part of the country, the other for Ulster.

King Edward VII died in 1910 and his son, George V, became king. His influence has been steadily exercised in the development of the more kindly interests of the people, in the encouragement of patriotism, especially during the war, and in drawing more closely the bonds between England and the other parts of the empire. In 1919 the Prince of Wales made a visit to Canada, Australia, and other colonies. The effect of the war has been to bring the self-governing colonies and the dependencies into greater and greater prominence. Their contributions of men and supplies were absolutely indispensable during the war, and their support greatly strengthened the moral position of the mother country. As a result of these conditions the prime ministers of the five self-governing colonial dominions and of India were invited to make up with the five members of the war cabinet of Parliament an "Imperial War Cabinet." This sat at London right through the war, and arrangements have been made by which it will become a regular part of the government of the empire even after the war. When the treaty of Versailles was signed the representatives of the principal colonial dominions signed it as though they were separate nations, and they are similarly represented in the Assembly of the League of Nations.

106. A Policy of General Social Reform. — Notwithstanding all the industrial advance that has been described and was still in progress, and notwithstanding all the combined action and all the favoring legislation that had been adopted, it was still doubtful whether the condition of the mass of the people had been appreciably improved. Certainly inequalities and evils were still everywhere conspicuous. Careful statistics worked out just at the beginning of this period, in 1909, showed that of the 44,500,000 people in the United Kingdom about 5,500,000, or about one-eighth, received about one-half of the income of the country, the other seven-eighths, or 39,000,000, received the other half. These 39,000,000, taking men, women, and children, received an average annual income of less than $125 apiece. More than half the male workmen in the country were receiving wages of less than $7.50 a week, and about ninety per cent less than $10 a week. There was much unemployment, and prices were rising. Real wages, allowing for the increase of prices and for unavoidable unemployment, were at the beginning of this period, in 1906, somewhat below what they had been ten years before, and five years later they were lower still. No one could look seriously into the condition of the masses of the English people and not be impressed with its deeply unsatisfactory character. It was a sad thought that all the triumphs of modern invention, organization, and effort had left so much misery in the richest country in the world.

The belief that this poverty, distress, and lack of opportunity could be overcome by the individual exertions of those suffering from it was becoming constantly weaker; the belief that these evils could be largely removed by general effort through the action of government was growing in strength. Many social reforms had long been acknowledged by all parties to be necessary or desirable, and had even been brought up for discussion in Parliament. These had not been adopted, either because there was too much difference of opinion as to how far they should extend, or because the ministry and Parliament felt it necessary to give precedence to other matters. The new Parliament that met early in 1906 had, however, been elected largely on a platform of the adoption of such social reforms. Democracy was turning in the direction of improving the condition of the mass of the people. The prime minister, Campbell-Bannerman, the two most prominent members of the cabinet, Asquith and Lloyd George, each of whom in succession later became prime minister, as well as several other members of the ministry, were devoted to the cause of social reform. Indeed, Mr. Asquith declared that "political machinery is only valuable and is only worth having as it is adapted to and used for worthy social ends." The Labor party members were an important element of the majority in Parliament and they, of course, insisted on attention to reforms which were of particular interest to the working classes. The result was that between the years 1906 and 1914 measures of social reform greater in number and more far-reaching in importance were carried through Parliament than at any other time in English history.

Some of these measures were merely extensions or codifications of laws already in existence, the original adoption of which has been described in earlier chapters. In 1906 immediately after the opening of Parliament a much more liberal and inclusive workmen's compensation act was passed. It repealed the earlier laws on the subject and established what was practically a code of workmen's compensation. Its pro-

visions were extended beyond the classes formerly
to apply to seamen, domestic servants, and all emp......... ...
the government except those in the army and navy. It was
also made to include protection from certain forms of poisoning
or other diseases resulting from industrial causes, and power
was given to the authorities to extend this list of industrial
diseases. The law provided that any workman injured in the
course of his work or suffering from certain diseases as a result
of his work should receive from his employer as long as the
results of the injury or the disease continued an amount equal
to about half his previous earnings. In the case of an accident
causing death, an amount equal to three years' wages should
be paid to his widow or other dependents. Industrial insurance
is taken to cover these losses.

In each of the four years 1906, 1907, 1908, and 1909 a bill
was passed for the special welfare of children. By these
measures the school authorities were required to give or sell
meals to those who came to school underfed; playgrounds and
medical inspection were provided for; juvenile courts were
established; children were better protected from cruelty, and
many other arrangements made for the children of the common
people who were apt to have little opportunity otherwise to
grow up with bodily and mental health and training and capable
of enjoying and profiting by their life.

In 1912 there was a further extension of the old factory
acts. A law was passed which required all retail stores, —
called in England " shops," — all restaurants, and similar
establishments, to close one half day in each week, besides
Sunday. It also limited the hours of employment in such
establishments to sixty hours a week and made various other
provisions about time of closing, comfort of employees, and
such matters. These laws and a number of others either
passed or introduced into Parliament for discussion did not
involve any new principle, and were not seriously opposed by
any political party. Others, however, of the same general

z

character but introducing more of government action, or interfering more extensively in what had previously been considered private affairs, were carried against considerable resistance. The three most important and hard contested of these will now be described.

107. Old Age Pensions. — Neither the reformed poor law of 1835, the workhouse test introduced in 1871, the outdoor relief provided for in 1895, individual savings, nor private charity had solved the problem of providing satisfactorily for the support of old people of the poorer classes. Wages were, as has been pointed out before, so low in most cases that it could not be expected that workingmen should save enough for old age, or that younger people could support their parents when they became too old to work. In addition to the statistics already given it may be stated that in 1886 average wages were only about $6.00 a week, and many were getting far less than that sum. In 1917 more than four million full-grown men when regularly at work were receiving less than $7.50 a week. In the same year almost two-thirds of the farm laborers of England got less than 18 shillings, about $4.50, a week, and almost one-half of the women workers in the industries in which the largest number of women worked were paid an average of less than $3.00 a week. In 1894 almost one-third of the people of England above sixty-five years of age were in receipt of public relief.

Conservatives and Liberals alike had sought a satisfactory plan for the support of the aged poor. Suggestions were made from 1879 onward for some general legislation on the subject, and various measures had been introduced into Parliament, but had failed for one cause or another of adoption. The Labor party had declared some years before for a simple direct pension of five shillings a week, paid from the national treasury, for the support of all aged poor persons. The ministry now took up this plan and after long debates carried it through Parliament in 1908. It provided that every man or woman who has reached the age of seventy years, whose means of support do not amount to more than £31, 10 s., about $155, a year, and is not receiving parish relief, shall receive a pension from the national government. This pension varied in amount from one to five shillings a week according to the income which the person receiving the pension had from other sources. Claims for a pension could be made, and the pension paid through the nearest post-office. Within five years of the passage of the act almost a million old men and women were receiving government pensions, nearly all of them of the maximum amount, that is to say, five shillings a week. The cost to the government was about $60,000,000 a year. It was urged by some that the age limit should be reduced to sixty-five years, but this would have cost $35,000,000 a year more, and it was not adopted.

It was carefully provided that the receipt of these old age pensions should not carry any stigma, and the recipients are spoken of as "pensioners," not paupers. As a result of this and other causes a great many old people gave up their parish relief and applied for government pensions. In 1911 the disqualification of those receiving parish relief was removed entirely, under the belief that none would apply for local relief, with all its traditional disgrace, if they could avoid it. From 1906 to 1915 the number of paupers above 70 years of age receiving local relief was reduced from more than two hundred thousand to about fifty thousand. Most of these were in institutions, and by the end of 1917 scarcely more than a thousand aged people in all England were left to receive outdoor relief from their local boards.

In 1916, on account of the increase of prices for food and other necessaries due to the war, grants of weekly payments of two shillings and sixpence were added to the old age pensions. At the close of the war a committee of Parliament was appointed to look into the whole subject, and in accordance with their report, in December, 1919, the weekly payments were raised to ten shillings, about $2.50, a week. This adds an additional amount of about $50,000,000 a year to the cost of old age pensions. The problem of pauperism of those not above the age limit is still a serious one. Just before the war there were about 600,000 paupers in England, who were receiving from taxes about $75,000,000 a year, an average of about $2.00 apiece from every person in England. How to remove this expensive and demoralizing burden is still being studied.

The debate on the pension bill of 1908 brought up discussion of many similar questions. The Labor members claimed that aged working people ought to be looked on as " veterans of industry," whose labor had been the chief factor in the winning of England's wealth, and who could therefore claim support in their old age as a right, not merely as a charity. If this were so, their pensions should be much larger, but for this the majority in Parliament was not ready. Mr. Asquith, however, who had just become prime minister, said concerning the act, " beyond this there lies the whole still unconquered territory of social reform." Soon afterward, in 1909, a commission on the poor laws which had been making investigations and taking testimony for the preceding three years made its report. It recommended a large number of changes in the laws, and the minority of the committee made a separate report, urging still more extensive reforms. This " Minority Report " of 1909 has become a sort of program of projects for social betterment.

108. Government Labor or Employment Exchanges. — One of the constant difficulties of modern times is unemployment. Quite apart from the idle, dissolute, or otherwise incapable and from men temporarily out on strike, there is always a greater or less number of competent persons anxious to obtain positions but unable to find them. In peace time between three and ten per cent of workingmen are always out of work. At certain times the number increases materially. Some trades are " seasonal," that is to say, they are active during part of the year, dull at another part. Such are coal mining, clothing manufacture, candy making, and others. At the active periods in these industries there is work for everybody, at the dull periods of the year for very few. In the coal mines, for instance, the number of days in a year a man can obtain employment varies from one-half to two-thirds. At more irregular intervals there is the same lack of work in occupations dependent on the weather, such as bricklaying, bridge-building, railroad track laying, general labor, and other outdoor work. A great deal of unemployment results from the alternation of good times and bad times, from commercial or financial panics that close up many industrial establishments, and from the introduction of labor-saving machinery that throws men out of employment, at least for the time. It is a sad fact that thousands of workmen, sometimes hundreds of thousands, ready and willing to work, from causes entirely beyond their control and notwithstanding their utmost efforts, are sometimes without occupation or wages for days, weeks, and months. In the longer periods they tramp from town to town in search of work, their savings are exhausted, their families suffer, they run into debt, regularity of habits is destroyed, and hope lost. One of the means by which these evils could be prevented was considered by some to be by improving the means by which employers and employees should be brought together. At the same time some workmen were seeking work, some employers might be seeking workmen, and no very satisfactory method existed of making them known to one another. To accomplish this result certain cities in England, following the example of German cities, from about 1892 onward established municipal " labor exchanges." By 1905 there were some twenty-five such exchanges in existence and they were filling 15,000 or more places a year.

In 1905, while the old Conservative ministry was still in power, an " Unemployed Workmen Act " was passed authorizing cities to enter more extensively into such plans and to lay certain taxes for their support, to which Parliament would add special grants. These plans were to be carried out largely by voluntary local "distress committees," and were therefore bound up closely with charitable efforts. Only London followed the recommendation and the results were generally felt to be unsatisfactory. In 1909 the Commission on the Poor Laws referred to above proposed that this work should be taken in charge by the national government, and in the autumn of the same year a law was passed by which the ministry was authorized to take over all city offices of this kind and to establish a system of national government labor exchanges. They were defined as agencies intended to bring together workmen needing positions and employers needing workmen, to aid workmen to reach places where their services were in demand, to give information about opportunities for work and for other similar purposes. The ministry made immediate use of this authorization by Parliament and of the appropriation granted at the same time. Within six months eighty of these government employment offices were opened in various cities; in 1912 there were more than four hundred in existence in cities and large towns, besides more than a thousand branches in small towns and industrial suburbs open only a day or two a week, or for part time. They were carefully organized. The whole country was divided into ten districts for their administration, each with a central office, and there is a main central office in London. From this central office is sent out each day to each labor exchange in the country a list of several thousand openings for workmen in all parts of the country. Their officials are assisted by voluntary local committees, and they work as far as possible in connection with trade unions and similar bodies. At first some employers opposed the exchanges on the ground that they were unduly favorable to the workingmen, but most of this opposition has passed away. Indeed many employers have entered into agreements to secure their employees only through the labor exchanges. Much attention is paid to placing children and young persons coming under their charge in suitable positions, and the voluntary committees agree to keep an oversight over young persons in the early years of their employment.

The exchanges do not guarantee the competence of the workmen for whom they secure positions, nor do they go into the question of good wages or working conditions, or whether the applicants are on strike or not. On the other hand, the voluntary advisory committees include both employers and employees, with the object of bringing these two classes together in the management of the offices and consequently into closer touch with the problems of industry common to both in the locality. Early in 1917 charge of the labor exchanges was transferred from the Board of Trade to the Ministry of Labor, and it was then provided that the government should be represented on the advisory committees, though never with a majority of members. It was hoped that this system of local voluntary boards would prevent the exchanges falling into the hands of a settled bureaucracy, as has been so disadvantageous in some other countries. During the war the labor exchanges did a great service in securing workers for the government munition works and for agriculture. In 1917, 2,837,650 separate individuals were registered, applications were received from employers for 1,999,444 vacancies, and 1,555,223 positions were filled. Early in 1919, soon after the close of the war, there were something more than a million names inscribed on the registers of the exchanges, about 40,000 vacancies a week were being notified to workmen, and about 30,000 vacancies a week were being filled. Some 3000 workingmen and women weekly were being helped by loans of money or car tickets to pass from one district to another to secure positions.

109. National Insurance against Sickness and Unemployment. — Labor exchanges would bring employers and employees together and would no doubt lessen the amount and duration of unemployment, but they could hardly get rid of it altogether. A certain amount of irregularity of employment would have to be counted on. To relieve the distress caused by this the plan of insuring against it, as is generally done against other forms of loss, had been advocated for some time. It was in force in Germany and it was announced by the ministry as part of their plan, although it was not followed up, when the bill for labor exchanges was carried in 1909.

Another form of insurance was also pressing for consideration about the same time. The mutual insurance companies for the payment of sickness and death benefits, " friendly societies," as they are called in England, seemed to have about reached their limit, and yet a great proportion of the lower classes had no provision for support during periods of sickness or for the expenses and protection of their families at time of death. This condition of affairs had come up for consideration repeatedly in connection with workmen's compensation, old age pensions, and other social reforms. These two needs, insurance against disease and against unemployment, were now combined in one extensive measure and carried through Parliament, after considerable opposition, in December, 1911. Sick insurance, according to this plan, is compulsory for all workingmen and women receiving less than about $800 a year, and unemployment insurance for all workmen in certain trades, which were chosen partly for experimental purposes, partly because of their " seasonal " or irregular character and their consequent special need. They were principally the building and engineering trades, including perhaps a sixth of all industrial workingmen.

The fund for allowances during sickness was made up by payments of 2 pence a week by the employer and 3 pence by the workman, during every week he is at work. These payments are made through the post-office by buying stamps and fixing them on a card kept by the workman. The employer is bound to see that the workman's payments are made and can deduct the amount from his wages, but is forbidden to diminish the workman's wages to cover his own contribution. The benefits resulting from this insurance are free medical attendance, sanitarium treatment for consumption, maternity benefits for women, and a payment for support in ordinary sickness, after the first week, for half a year of about ten shillings a week, and afterward indefinitely of five shillings a week. There are some differences between the payments and benefits of men and women, of higher and lower paid men, and other variations. About a quarter of the sum paid was contributed by the government, and the payments were mainly made through the friendly societies. Death benefits were not included in this scheme of government insurance because they were so much more generally provided for already through other forms of insurance, through friendly societies, and through the trade unions.

The fund for unemployment insurance was made up by a payment of 2½ pence a week each by employers and employees in the trades to which it applied. The government added a penny more a week and agreed to bear the cost of administration. After one week of unemployment a man or woman can begin to draw about seven shillings a week and can continue to do so for fifteen weeks in any one year, with the restriction that he cannot draw more than one week's pay for every five weeks for which he has contributed. For unemployment due to strikes, lockouts, or other preventable causes payments are not allowed. There are provisions for recovery of the amount paid by both employers and workmen in case of long continuous employment, and other careful modifications exist. Payments of unemployment insurance are made through the labor exchanges. Within a short time some 15,000,000 persons were in this way insured against sickness and 2,500,000 against unemployment. The sickness, maternity, and total disablement allowances made under this act amount to about $40,000,000 a year.

110. Trade or Minimum Wages Boards. — Workmen's Compensation for Accident, Old Age Pensions, Unemployment and Sickness Insurance, and Labor Exchange acts all were concerned with what might be considered accidental evils in industrial society, although so constantly recurring as to call for general legislative and administrative treatment. In the field of ordinary wages there was much that was as unsatisfactory as were these irregular occurrences.

One of the most conspicuous of these difficulties was the so-called " sweated industries." These were certain occupations where there were no trade unions, where women's labor predominated, where in some cases at least there was much foreign labor, and where the labor was largely unskilled. As a consequence of these conditions low rates of wages, long hours, and bad surroundings prevailed. In some of these industries much of the work was done in the homes of the workers. In the ready-made clothing industry, for instance, two-thirds of the women employed earned less than fifteen shillings, $3.75, a week, hours of labor were very long, and sanitary and other living conditions notably bad. The " sweated trades " were long a subject of inquiry and discussion. It was generally felt that every one should have a living wage, which many of these workingmen and women certainly did not have. A committee of the House of Lords published reports on the subject as early as 1890, a Women's Industrial Council and an Anti-Sweating League were formed shortly after that time, and various measures intended to improve conditions were introduced into Parliament between 1895 and 1905. A characteristic tendency of this period was to bring up such questions of social reform, but sufficient pressure was not exerted by the ministry to overcome the conservative tendency of their party and to pass them.

In 1908 and 1909, however, in addition to a number of private bills on the subject the ministry brought in one of their own and in 1909 carried it through. This law required that in each of a number of trades of the nature described above, especially ready-made clothing, paper box making, artificial lace making, and some others the Board of Trade should appoint a body to be known as the " Central Trade Board." This board should consist in each trade of an equal number of representatives of the employers and the employees, with a representative of the government added. The central boards were required to appoint boards of the same nature in each locality where the industry was carried on. Each such local board should then establish a schedule of minimum wages in its industry in that locality. Compulsion was to be introduced only gradually. Time for protest was allowed, a " white list " of those willing to pay the rates voluntarily was to be formed, the established rate was to be paid by the government to its employees and to be required from all government contractors; finally, after six months, the rate established by the board was to become compulsory. The rates were to apply to home as well as factory work, and inspectors under the boards had a right of entrance to any place where work was done at any time. Within four years such boards had been established widely in the industries named, and extended to candy making, food preserving, shirt making, and a number of other trades, embracing about 400,000 workers. Wages established were seldom very high, indeed they were often deplorably low; they ranged from about $3.75 a week for women to about $7.50 a week for men.

This act represented a greater change of principle than any that has been recorded in this or the three preceding chapters. It was practically a return to the principle of legal regulation of wages, which was the basis of the old Statutes of Laborers and of the Statute of Apprentices.[1] There were, however, two striking differences. In the first place this was a plan to keep wages up, whereas the earlier statutes were to keep them down; secondly, in the earlier forms of regulation the working people had no representation; on the Trade Boards they were fully represented. The essential principle, that wages might be fixed and then enforced by the government, was a new principle so far as the economic history of the last one hundred years was concerned. Although there was some

[1] See pp. 91–94, 148–150.

opposition in Parliament to this law on the theoretical ground
that it was socialistic, and some on the practical ground that
it would put England in a disadvantageous position in international competition, there was on the whole but little opposition to the principle involved. By most it was strongly
supported on the ground that it was necessary in order to keep
up the physical and mental powers of the people, that the community would otherwise have to make good the inefficiency
that sweating produces.

It was not likely that this principle would halt at the sweated
trades. The coal miners were well organized into trade unions,
and rates of payment had long been arranged with the coal
mine owners either by direct negotiation or, after 1893, by
Conciliation Boards. These boards worked on the basis of
an agreed upon minimum piece rate system, ordinarily so
much per ton for each ton hewn, but the men declared that
the irregular nature of the work prevented this in many cases
from being a living wage. In January, 1912, the Miners'
Federation determined by an overwhelming majority to strike
for a national minimum daily wage of 5 shillings, about $1.25,
for men working underground, with corresponding piece rates.
Many of the employers were willing to agree but many were
not, and a long and bitter strike took place. There was no
appreciable disorder, but the cessation of production of coal
closed so many industries and brought so much suffering on
the country that it seemed necessary to take any steps possible
to bring it to a close. The ministry therefore in March rather
reluctantly carried through Parliament a bill providing for the
appointment in each of the coal districts of a joint board of
employers and miners with a chairman elected by the two
parties, or, in case of their failure to elect, appointed by the
government. These boards should establish in each locality
a legal minimum rate of wages, less than which the employers
must not pay or the miners accept. In case of non-agreement
the chairman had a deciding vote. The minimum rates estab-

lished by these boards were generally a disappointment to the men, though circumstances seemed to require agreement to them. The rates were in some cases increased by later negotiations, but the settlement remained on the whole unsatisfactory. The extension of the principle of a legal minimum wage to agriculture was widely advocated at the same period in the form of Agricultural District Wages Boards, but it was not introduced until, during the Great War, such boards were established temporarily as a means of encouraging agricultural production. In 1911 a Labor member of Parliament urged upon the ministry the introduction of a government minimum weekly wage of 30 s. for all its employees, preparatory to introducing a measure for making this a general national minimum wage, but a representative of the ministry announced their unwillingness to take action, declaring that they had statistics of wages of about 3½ million workmen and that more than sixty per cent of them were getting less than the proposed rate. To adopt even the sum of $7.50 a week, therefore, would increase the national wage bill by about $440,000,000. Such a national minimum has, however, continued to be advocated by many influential bodies.

111. **New Legalization of Trade Unions.** — At the beginning of this period the trade unions were in a peculiar legal position. Since the passage of the laws of 1871 and 1875 they could not be treated as criminal organizations, nor could their members or officers be punished. They were under no disabilities so far as the criminal law was concerned. They had also so many forms of legal recognition that it was generally supposed they were fully protected by the law in all their civil functions. Efforts were made, however, from time to time to hold them liable for loss or damages due to strikes. Finally, in 1901, the House of Lords, the highest court of appeal in England, in the "Taff Vale Case," a suit for damages by a railway company against a miners' union, decided that

trade unions could be sued and made to pay damages for loss brought about by strikes ordered by their officers.

This decision was a great surprise and at the same time a shock not only to members of trade unions but to others as well because the great trade-union funds, collected for purposes of insurance and other uses, might now be levied on in any trade dispute that caused loss to the employers of the men in the union. There was a widespread belief in the community that if this was the state of the law it should be changed, and in 1905 the Conservative party introduced an amending act but did not succeed in passing it. In 1906, immediately after the assembling of the new Parliament, the Liberal ministry and the Labor party representatives each introduced a bill on the subject. These were later combined and, although there was much opposition, a law was passed within the same year, known as the Trade Disputes Act. This practically reversed for the future the Taff Vale decision. It provided that suits for damages could not be brought against trade unions for any action taken in connection with a strike or other trade dispute unless the action was itself illegal. A trade union as a whole could not be sued for any action taken by its officers. To settle the question of legality or illegality of " picketing," the right to stand near any dwelling house or any business place for the purpose of persuading any one not to work during a strike was especially guaranteed. No act done during a strike should be declared illegal just because it brought about a breach of contract or interfered with a man's freedom to do what he would with his capital or labor. By these provisions trade unions were protected from suits for money damages in their disputes with employers as completely as they had been thirty years before from criminal punishments.[1]

In December, 1909, another decision on trade unions was made by the House of Lords, known as the Osborne judgment.

[1] The group of acts of 1871, 1875, 1876, and 1906 are conveniently given in Hayes, *British Social Politics*, pp. 85–101.

This was to the effect that trade unions are recognized by the law of 1876 as being practically corporations, but incorporated for the purposes indicated in the definition of a trade union given in that law and for those purposes only. As the purposes mentioned are only those connected with industrial disputes or regulations, it is illegal for trade unions to use their funds to pay members of Parliament or for any other political purpose. This was a hard blow to the new Labor party. Members of Parliament received no salary from the government; the Labor party members, who were not men of private means, were supported and the expenses of their election paid by the trade unions which were interested in sending them to Parliament. In 1911, therefore, at the request of the Labor party members, the prime minister carried a measure for the payment of salaries to all members of the House of Commons. The Representation of the People Act of 1918 provided for the payment of election expenses by the government, so that members of all parties may now be chosen and serve without serious expense.

The larger restrictions on the activities of the trade unions implied in the Osborne decision were still unsettled. That decision practically forbade educational and other such functions as well as their political activity. In 1913 a new Trade Union Act was passed. It practically reversed the Osborne decision, much as the Trade Disputes Act of 1909 reversed the Taff Vale decision. It provided that a trade union could use its funds for practically any purposes it wished, on condition that its members voted by a general ballot for the object, and that no member should be compelled to make a contribution for a political object. Trade unions were newly defined in this law so as to include any bodies that had to do with the regulation of trade, whatever other objects they had in addition.

112. Advance of the Labor Party. — The alliance of the various groups of Labor members of Parliament with the Liberals and Nationalists during the period in which the social reforms described above were being carried was a natural and easy one. They supported the Liberals also in the adoption of the new forms of taxation in 1909 and the Parliament Act of 1911, and did not oppose them in the two elections of 1910. But the desire of the trade-union leaders who had advocated the entrance of workingmen into the political field in 1899 was for an entirely separate party, and, as already stated, in 1906 they took the name " Labor Party " and adopted a full party organization. In the Congress of the party in 1907 they adopted a set of principles largely socialistic in nature, declaring for " the socialization of the means of production, distribution, and exchange, to be controlled in a democratic state in the interests of the entire community." In 1910 the party adopted a more definite constitution. They declared themselves to be a federation of trade unions, trades councils, socialist societies, local labor parties, coöperative societies, and women's organizations, so far as these accepted their principles. They had a centralized executive council in which these various classes were represented. They placed their candidates as in the case of similar bodies under very strict regulation. They required them to accept the constitution of the party, appear as candidates of the Labor party only, and vote according to the decisions of the organized party. This requirement of a pledge of obedience to party decisions was widely criticized and was made less strict, though not actually withdrawn, in 1911.

During the war, as already stated, the Labor party acted as part of the Coalition government and there were several Labor members in the ministry. But relations were rather strained. The Coalition ministry contained some of the bitterest opponents of the fundamental principles of the Labor party, and Labor members found it hard to work with their old antagonists. The prime minister himself adopted many points of policy to which they were opposed. The Labor members, therefore, withdrew from the ministry as soon as the war was over. The party became steadily more assertive and ambitious and in January, 1918, adopted, provisionally at least, a full and far-reaching statement of principles and plans for reorganizing much of society. This programme as it was presented to the Congress of the party by its executive committee was called " Labor and the New Social Order." It represented the views of the " left " or progressive element in the party, and many of the trade unionists of the older type were not very much interested in some of its socialistic proposals or perhaps even disapproved of them altogether. On the other hand, this programme attracted much attention from men of other classes and was republished and read widely in England, America, and other countries.

When the Representation of the People Act was passed in 1918 and it became evident that women would be given the right to vote and that all voting would be placed on a more democratic basis, the Labor party, at a meeting in February, 1918, reorganized inself on a broader basis, made a special bid for the new voters, planned to put up a candidate in each district and appealed to all workers " by hand or by brain " to support them. Later a definite platform was adopted on the basis of " Labor and the New Social Order." When the new elections were held in December, 1918, the Labor party elected fifty-nine members, polling more than two and a quarter million votes. During the year 1919 four additional Labor members were elected at " bye-elections " to fill vacancies, and by the middle of 1920 it has come to be considered not unlikely that at the next election the Labor party will be in a majority in Parliament.

113. Effect of the War on the Trade Unions. — In the years 1911 and 1912 there were serious and long-continued strikes, especially that of the miners already referred to, the railway men, and the dock workers. The first of these might have been considered a success for the men, the second a drawn battle, the third a failure. But all of them alike left the workmen deeply dissatisfied. " Labor unrest," as it has come to be called, was already widespread. Events in-

2 A

creased its extent and intensity.   When the war broke out, in August, 1914, it was evidently necessary to augment as rapidly as possible the production of munitions and many other requirements for the government in carrying on the war. The rules of the trade unions, although formed primarily for the protection of the standards of life of the workmen against the destructive effects of business competition, stood in the way also of increased production.   On March 17, 1915, at a meeting between the prime minister and thirty-five trade union officials, yielding to war requirements, the union representatives agreed to suspend all union rules till after the war, and not to enter upon strikes during its continuance.   Thus the great structure of agreements and restrictions of all kinds which had been built up through more than a half century of effort was suddenly pulled down.   Women, boys and girls, and untrained laborers were poured by hundreds of thousands into the old skilled trades; hours, piecework, apprenticeship, and scores of other rules disappeared, so that it seemed that trade unionism had suddenly and for the time disappeared from the industrial world.

Other conditions made workingmen restive.   It was a hard time for everybody.   The cost of living began to rise rapidly, and although wages were raised by private employers, and the government paid a bonus in addition to the old wages in industries under its control, the men did not consider this increase proportionate to the increase of prices.   Those workingmen, like people in other classes, who had small families or were favorably situated, were better off than before, but a vast number of others were worse off.   There was a restless doubt among the men as to the real objects of the war, and many believed that fundamentally it was a " capitalists' war." As the war dragged on year after year, trade unionists saw their old rules left farther and farther in the background, and began to lose faith in their restoration after the war.   At the same time the constant official appeals to their importance in providing the equipment for the war and the general awakening of thought by the discussions of the times led to a widespread acceptance of much more far-reaching plans than the old trade-union principles. The rank and file of the trade unionists came to be less and less under the influence of their leaders and frequently disregarded their advice or control. What were known as "shop stewards," local officials of the unions, began to exercise more influence than the national officers. Strikes were threatened among the ship-builders, miners, dock laborers, and others who had not entered into the arrangement of March, 1915, or who did not feel bound by the agreements of their officers. Many disputes occurred with the representatives of the government, which was now controlling so many industries. In general, workingmen were during the later years of the war sore, suspicious, and dissatisfied, and labor unrest became more marked than ever.

Just before the war what was called the "triple alliance" was formed, consisting of the Miners' Federation of Great Britain, with 800,000 members, the National Union of Railwaymen, with 350,000 members, and the Transport Workers' Federation, or port laborers, with 250,000 members. In April, 1914, representatives of these three great unions, numbering together some 1,600,000 workmen, entered into an agreement which bound them to confer together from time to time and to take common action whenever the three partners should agree upon it. There was no such common action during the war, nor indeed has there been since; but the possibility of a joint strike in these three basic industries, which would reduce England to famine and put a stop to all industry until a settlement of some kind was reached, has been constantly in the minds of all workingmen, employers, and representatives of the government, since the formation of the "triple alliance."

The close of the war, in November, 1918, was marked by a large number of detached labor outbreaks and the presentation of demands upon either their employers or the government from the three great industries just named. The railway men's claims dated from their dissatisfaction with the settlement of the strike of 1912. They now put forward a number of proposals, including one that was new. This was for representation on the governing boards of the railways. The long and what the workmen considered dilatory negotiations which followed at last broke down and a ten days' strike occurred at the close of September and the beginning of October, 1919. The government showed unexpected vigor and resource; many men and women not of the working classes volunteered for railroad work, and the general community, alienated by the suddenness of the strike and the obscurity of its causes, gave little support to the strikers. Some of the men's demands, however, were granted at the time, others, after further discussion, were finally agreed upon in January, 1920, although even this settlement was not entirely satisfactory to the men.

In January the miners presented a series of proposals mostly connected with wages, hours, and working conditions, but including also a demand for nationalization of the mines. When these demands were not granted by the government, which was carrying on the mines, a strike was determined upon by the miners by a vote of nearly five to one, to begin on March 15. To avoid this the government, with the agreement of the miners, appointed a Coal Commission consisting of three men each from the mine owners, the mine laborers, employers in other industries appointed by the government, and expert economists appointed by the men. This commission of twelve men was presided over by Justice Sankey. The chairman, with the majority of the commission, reported in favor of the government buying out the mine owners, retaining control of the mines, and carrying them on in conjunction with representatives of the operators and the miners, with various improvements of hours and wages. The ministry did not accept this " Sankey report," but proposed instead a plan for buying out the holders of the royalty rights in the mines only, the improvement of working conditions, and representation of men on the boards that should work the mines. The men have continued work at the mines while these conditions have been in process of introduction, but have not given up their demand for the complete nationalization of the mines.

While these two contests were in progress, the transport workers, the third member of the "triple alliance," were carrying on a dispute with the port authorities and their employers which for a while threatened a great strike in the shipping world but which was compromised in March, 1919. During the period of these disputes there was constant fear that the workmen in the three great industries would make common cause with one another and force the issue by a general strike; but the moderate attitude of the officers of the unions, the conciliatory policy of the government and of many of the employers, and the prospect of some more complete reorganization of industry combined to prevent an outbreak of more serious proportions. Nevertheless it became evident that new ambitions and new ideas were at work among the men. The demand for representation of the workingmen on the boards that should in future administer the railroads and the mines indicated the passage of many workingmen from the old ideals of the trade unions, which were so largely restrictive, to a new plan in which they themselves would take more part in the carrying on of industry. This became the acknowledged desire of the government also as embodied in the industrial councils which were set up at this time with government approval and encouragement. The demand for actual government ownership of mines and railroads is a still larger proposal. Before, however, describing the activities of the government since the war, a movement in the same general direction emanating from some of the older trade unions must be explained.

114. National Gilds or Gild Socialism. — About 1906 a plan was proposed to improve modern industrial conditions by reëstablishing bodies somewhat similar to the mediæval gilds. These proposed modern gilds would, however, differ from those of the Middle Ages in several important respects. They would be national, not local, in character ; the workingmen and technical experts, not the " masters " would make up the gild; and, ultimately if not immediately, the whole community, not private men, would own the capital and other material requirements for carrying on the business. The men who provide the essential labor, both of hand and brain, in any line of industry, would according to this plan be organized as a national body or gild to administer that industry. Those industries which are in their nature public or already largely under public control, such as mining, railways, ship-building, the production of electricity, would be owned by the public, and administered under government supervision by the gild or association of the men who at present do the actual work of carrying them on, including workingmen, foremen, managers, clerks, technically trained experts, engineers, and all others actually engaged in the industry, except the representatives of capital. Ownership in such industries would be in the hands of the public, administration in the hands of the workers.

Industries not suited or not yet ready for public ownership would be similarly administered, each by its national gild, the man or men who provide the capital being paid interest but having no control of the industry, foremen and other managers being chosen and paid by the gild, not by the capitalist. In both these classes of industries the control of the community over wages, prices, rate of interest, and other conditions would be so large that the plan might be described as an industrial partnership between workers and public. The ownership of industries by the government distinguishes this plan from " syndicalism," a plan advocated by many of the French trade unions and put forward by a few men in England, which would put both ownership and administration in the hands of the workers.

It is evident that these national gilds, if they are to come into existence and take over the industries, must be built up on the present trade unions. This can be done by bringing into the unions foremen, managers, technicians, and others who work principally by brain, in addition to their present members, those who work principally by hand. The unions would also have to take the form of industrial rather than craft unions, all workers in any one industry being amalgamated into one body as is already practically true of the railway men, transport workers, miners, and workmen in some other fields.

In this way, it was contended, there would be larger production, since workingmen would be interested in their industry; there would be more good will and more coöperation in effort, and ability would be more successfully discovered and utilized. Another advantage would be still more important. Men would have industrial as well as political freedom. In a democracy, the individual citizen should be self-governing in his economic life, as a producer, as well as in his political life, as member of the state. The long standing problem of how to attain political freedom while remaining under practical economic subjection would thus be solved.

For about ten years these ideas and plans interested only a comparatively few educated people, but in the spring of 1915, as a result of the agitations connected with the war, the " National Gilds League " was formed. It defined its object in its constitution as " the abolition of the wage system and the establishment by the workers of self-government in industry through a democratic system of national gilds working in conjunction with a democratic state." These ideas were vigorously put forward and have spread rapidly among trade unionists and persons interested in industrial reconstruction. The number of members of the League is not large but many of them are in positions of much influence in the larger trade unions and in government office. The demand for the nationalization of the mines by the miners in their threatened strike

of 1919 and for the formation of joint boards of control of the
railways by the railway men at about the same time are closely
connected with this movement.

In some fields of industry such gilds are actually at work.
" Building Gild Committees " were formed by the builders'
trade unions in the latter part of 1919 and the early part of
1920 in Manchester, Warrington, and other Lancashire towns,
and in London, and have offered, in the existing shortage of
houses, to provide labor, management, and materials and to
contract with the town councils for the complete production
of workingmen's houses. In one town a contract has been
actually signed for the completion of 500 houses in 1920 and
500 more the next year, the Building Gild providing the labor
and materials at the usual market rate, charging 2% for management and 8% more to provide for the necessary plant and to
pay their own members full weekly wages instead of only for
days of good enough weather for outside work. The committees of the building trade unions are planning to form a
National Builders' Gild.

The importance of the plan of drawing into the trade unions
all the present employees of whatever grade, with a view to
their carrying on the industry under government ownership and
control, lies not only in the extent to which it is actually introduced but also in the degree to which its discussion is transforming and clarifying trade union and public opinion concerning the problem of economic production.

There has been a general revolt against the treatment of
labor as a commodity. The older trade unions claimed only
that they should get a fair price for the commodity they had
to sell, labor, just as the capitalist had a right to a fair profit
on his commodity, capital. " A fair day's wages for a fair
day's work," was a popular saying among trade unionists.
Workingmen now, however, have come to believe that they do
not sell their labor power for wages in such a way as to let it
go out of their own control; that their labor is inseparable

from their personality and that they have continuing rights and responsibilities for the use of it in the industry in which they are engaged. This principle has become more and more widely recognized and has been recently officially accepted by the British government and others. Among the general principles laid down in the labor clauses attached to the Treaty of Versailles of 1919 it is declared that " labor should not be regarded merely as a commodity or article of commerce."

The same principle has been accepted by many private and corporate employers in Great Britain. Within the last few years, at the suggestion of the twelve principal trade unions in the building industry, an " Industrial Council for the Building Industry " has been formed, consisting of 132 members, 66 elected by the twenty-two existing trade unions in that industry, the other 66 by the seventeen associations of building trades employers. This council, half of employees, half of employers, has joint control of a great number of matters of common import to all its members and is an effort to bring the whole industry under a general and efficient management.

115. Whitley Councils. — Among the sub-committees appointed by the government for its assistance during the war was one on " Relations between Employers and Employed," under the chairmanship of J. H. Whitley, a member of Parliament. The committee included several large employers and several trade unionists. During the serious outbreak of labor unrest in 1916 and 1917 this committee was asked by the government to consider suggestions for " securing a permanent improvement in the relations between employers and workmen." In response to these instructions, what have become known as the " Whitley reports," were made in the year 1917. They recommended that the government should encourage the formation of joint industrial councils in each industry, such as that which has just been described in the building industry, to consist half of members elected by the employers' associations, half by the trade unions. In industries in which either the employers or employees were insufficiently organized they recommended that a government representative be appointed to bring such a council into existence; and in industries in which there was no organization at all trade boards should be formed under the law of 1909. These joint industrial boards in each industry should meet as national boards, and as soon as possible organize district councils in each region of the country and workshop committees in each industrial establishment. All should be formed on the same basis of election, half by the employers, half by the workmen. They should take up matters of general interest in the trade, wages, piecework, improvements, technical training and research, legislation affecting the industry and such questions.

The ministry adopted these recommendations, issued an invitation to the trade unions and employers' organizations of the country to organize what have come to be known as Whitley Councils, and explained that the plan was intended to admit work people to a much greater share in the management of industry. The invitation was widely accepted. One industry after another, on the initiative either of the unions, the employers, or a representative of the government, organized such a national council, and in some cases proceeded rapidly to complete the scheme by forming district and workshop committees. The first to be formed was in the pottery industry, in which a council consisting of thirty representatives of the employers and thirty of the employees was formed, with the manager of the old Wedgwood pottery as chairman. By the spring of 1919 some forty-two trades had been organized and thirty-five were being aided in organization by government officials. Some bodies already in existence, such as the building trades council already described, were taken over and considered as part of this scheme. The ministry announced early in 1919 that it proposed to organize the industrial and administrative branches of the government departments along the same general lines. Later in the year rules were issued for their formation, but it was declared that these councils were only for purposes of consultation, all ultimate control of government departments being in the hands of Parliament.

116. The Permanent National Industrial Council. — Although these councils bade fair to settle many trade questions and to lay a foundation for happier relations in many trades they did not exist in the unions of the " triple alliance " or in some of the other most troubled industries. There was besides no means of bringing all industries together so that matters common to all might be considered. In February, 1919, when such bitter and widely extended strikes were threatened, the government took a further step in this direction and summoned a joint industrial conference of employers and employees of all trades to consider some more far-reaching scheme of industrial peace. This meeting, numbering some 500 representatives of labor and 300 of employers, met at Westminster, February 27, 1919, and was attended officially by the prime minister and the minister of labor. On the recommendation of a large joint committee of employers and employees on organization, presented after a month of discussion, the conference decided unanimously on the formation of a permanent National Industrial Council of 400 members, 200 to be elected by employers' organizations, 200 by trade unions, to be presided over by the minister of labor or his representative. The Council must meet at least twice a year, and a large standing committee is to meet once a month. All actions of the Council to be valid must have a majority vote of both the employers' side and the employees' side taken separately. The government will provide officers, quarters, and such information as the Council may wish and government departments can furnish. The government through the prime minister and the minister of labor agreed to recognize the National Industrial Council as an official consultative authority upon industrial matters and to seek through it information and opinion on all questions in which industry as a whole is concerned. The Council was also authorized to issue statements for the guidance of public opinion.

The most striking facts about this establishment of a National Industrial Council are, first, its close connection with the government; secondly, the unanimity of its acceptance by representatives of both employers and employees; thirdly, its requirement of the complete organization of the working classes as trade unions and the employers in employers' associations. No provision was made in the work of this conference for the exercise of any influence on industrial affairs by non-union workmen or by unorganized employers. Further it might be noted that a number of women participated in the conference.

In addition to the formation of this permanent Council and a declaration in favor of a legal maximum eight-hour day, a legal minimum wage in all trades, universal recognition of trade unions, and certain schemes to prevent unemployment, each " side " of the conference undertook to draw up a series of recommendations from the point of view of its own special needs. The employers announced their intention of presenting a full report concerning the need for output or production, but required more time for its preparation than the brief period of the conference allowed. The workingmen presented a long memorandum on the causes of industrial unrest. Besides a number of complaints, which are much the same as those put forth in the platform of the Labor party, and a statement of the low prevailing rates of wages in many industries, they stated as their main conclusion that the real difficulty in solving the labor question was a growing opposition on the part of the working classes to the whole existing structure of industrial society based on capitalism, their belief that production primarily for profit, as carried on in the past, was a bad system, and their determination to substitute to a much greater degree public service for private gain as a motive, and to establish " democratic control over industry." The word socialism was not used in these discussions, but these principles are nevertheless obviously socialistic.

117. Extension of the Functions of Government. — The progress of invention, business organization, legislation, and opinion, as it has been described in this chapter and the chapters immediately preceding, had reduced the *laissez-faire* theory of government to unimportance. What few remains of economic individualism still survived were swept away in the World War. But the tendency in this direction was already perfectly clear before the war. To the older forms of government regulation, control, ownership, and aid were added, after the opening of the twentieth century, old age pensions, government insurance, government labor exchanges, government assisted trade boards, and after the outbreak of the war Whitley Councils and the National Joint Industrial Council.

In 1909 a Housing and Town Planning Act carried much farther the principle of the Housing of the Working Classes Act, passed twenty years before. This later law had been suggested and the way for it had been prepared by the establishment of several privately owned and planned model towns or settlements, usually in connection with some large industrial concern. In these, instead of the profit of the investor, the comfort and opportunities for enjoyment of the inhabitants had been the primary consideration. One of the earliest of these was Port Sunlight, built by William Levin in 1887, another the " Garden City " at Letchworth, laid out about 1900. It was obvious that if such towns, suburbs, or other settlements could be built by private persons for other than profit-making motives, the same thing might be done by municipalities or other public bodies, if they were given by Parliament adequate powers. Such sanction was given by the act of 1909. The local authorities, or in case of their neglect, the central government, was given the power to secure ground by compulsory purchase, to tear down buildings that interfered with the approved scheme, and to construct any kind of buildings or a settlement, with water supply, drainage, lighting, parks, and all other requirements for a town. The only way such a suburb, extension, or new settlement would differ from any other was in the fact that it was put up by public authority with public funds, and presumably from motives of public advantage, not for the sake of profit.

Late in the same year, 1909, a measure for much more extended public ownership was adopted. This was the " Development and Road Improvement Act." So far as roads were concerned, this was nothing more than a somewhat wider extension of the well-established responsibility of government for the creation and maintenance of roads. The " development " part of the bill created a government board to be known as the "Development Commissioners," to be provided with money by Parliament, to carry out drainage schemes, harbor improvements, forest planting, fisheries, the building of what are called in England " light railways " for local traffic, and other minor public industries. They should also carry on instruction, research, and experiment helpful to rural development. The Commissioners could acquire land by compulsory purchase for their purposes and could use any profits which resulted from their operations for the same purposes. They must, however, report to Parliament every year what they were doing, and their activities could of course be controlled at any time by parliamentary action. In the years immediately following the adoption of this law, the boards provided for in it carried on some quite extensive operations in automobile road building and gave assistance to local bodies in experimentation and instruction in forestry, agriculture, stock-breeding, and harbor development. From 1912 to 1914 the Development Commissioners spent about $7,000,000.

The oncoming of the war limited for the time these activities; money and energy were needed in other directions. In these very directions, however, there was a sudden and unparalleled extension of the field of government control and even ownership. August 5, 1914, the day after Great Britain declared war against Germany the government took over the twenty-nine railroads of the country, and they are still, in July, 1920, in government hands. They are administered by the President of the Board of Trade, one of the ministers, through a committee of railway officials, the stockholders being guaranteed the same income as in the year 1913.

The extension of government control proceeded rapidly. All factories actually engaged in the manufacture of war materials were taken into the hands of the government by the Defense of the Realm acts, August 7–20, 1914. In March, 1915, by a new act, all other industrial establishments which could be utilized for munitions of any kind were made government works. As to other industries, the government tried to avoid control and only interfered slowly and reluctantly. Generally speaking, in 1914 and 1915 an attempt was made to meet the exigencies of the war by government pressure exercised on private owners; in 1916 detailed regulation was established to which all must conform; before the close of 1917 all forms of industry required for the service of the government or the well-being of the community in war time had been taken into the possession of the government or placed absolutely under its control.

Early in 1916 the government took by compulsory purchase all the wool crop in England, and later in the same year all that of Australia and New Zealand, rationing to manufacturers what was not needed for government work. The same action was soon taken for hides and leather. In 1917 the government took control of the coal mines. By a series of proclamations all merchant shipping was placed at the disposal of the government, the necessary space for government needs requisitioned, and other goods permitted to be shipped only with a government license and at a rate of freight fixed by the government. The distribution and consumption of meat, flour, sugar, and many other foods and necessities of life were placed under government control.

Since the war some things have been restored to their pre-war conditions. But in many ways the war simply made changes in the industrial world which were already in progress more rapid and complete. Many representatives of capital as well as of labor, and thinkers coming to the question from many points of view, had declared their conviction that our present economic organization was unsatisfactory. Interference in capitalist control of industry by government regulation in the interest of the community on the one hand, and by the organized power of the workingmen in the interest of their class on the other, had gone so far that it was irreversible. The necessity for the government to take over the control of so many lines of industry to meet the exigencies of war shook still further men's confidence in the capacity of capitalist industry to meet altogether satisfactorily the requirements of peace. Few business organizations seemed willing to declare themselves able to act entirely without support or direction from the government, and the Labor party, the most vigorous and constructive of the political parties, declared that capitalist production based on the private ownership and competitive administration of land and capital had broken down and that society itself needed reconstructing on more coöperative lines. Production was evidently being limited by the chronic discontent of labor, and by the failure to use land efficiently; equally injurious results were threatened by the manipulation of banking capital and the economic power of " big business."

Among enlightened business men, as well as among workingmen, statesmen, and writers on social subjects, there is a widespread tendency to look for some kind of reconstruction that will carry industrial and social life forward to a more satisfactory state rather than to restore it to any earlier condition. Where the changes which England and other countries are now undergoing will lead and how far they will be beneficial depend on the thought and efforts of those now living.

Democratic Influences on Industrial Life 369

118. BIBLIOGRAPHY

Monthly Bulletin of the United States Bureau of Labor Statistics, Washington.

This publication, which will be sent almost free to those asking for it, contains much information concerning recent movements in British industrial life. Among its special reports are:
No. 102, British National Insurance Act, 1912.
No. 133, Inquiry into Industrial Agreements, 1913.
No. 237, Industrial Unrest in Great Britain, 1917.
No. 255, Joint Industrial Councils in Great Britain, 1919.

British Labour Gazette, London, published monthly by the Ministry of Labor.

British Labour Year Book.

Hazell's Annual.

These two publications give recent information concerning economic and social movements.

Schloss, D. F.: *Insurance against Unemployment.*

Beveridge, W. H.: *Unemployment,* 2d ed., London, 1912.

Chapman, I. J.: *Work and Wages,* Pt. II. *Wages and Employment,* London, 1908.

Gray, H. L.: *War Time Control of Industry, The Experience of England,* N. Y., 1918.

Kellogg, Paul U., and Gleason, Arthur: *British Labor and the War,* N. Y., 1919.

Gleason, Arthur: *What the Workers Want,* N. Y., 1920.

Henderson, Arthur: *The Aims of Labor,* 1918.

MacDonald, J. R.: *The Social Unrest, its Cause and Solution,* London, 1913.

Clay, Sir Arthur: *Syndicalism and Labor,* London, 1911.

Hobson, S. G.: *National Gilds; an Inquiry into the Wage System and the Way Out,* London, 1917.

Cole, G. D. H.: *Self Government in Industry,* London, 1918.

Meakin, B.: *Model Factories and Villages,* London, 1905.

Lord Avebury: *Municipal and National Trading.*

2 B

INDEX

Accidents, industrial, 315; legislation concerning, 315-317; provisions of workmen's compensation act of 1906 regarding, 337.

Acre, the mediæval English, 31.

Adventurers, term applied to English foreign traders, 140-141.

African slave trade, 166.

Agincourt, English victory at, 83.

Agricultural District Wages Boards, 349.

Agricultural Holdings acts, 303-304.

Agriculture, in Saxon England, 10; mediæval system of, 31-35; changes in system of, in 14th century, 110-111; changes in, in 15th and 16th centuries, 120-125; government regulation of, in 16th century, 150-151; during 17th and 18th centuries, 158-160; revolution in, in 18th century, 185-188; government Board of, 186; advances in, during period 1848-1878, 257-258; most prosperous era of British, 258-259; decline of, from 1874 onward, 301-302; investigation of, by Duke of Richmond's Commission, 302; establishment of Department of, and appointment of Minister of, 302-303; question of small holdings and allotments, 303-306; minimum wage for those engaged in, 349.

Aids, meaning of, under feudal system, 20.

Alderman, presiding officer of gild merchant, 53.

Ale taster, petty manorial officer, 44.

Alexandria, Egypt, bombardment of, 300.

Alfred, King, reign of, 13.

Allotments, establishment and spread of, 305-306.

Allotments and Small Holdings Association, formation of, 305.

Alsace-Lorraine, seized by Germany (1871), 252.

Amalgamations of trade unions, 320.

Amerciaments, fines called, 44.

America, founding of English colonies in, 154; emigration to, due to religious persecutions, 156; extension of English colonial empire in, 158; importance of plantations in, for trading purposes, 165-166; revolution in, and loss of thirteen colonies, 173; early steamship lines between Great Britain and, 217-218; British sympathy with South during Civil War in, 252; treaties between Great Britain and, 252-253.

Anderson, James, *Political Economy* by, quoted, 198-199.

Angevin kings, period of the early, 21-28.

Angles, invasions of Roman Britain by, 8; numbers and spread of, 9-10; give name to England, 10.

Aniline dyes, manufacture of, 256.

Anne, Queen, reign of, 158.

Annual Trade Union Congress, meetings of, 292-293, 322-323, 328.

Anti-Corn-Law League, organization and work of, 221-223.

Anti-Sweating League, organization of, 346.

Antwerp, rise of, as commercial city, 140.

Apprentice houses for child laborers, 233.

Apprentices, Statute of (1563), 134, 150, 163, 196-197, 226.

Apprenticeship under gild system, 56.

Arable land, meadow, and pasture land, in mediæval system of agriculture, 31-33, 40.

Archbishops, in early organization of church, 11.

Architecture, Norman, in England, 15.

Index

Hudson, George, so-called "railway king," 213–215.
Hughes, Thomas, a Christian Socialist, 271.
Huguenots, immigration of, into England, 160–161.
Hundred, governmental district of Saxon England, 10.
"Hundred Rolls," compilation of the, 26.
Hundred Years' War, 83–84.
"Hungry forties," period called, 224.
Hyndman, H. M., organizer of Social Democratic Federation, 326.

Imperial War Cabinet, sittings of, 334–335.
Income tax, adoption of, 223.
Independent Labor party, organization of, 322; growth in strength of, 328.
India, East India Company in, 154; English predominance in, 158; trade to, opened to outsiders, 198; Sepoy Rebellion in, 251; made a direct dependency of British crown, 251; Queen of England given title of Empress of, 252.
Individualism, growth of theory of, in economic life, 198–201; more than a mere *laissez-faire* policy of government, 200; disappointing results of, 201–203; period of predominance of ideal of (1820–1848), 205–249; sweeping away of economic, in Great War, 365.
Industrial and Provident Societies acts, 270.
Industrial Council, National, 363–364.
Industrial revolution, meaning of, 184–185.
Industrial unionism, 318.
Insurance, a feature of certain mediæval gilds, 61; origins of fire and life, 171; new form of, due to Workmen's Compensation Act, 317; national, against sickness and unemployment, 343–345.
Intercursus Magnus, treaty known as, 144.
Interest, payment of, on loans, 147–148.
International Workingmen's Association, 325.
Inventions, great mechanical, of 18th century, 176–182.

Ireland, beginning of conquest of, 22; English policy toward, 154; English and Scotch settlers in, 165; united with England and Scotland, 176; troubles with, 253; home rule bills of 1886 and 1892, 297, 299; disturbances in, during Great War, 333; Sinn Fein activities and successes in, 333–334; separate Parliament for, organized in Dublin, 334; disorder and assassinations in, 334.
Iron, 2; production of, in 18th century, 184; increased demand for, due to growth of railways and steamships, 218–219; production of, tripled in period 1848–1878, 256.
Iron workers' coöperative associations, 268.
Italy, English trade with, in Middle Ages, 72; bankers of, in England, 78; influence on English literature and intellectual interests in 15th century, 116; war in, in 1859, 252.

James I, reign of, 153–154.
James II, 157.
Jews, in mediæval England, 51; admission of, into Parliament, 255.
John, King, reign of, 23–25.
Joint Industrial Councils, 363–364.
Joint stock companies, 306, 307.
Journeyman, grade of, under craft gild system, 56; change in position of, 129.
Journeymen gilds, formation of, 127.
Jury system, introduction of, 23.
Justice, Socialist newspaper, 327.
Jutes, in Roman Britain, 8; kingdom of Kent established by, 9.
Juvenile courts, establishment of, 337.

Kay, John, drop box and flying shuttle invented by, 179
Kempe, John, Flemish weaver in England, 81.
Kings. *See* Royal government.
Kingsley, Charles, interest of, in working-class movements, 288; one of founders of *Christian Socialist*, 324.

Labor and the New Social Order programme, 353.

Profit sharing, difference between coöperation and, 273–275.
Progress and Poverty, Henry George's, 326.
Public ownership, progress in, 365–367.
Puritans, rise of the, 120.

Queenwood, coöperative community at, 247.
Quia Emptores, Statute of, 26.

Radical movement, beginning of, 207.
Railway mania of 1845, 212–213.
Railway strike of 1919, 356.
Railways, era of development of, 208–215; slight government control of, 215–217.
Reaper, a manorial officer, 44.
Reeve, office of, 36, 44.
Reform Bill, of 1832, 207–208; of 1884, 296–297. *See* Parliament.
Reformation, the, in England, 118–119; effects of, on gild organizations, 135–136.
Regrating, meaning of, 57.
Regulated companies, 163.
Relay system in factories, 276.
Relief, payment to landlord called, 20, 37.
Religious gilds, 60.
Religious observances of craft gilds, 58.
Rents of assize, 37.
Representation of the People Act, 332, 351.
Restoration, the, 156.
Revolution of 1688, 157.
Ricardo, works of, 194.
Richard I, 24.
Richard II, 85; and the Peasants' Rebellion, 98, 102–105.
Ring spinning, use of, 255.
Rivers of England, characteristics of, 2.
Roads, Roman, in Britain, 6; improvements in modern, 184–185.
Rochdale Pioneers, account of, 263–265; followers of, and variations of plan of, 265–267.
Rocket, Stephenson's locomotive, 211.
Rod, the mediæval English, 31.
Roebuck, promoter of blast furnace, 184.
Roman Catholics, favored by James I, 154.

Romans, in Britain, 5–8.
Rood, meaning of, 31.
Royal African Company, 165.
Royal Agricultural Society, founding of, 258.
Royal government, increase in strength of, begun with Edward IV, 117; paternal form of, 148–151.
Rural life and organization in 13th and 14th centuries, 29–46; effects on, of pestilences of 14th century, 88–91; changes in, in 14th century, 107–113.
Russell, Lord John, Liberal leader, 255.
Russia, war against, in 1854, 251; war between Turkey and (1877–1878), 299.
Russia Company, the, 142–143.

Safety lamp, Davy's, 184.
St. Albans, occurrences at, during Peasants' Rebellion, 102.
St. Ives, fairs held at, 64.
Salle, Sir Robert, victim of Peasants' Rebellion, 101.
Salvation Army, founding of, 326.
Sankey report, the, 356.
Savannah, first steam vessel to cross Atlantic, 217.
Saxons, Roman Britain invaded by, 7–8; petty kingdoms established by, 9; South, West, East, and Middle, 9; supremacy of West Saxons, 9; defeat of, by Normans at Hastings, 15.
Scandinavia, early immigrations into England from, 12–13.
School lunches, legislative bill requiring, 337.
Scotland, English interference in affairs of, 22; failure of England to absorb, 23; union of England and, 176.
Scots, early invasions of Britain by, 7–8.
Screw propeller, invention of, 217.
Senlac (Hastings), battle of, 15.
Sepoy Rebellion, the, 251.
Serfdom, in England in 13th century, 40; removal of burdens of, an aim of Peasants' Rebellion of 1381, 106–107; reasons for disappearance of, 111–113.
Seven Years' War, the, 158.
Shakespeare, period of, 156.
Sheep-raising, changes in agricultural system caused by, 120–125; government regulation of, 150; ceases to be

2 C

Workmen's Compensation Act, passage
of, 316–317; a new, in 1906, 336–337.
Wrawe, John, leader in Peasants' Rebellion, 101.
Wycliffe, John, work of, 84–85; social
trend of teachings of, 95.

Yeomen, class of farmers called, 111;
disappearance of, 202; transformed
into farm laborers, 206.
Yeomen gilds, formation of, 127.

York, bishopric of, 11; population of
city, in 13th century, 50; craft gilds
at, 55; mystery plays at, 59.
York, house of, defeat of house of Lancaster by, 86.
Young, Arthur, agricultural observer and
writer, 185; criticism of government
policy by, 193.
Young Ireland party, 253.

Zealand, artisans from, in England, 81